YEN!

*Japan's New Financial Empire
and Its Threat to America*

Daniel Burstein

Simon and Schuster
New York   London   Toronto   Sydney   Tokyo

Simon and Schuster
Simon & Schuster Building
Rockefeller Center
1230 Avenue of the Americas
New York, New York 10020

Designed by Irving Perkins Associates
Manufactured in the United States of America

10 9 8 7 6 5 4 3 2 1

Library of Congress Cataloging-in-Publication Data

Burstein Daniel.
Yen! : Japan's new financial empire and its threat
to America.

Includes index.
1. Financial institutions—Japan. 2. International finance. I. Title.
HG187.J3B87 1988   332.4′560952′073   88-28494

ISBN 0-671-64763-6

For Julie, whose love shone like the sun
on the hardest moments of this project,
and who shared everything great and
small along the seventeen-year journey from
Málaga to Tokyo.

Contents

Part I

TOWARD THE
JAPANESE CENTURY

Prelude:
A Twenty-first-Century Scenario

Under your strategy, Japan in the postwar period mobilized all the wisdom it had accumulated over its long history to achieve economic reconstruction. The product of this is a boy with a huge body, who, head stooped, walks around in the world.

"Hey, boy," you still call out to him, but he is no longer willing to do all you want him to do.... Under the mask you gave us, our own physiognomy is taking shape.... We feel the time has come when we should show it to the world.

The real face is our own global strategy.
                                        —Jun Etoh, Japanese social critic[1]

November 2004. America, battered by astronomical debts and reeling from prolonged economic decline, is gripped by a new and grave economic crisis. Like all such events, the causes are multiple and complex. But the president-elect and the voters who chose him by a landslide see only a single cause and a single culprit for America's problems: the Japanese.

What the president will do when he takes office in January is at first unclear. His campaign was long on rhetoric about "standing up to the Japanese" and short on specifics. He has vowed to bring an end to what he calls "the historic pattern of underestimating the Japanese menace."

The litany of erroneous estimates is a painful one for early twenty-first-century Americans. They find it hard to believe, for example, that the U.S. Congress of the 1950s was actually worried enough about Japan's chronic trade and budget deficits to recommend plans to help Japanese industry develop exportable products. It is inconceivable now that in the 1960s Detroit's moguls laughed at the funny little Japanese cars in California showrooms and ignored the possibility of a competitive threat to the mighty American automobile industry. Or that Silicon Valley's wunderkinds of the 1970s believed the Japanese incapable of competing with the research that made America number one in technology. Or that Wall Street's shrewd minds of the 1980s couldn't foresee that when their demand to open Tokyo financial markets was met, a torrent of capital would be released, and Japanese financial service companies would emerge as world leaders.

How tragically short-sighted it now seems that during those years, the Reagan administration halved the value of the U.S. dollar in the vain hope of restoring "competitiveness" to American manufacturing and reducing the massive trade deficit. Didn't they realize how much less competitive American business would become over time against Japanese rivals whose yen-based financial resources doubled when the dollar fell? Apparently not. They believed American wealth and power were God-given birthrights.

But now, in 2004, Japan is the richest country in the world. Like Americans of another era, the Japanese now have the world's highest living standards. They enjoy the latest high-tech household conveniences, international luxury products, and vacation homes in Hawaii and other Pacific resorts served by supersonic Japanese airlines. Indeed, ordinary Japanese now live a life-style to which only affluent Americans can aspire.

Japan has experienced few of the vexing social problems that are increasingly pitting American "haves" against "have-nots." Data from the 2000 census indicate that 15 percent of Americans are now in the "underclass"—without visible means of support, usually illiterate, and, in five million cases, homeless. They are victims of slashed programs that once made up the "safety net." Census statistics suggest that the large American middle class is still reasonably secure. But many would dispute that notion. Only a shrinking minority of American families believes they will ever be able to own their own home, send their children to college, or assume responsibility for aging parents no longer covered by Medicare after age eighty or Social Security after eighty-five. Americans have lost the optimism that once defined their national character.

To be Japanese in the early twenty-first century, on the other hand, is glorious. Known in the 1970s and 1980s as the world's most efficient workers, the Japanese have now become the world's most efficient managers, marketers, traders, and, most of all, *financiers.* From their headquarters in Tokyo, Japanese financial institutions control the strategic resource of capital the way OPEC once controlled the world's oil supply.

The U.S. dollar is still an important currency, but the biggest chunk of world business is yen-denominated. English is still the world's common business language, but all over Europe and Asia, and even in the United States itself, young people are studying Japanese. In Los Angeles, New York, London, Paris, and Hong Kong, Japanese businessmen live at the best addresses. Throughout the world, Tokyo's fashions, popular culture, and ways of doing business are admired and emulated.

Almost every major economy relies to some degree on attracting Japanese money, but the United States is the most dependent. Even Washington's austerity budgets cannot be financed without large-scale Japanese capital infusions. The same is true for many state governments. The U.S. economy as a whole is depressed; the bright spots of revitalization are frequently Japanese-owned.

America's great military machine now survives in part because of Japanese subsidies. Early in the 1990s, Congress decided it was foolish to continue underwriting Japanese defense when Japan itself had become so wealthy. Tokyo agreed to undertake a partial remilitarization—enough, in fact, to make the Japanese archipelago virtually impregnable from conventional attack. In addition, Japan agreed to pay "user fees" for continued reliance on U.S. nuclear deterrence. The Department of Defense now depends on Japan for a quarter of its annual budget.

The story of how America became so dependent has its roots in the 1980s when the Reagan administration turned the United States into the biggest debtor nation in history. "Spend, consume, and borrow" was the order of the day—an agenda made possible by the ready availability of foreign investors. Foremost among America's foreign bankers were the Japanese, who were then just learning to use their massive capital surplus to sow the seeds of empire.

America's dependency on Japan grew rapidly, invisibly, and nearly silently. A few American financial wizards worried out loud about the trend: "We have made ourselves hostage to the Japanese, and now we better keep them happy," was the sentiment expressed by one former Reagan aide turned investment banker.[2] But U.S. capital shortages and Japanese surfeits were institutionalized before most Americans had the chance to understand what was happening.

By the late 1980s, however, the combination of a stock market crash, a weakened dollar, and an intractable U.S. trade deficit began to convince many people that something was fundamentally wrong. In response, budget-cutting rhetoric became politically popular. Trims were made here and there, even significant ones. But no politician was really ready to say the United States couldn't afford military leadership anymore; none wanted to cut into the pocketbooks of senior citizens, and most saw no practical alternative to the "big government" they incessantly decried. Even those who in prior years would surely have argued for higher taxes now found such a campaign politically impossible, despite the fact that the United States had instituted one of the lowest personal income tax structures in the industrial world.

As a result the country moved steadily deeper into debt in the early 1990s. Soaring debt, in turn, made it impossible for the government to invest heavily in future-oriented programs for building infrastructure or carrying out scientific research. Funding for education dried up, even though everyone knew that America's future ability to compete in a "brain-intensive" global economy depended directly on it. American productivity, once the highest in the world, rates only seventh in 2004, in large part because workers lack the functional and technological literacy necessary to operate today's standard equipment.

Reliance on foreign capital also crippled American negotiators trying to take a "tough" stance with Japan on trade matters. Indeed, throughout the 1990s Washington and Tokyo played a perennial game of chicken, with American leaders threatening and sometimes taking protectionist actions against the Japanese, and the Japanese quietly replying by boycotting Treasury refundings, turning the screws on the dollar in world currency markets, and summarily moving large portfolios out of U.S. stock markets.

But that was not the worst of it. Washington's addiction to debt arose in a time of relatively low oil prices, low interest rates, and strength of the U.S. dollar. As the mountain of American debt expanded, however, the world became more uncertain about America's much vaunted stability. A wave of junk-bond defaults frightened foreigners. Interest rates had to rise continuously to attract new capital from abroad. Even as budget cutters finally shaved government spending down to true austerity levels, rising debt service costs over-whelmed them. To finance a $200 billion deficit at 7–9 percent inter-est rates in the 1980s was one thing; it was quite another to attempt to finance even larger deficits in the 1990s at rates of 14–16 percent. Debt service became the biggest chunk of the budgetary pie—far bigger than military spending or Social Security. Two-fifths of new government spending now goes to pay back debts inherited from bloated budgets of prior years.

Americans have become indentured servants of a new kind. The average worker labors five months of the year just to pay his taxes. Every single American works an entire month for no other purpose than to pay off debts owed to Japanese and other foreign creditors.

The Japanese still dominate the "old" industries that propelled them to superpower status—automobiles, steel, and microelectronics. But manufacturing has been shifted abroad to regions that have sizable local markets and offer cheap land and labor—especially the United States. Throughout the late 1980s and 1990s, the weak dollar made it cheap for Japanese investors to buy up American companies, real estate, and every kind of asset. Of the still venerated *Fortune* 500, one hundred are now Japanese-owned.

Although Japanese capital was credited with sparking a wave of American reindustrialization in the 1990s, profits from Japanese-owned enterprises are now taken out of the U.S. economic loop and repatriated to Japan. The largely nonunion American work force at Japanese companies has also learned about the Japanese philosophy of "sacrificing for the company." Even during the current downturn, Tokyo still expects foreign subsidiaries to return profit quotas. The usual way to do that is to lower wages.

As a group, U.S. workers now earn far less than their counterparts in Japan—and less than Germans, Swiss, Norwegians, Swedes, and Canadians as well. Americans don't take comfort from the fact that they are still better off than the British, French, and Italians, to say nothing of most of the rest of the world. Nor does it really matter that they own more material goods than Americans of the 1980s. Instead they look with envy on how well the Japanese live and resent it fiercely.

Inside Japan, a whole new domestic economy has been built based on the advances of the information age. Japan has leapfrogged ahead of the United States to become the dominant force in such businesses as superconducting materials and processes, bioengineered food and pharmaceutical products, robotics, high-speed transportation systems, and computer services. During the 1990s, it became clear that the scale of scientific research and the cost of commercializing new breakthroughs had become so great that only the biggest, best-capitalized companies could compete seriously and even then only with massive government support. These new realities are destroying much of what is left of American leadership in science and technology.

The trigger on the current economic crisis was pulled last year when simultaneous terrorist attacks on oil depots across the Mideast led to the first big oil price run-up in twenty years. Japan, for once, has not been severely affected since it now satisfies most of its energy needs from nuclear, solar, and other high-tech generating systems. The oil it needs for less-efficient factories in other parts of the world is obtained under long-term stable supply arrangements with China.

In the United States, however, the effects have been devastating. Despite bitter past experiences, America allowed itself to become reliant on "cheap" Mideast oil once again. In the current crisis, as in the 1970s, skyrocketing oil prices have carried interest rates and inflation along with them. Yields on U.S. bonds leaped to an all-time record 21 percent. Yet even at 21 percent, Japan is loath to continue lending money. Japanese economists believe Washington will soon default on a substantial portion of its obligations. The "full faith and credit" of the U.S. government has become empty rhetoric.

Over the last few months Japanese negotiators have put forward a proposal to resolve the situation. Nothing like it has ever been seen in the history of international relations. It is extraordinarily complex, but the essential point is clear: the price of further Japanese capital is an agreement that if the U.S. defaults, Japan will effectively put America into "receivership." A joint U.S.-Japan condominium will be established on American soil, with the Japanese side holding temporary veto power on matters of budgeting, finance, trade, and industrial policy until solvency is restored. Existing Japanese investors will be allowed to exchange U.S. bonds for tracts of federal land and other assets. Japanese companies will gain unrestricted access to the American market, along with unrestricted immigration for their workers. A new American currency will be issued with its yen conversion rate set by Tokyo.

The outgoing president and his chairman of the Federal Reserve are reluctantly recommending acceptance of the plan. Some Americans even welcome it, arguing that only the Japanese can help get America's house in order again. But to the incoming president, the whole idea is synonymous with treason. He will not only refuse it, he will implement a diametrically opposed plan of his own. He and his brain trust have charted a first one hundred days of action that will be the most decisive in American history.

On taking office, the new president will declare a moratorium on interest payments due Japanese investors for all American debts, public and private. He will announce measures forcing Japanese companies to sell majority interests in their U.S. facilities to American partners at fractional market values. He will impose a freeze on the repatriation of profits earned by Japanese companies. And much more—all part of the crusade he will launch in his inaugural address to free the U.S. economy from "the tentacles of the Japanese empire."

In Tokyo they know what is coming. Ever since Richard Allen, Ronald Reagan's first national security adviser, the Japanese have found ways to infiltrate the inner chambers of Washington. They also know exactly how they will respond. A long-standing contingency plan will be put into action. The Japanese will not spend the eight weeks that remain before the inauguration idly waiting for the value of their holdings to be destroyed or hoping for an American change of heart. Instead they will immediately pull out every investment they can from the United States, taking whatever losses are necessary to liquidate such huge portfolios. This will throw the U.S. economy into chaos even before the new president takes office. It will undermine whatever ability he might have had in moderating the anarchy of financial markets gone berserk.

Japan will immediately suspend "user fee" payments due the Pentagon and announce an independent military policy. To allay Soviet and Chinese fears, Tokyo will open negotiations on mutual nonaggression pacts with both countries, sweetening the deals by offering to loan, invest, and donate most of the funds recovered from the sale of U.S. assets.

Finally, in the tradition of Japan's many fanatical national campaigns, the whole country will be thrown into a massive rearmament drive. Secretly Japanese scientists are already close to perfecting a "Star Wars"–type defense system. This effort will be speeded up, as will development of Japan's own nuclear arsenal.

The Japanese people will suffer greatly, but their leaders have prepared them well for this eventuality. The pain will be far worse in the United States and other Western countries, which are unprepared. There, banking systems will collapse, currencies will lose their value, whole nations and industries will be bankrupted. Panic will be everywhere as the basic underpinnings of the global economy are violently ripped apart.

When the pandemonium dies down, Japan will emerge as the winner. It will no longer be simply the richest country in the world—it will also be the strongest.

Introduction:
Avoiding the Apocalypse

The United States, the creator of the postwar economic system and home of the world's key currency, has become the
largest debtor nation ever known to mankind.... Japan,
widely viewed as a developing country only a generation ago,
has become by far the largest creditor.... The forces set in
train by these historic changes will dominate the course of
global economic events for the next five to ten years.
                              —C. Fred Bergsten, director,
                              Institute for International
                              Economics[1]

The scenario in the first pages of this book is fiction. But it is not
beyond the realm of possibility. Its elements are drawn from today's
real-life issues, ideas, trends, and fears. Thoughtful people on both
sides of the Pacific, while wishing for a workable U.S.-Japan symbiosis, have been compelled by recent events to grapple with the
horrifying idea that "the world's most important bilateral relationship"[2] could be torn asunder by contradictory economic forces now at
work within it.

At the moment, those forces are juxtaposed sufficiently sharply for
some scholars to forecast a rupture sooner rather than later. John Zys-
man, a Berkeley political scientist, warns that a U.S.-Japan "divorce"
could come in the early 1990s. Robert Gilpin, a Princeton political
economist, believes that world stability cannot rest much longer on
"Japanese-financed American hegemony." If the U.S.-Japan relationship collapses, "the possibilities of a stable international political
order" may vanish as well, he has noted.[3] George Packard, the dean
of The Johns Hopkins School of Advanced International Studies, predicts that if current policies don't change, the U.S.-Japan relationship
will descend into protectionism, "retaliation, recrimination, and a

search for different partnerships." Japan would then link its destiny to the Chinese or Soviets, seek to expand its "widening economic sphere in Asia and the Pacific," and end up "in direct confrontation with the United States."[4]

One doesn't have to listen very hard to hear the danger signals. "God bless Harry Truman," declares Texas Congressman Jack Brooks, praising the two bombs dropped on Hiroshima and Nagasaki at the end of World War II. Truman's mistake, he concludes, was that "he should have dropped four."[5] In the shadow of the Capitol Building, a group of otherwise intelligent American legislators viciously smash a Toshiba boom box to bits with a sledgehammer in order to "send a message to Japan." Washington names a new commerce secretary, and just before he departs for his first round of trade talks, he rekindles wartime hostilities by publicly referring to those who will receive him in Tokyo as "the Japs."[6]

Jingoistic Americans bash Japan, unaware that on the other side of the world their counterparts are bashing America. In Tokyo's bookstores some of the hottest-selling titles on current affairs translate as *Traps Set by America, The Bad One Is America, Not Japan, The Japan-U.S. War Has Not Ended, Can America Be Trusted?*, and *The Battle for the American Continent.*[7] Farmers hang Ronald Reagan in effigy at a mass rally. An opinion poll reveals that more Japanese young people believe Japan will fight its next war with the United States than with the Soviet Union.[8]

No one knows what real U.S.-Japan fission would look like. But whether the impetus comes from an expansive Japan pushing too far or from a wounded America lashing out violently at Japan, most experts agree the impact would be apocalyptic. That is because today's global prosperity hinges as never before on a delicate set of balances, interdependencies, and confidences. And the U.S.-Japan relationship lies at the very nucleus of that belief system.

With just 7 percent of the world's population, the two economies produce 30 percent of the world's goods and control a similarly disproportionate percentage of global trade. Together the two countries account for nearly three-quarters of world stock and bond market value and half of all bank lending. They issue 80 percent of the money used by other nations as reserve currencies.

The instruments of debt and equity that flow instantly across borders these days are so sophisticated that it is easy to forget how conditional their value is on the unspoken assumption that the rules of the global economic game will be the same tomorrow as they are today. But if the U.S.-Japan relationship is severed and the two sides are thrust into conflict, many of those rules will be thrown open for question. Therein lies a recipe not only for panic, but for global economic meltdown.

At the moment, U.S.-Japan economic activity remains symbiotic, if grudgingly so. A few skirmishes have been fought, giving world markets a faint hint of the dangers inherent in any sort of full-dress showdown. But to date no credible political or economic faction in either country actually advocates or desires a rupture.

That is the good news. The bad news is that forces of national interest are likely to prove more powerful determinants of the future than the wishes or intentions of today's decision makers. The argument of this book is not that such a confrontation is inevitable. Rather, it is only inevitable if we ignore it as a possibility and fail to take preventive action, or if the preventive action we choose to take is of the knee-jerk, protectionist type that could serve to bring the clash on sooner and more destructively. And here lies the great American quandary: we are being pushed and pulled between two political and economic trends of thought, both of which are dangerous and neither of which is addressing the fundamental problem.

The leading trend in the 1980s has been to ignore the depth of the threat. According to this line of reasoning, America is still number one and always will be; a globalized economy benefits Americans who have the intellectual and technological powers to dominate it; the flow of foreign capital is a testament to American strength, stability, openness, and the general superiority of our system. Therefore we should maintain the status quo domestically. Our "competitiveness" problems should be solved principally by persuading foreigners to be more like us in their home markets.

The reality is that this rosy view, for reasons we shall discuss throughout this book, has already been responsible for a rapid decline of American economic vigor and a similarly rapid rise of Japanese power. To continue to pursue such policies invites the prospect not of *interdependence,* but of a one-sided and highly destabilizing U.S. *dependence* on foreigners whose agenda is different from our own.

On the other hand, many of those legitimately alarmed by Japan's growing strength advocate xenophobic, backward-looking protectionist policies that assume if the foreigners can just be kept out at the gates, the domestic economy will regain its vitality. Any blanket policy of protectionism is fraught with dangers, not the least of which is history's well-documented lesson that trade wars have a way of turning rapidly into global depressions and even shooting wars. Contemporary protectionists also tend to ignore just how much retaliatory strength Japan has already accrued as a result of last decade's policies and just how willing and able the Japanese might be, if pushed, to use their leverage over the American economy.

Although some strategic areas of national interest undoubtedly ought to be more carefully protected than they are now, such steps should be part of larger agreements with our partners and competitors, not the outcome of blind anger or brinksmanship. Ultimately, however, protecting American industries and businesses offers no solution unless such measures are connected to an industrial policy (which should, in reality, be a postindustrial policy) and a national economic plan that takes account of why the American side is less competitive than the foreign side in the first place and proposes ways to either ameliorate the differences or compensate the inefficiencies through other means.

And that is the final corner of the dilemma. We have leaders who want to keep things as they are, even though doing so means further decline. We have other leaders who are willing to provoke dangerous showdowns to try to stem the tide of decline. But we have comparatively few leaders willing to recognize that the world really has changed, and that to be competitive in it we must be willing to use our much vaunted American aptitudes for innovation, creativity, and flexibility to reconfigure the way America does business and is governed.

Having reached decade's end, the Hollywood-style fantasies that concealed the underlying crisis in the U.S. economy earlier in the 1980s are finally being challenged publicly in some influential quarters. "Wake Up, America!" say the editors of *Business Week*. "We have spent too much, borrowed too much, and imported too much. We have lived beyond our means, relying on foreigners to finance our massive budget and trade deficits. The bill is now coming due."[9]

When America does awaken, we are told by former commerce secretary and investment banker Peter Peterson, it will be "the morning after." We will face a country that has "let its infrastructure crumble, its foreign markets decline, its productivity dwindle, its savings evaporate, and its budget and borrowing burgeon." The "day of reckoning" will be at hand.[10]

We hear this talk, and even recognize a ring of truth to it, yet we still don't want to believe it. We cling to illusions about "rebuilding American greatness," but we fail to define what that means in light of today's changed global environment. As Nobel economics laureate Paul Samuelson suggests, the United States, responsible for around 20 percent of the world's output today, simply cannot expect to exercise the same kind of dominant role in the world that it did after World War II when it accounted for 40 percent.[11]

We continue to maintain an extensive military capability in far corners of the world, but Paul Kennedy, the historian who has made an academic career of studying rising and falling empires, hypothesizes that in so doing, we are falling victim to the classic syndrome of "imperial overstretch" that has doomed great powers throughout history.[12] By spending so much on armies and weapons systems, we are draining the economy of resources necessary to compete successfully with Japan and other less encumbered powers.

Hidden behind the glittery facade of the "Roaring Eighties" in American business lies the reality that the United States has lost control over the central features of its own economy, thereby foreclosing many of the potential solutions to current dilemmas. Interest rates, the value of the dollar, the financing of U.S. government operations, the flow of imports and exports—none of these areas of fundamental importance to national well-being can be fully controlled any longer by American policymakers, even in those rare moments when they can agree on policy.

It would be an overstatement to say that Japan now controls these strategic areas instead. Some of the power relinquished has gone to our other old adversary, Germany; some has been claimed by a diverse lot of other foreigners. Much of the economic architecture we once relied upon has simply broken down in the wake of volatility in the global marketplace. But having said that, it is still imperative to recognize that Japan has gained a measure of control over our economy unwise to cede to any foreign country, even the friendliest, best-intentioned ally.

No evil cabal in Tokyo planned things this way. Rather, it is a case of Americans willingly, if not always knowingly, surrendering our own destiny. It is an epic tale with a theme worthy of the Bible: the American Esau—a strong, prideful hunter—has sold his birthright to the Japanese Jacob—a quiet, clever strategist—in return for a mess of consumption and debt. Nothing in the Bible suggests that Jacob is to blame for taking advantage of Esau in this way.

In the case of Japan, moreover, it is not just any foreign country to whom we've sold our birthright. Japan is our mirror image and our fiercest competitor. Japan is strong precisely where we are weak; its economy reverberates with the equal and opposite reactions to our American actions. Thus, while the United States has become the world's leading debtor, Japan has become its leading creditor. While we consume more than we produce, Japan produces more than it consumes. While our dollar weakens, Japan's yen strengthens. While we lust for imports, Japan's passion is for exports. While we deregulate and fragment our society, Japan maintains a strong central plan and national cohesion. While we find ourselves unable to rebuild our industrial and social infrastructure, Japan embarks on what will likely be the world's greatest domestic expansion of the nineties. And while we withdraw from global obligations, Japan begins to assume them.

Blinded by wartime victory and our long-standing role as senior partner in the U.S.-Japan relationship, we ignore the obvious: Japan is becoming a global superpower in its own right. We casually acknowledge Japan as a great manufacturing and trading nation that has surpassed us in certain product areas. We even accept the idea that "Made in Japan" means higher quality than "Made in USA." But we still shrink from recognizing the essential reality. A Japanese empire is being born that will pose a fundamental challenge to American power in every sphere.

The central issue here is not which country can produce better-quality automobiles or pack more circuits on a computer chip, important though such talents are to a national economy. Instead, what is at stake is the power that allowed Britain to dominate the nineteenth century and the United States to dominate the twentieth, and will, in all probability, allow Japan to dominate the twenty-first. It is the power that, when possessed by a nation, propels it beyond all others in its wealth, standard of living, technological development, productive capacity, and even its art, culture, and intellectual life. And conversely, the kind of power that, when lost by a nation accustomed to thriving on it, triggers economic chaos, stagnates growth, deepens the cleavage between rich and poor, and induces a profound crisis of identity and national spirit.

Japan is not only our mirror image and our fiercest competitor, it is also the only country that has ever bombed United States territory. It is not necessary to believe in the cliché of a Japanese conspiracy seeking to win back what was lost in 1945 to recognize that Japan's great wealth is regenerating a new nationalism, an ugly arrogance, and a certain imperial swagger. It is possible that the Japanese will resist the temptations of this trend in favor of a course that could influence world history in a much more humanitarian way. The fusion of Japan's rich cultural legacy with its new financial power could create a socioeconomic model that would inspire the rest of the world in the next century. Japan could be the engine that pulls the Third World out of its misery and teaches the superpowers that the arms race and economic development are incompatible. But although such ideas are sometimes voiced in Japan today, current events are not moving in their direction. The logic of contemporary Japanese policy, coupled with the leadership's need to defend itself from the illogic of American policy, creates fertile ground for crystallizing the almost inevitable consensus that Japan must convert the economic empire it has obtained into a political and military one as well.

Today's financial world is the razor's edge in this explosive process of Japanese expansion and American decline. The U.S.-Japan trade war is fast becoming an issue of the past, won for all intents and purposes by Japan. Now, the financial war is brewing. By following the trail of dollars and yen, we can see the accelerating pace at which the new Japanese empire is gaining momentum and the American empire is losing ground.

Japan's new role as the leader of world finance isn't taken terribly seriously by Americans. There are the odd voices, to be sure, like New York Congressman Charles Schumer, who worries, "We lost automobiles to the Japanese, we lost steel, and now we're losing financial services—what will we have left?" But to most on Capitol Hill as on Wall Street, Japanese financial surpluses are merely "temporary aberrations." Tokyo's financial markets are judged to be hot-air balloons, due for puncture at any moment. Its bankers and brokers don't have "the right stuff" to go up against the freewheeling, risk-taking American bulls.

It is shocking how much this reasoning sounds like Detroit's auto

executives speaking about the threat of Japanese competition in the
1960s. What is even more shocking is how much greater the stakes
are now. Not surprisingly, the new dimension of the U.S-Japan rivalry
is better understood on the other side of the Pacific. Tokyo's chief
trade negotiator acknowledges that he is preparing for U.S.-Japan
"financial friction" to be worse than the acrimonious trade war of the
1980s.

An executive with Daiwa, Japan's second biggest securities house,
frames the issue bluntly: "It is one thing to compete for a share of the
automobile market, but it is quite another to compete on the financial
battleground. Money is the blood that runs through every economy,
carrying food to the nation's brain and heart. There are those who will
see competition in the field of finance as competition for control of
the body's bloodstream."

I am one of those people. And that is really what this book is all
about.

Before proceeding to analyze this competition, a few cautionary
words are in order. Writing about contemporary financial trends in a
world where volatility is the rule rather than the exception poses significant problems. It is possible, even probable, that major unforeseen
events will take place while this book is current. The U.S. economic
expansion of the Reagan years might continue longer than pessimists
believe possible, breathing renewed—if temporary—strength into
the U.S. dollar. The world economy could be plunged into recession,
with the result that Japanese surpluses shrink and the yen weakens.
The Tokyo Stock Exchange might suffer a catastrophic drop, and Japanese investment abroad could be curtailed. All this would appear to
be at odds with the powerful image of Japan presented here.

But if those events come to pass, don't be fooled. Japan has survived many "shocks" to its system in the last two decades: Nixon's
unilateral decision to scrap the Bretton Woods monetary system, the
first "oil shock" of the early 1970s, the second shock that followed
the revolution in Iran, and the strong yen of recent years which American experts erroneously predicted would devastate its export-reliant
economy. One could make an intriguing scrapbook out of American
press reports heralding the end of the Japanese miracle at each of
these junctures. "Japan's Troubled Future" was the *Fortune* cover
story in the first week of a 1988 fiscal year that would see the country
rebound robustly from the temporary slowdown brought on by the

strong yen.[13] The lesson is that even if Japan falls on hard times again, the gloom is likely to be short-lived. Unlike Americans, the Japanese have evolved planning capabilities and processes to carry out systemic structural economic readjustment to new conditions.

Throughout this book I have made references to "the Japanese" such as the one above, as well as to "Japan," to "the United States," "America," and "Americans." In using these incredibly broad labels for societies that are each so enormously complex, I am trying to isolate the essence of trends in national behavior. I am *not* trying to imply that there is only one exclusive national policy or personality in either country.

This distinction needs to be underscored with regard to *"the Japanese"* because of the tendency Westerners have to see Japan in monolithic terms. My own experience suggests that under the outward appearance of unity, sharply divided factions quarrel within most Japanese boardrooms and government organizations. Minorities, rebels, and unique individuals of all types exist in Japan, and the society as a whole is becoming more pluralistic than it used to be. The big banks want to abolish article 65 (Japan's equivalent of the American Glass-Steagall Act preventing banks from entering the securities business), while even the worldly securities firms that support deregulation in other spheres are trying to preserve article 65 as long as possible. The powerful farming lobby wants to retain today's massive agricultural subsidies, while industrial interests want to end them in order to open up real estate for housing and factories. Japanese workers want higher wages to better enjoy the country's wealth, but employers want them to continue laboring in an austerity mode.

The intrinsic power of the search for consensus is an overwhelming force, however. The weight of even 60 percent of the Japanese nation expressing basic agreement with a certain idea is preponderant, especially when compared with the highly fragmented American context. It is this Japanese majority to which I am referring when I talk about "the Japanese."

I am also aware of the impressive arguments made by many economists suggesting that increased global interdependence makes it nearly impossible to speak in categorical terms about "American" and "Japanese" interests when each side of the equation today includes so many elements of the other. On the symbolic level, the Japanese are crazy about McDonald's, and Americans are enthralled with sushi. On the substantive level, Nomura Securities takes Merrill Lynch's side in pressing Tokyo's Ministry of Finance to open up the stock exchange to foreigners, while AT&T lobbies Washington not to retaliate against its excellent supplier, Toshiba. Shuwa Corporation is a more important player in the U.S. real estate market than on its home turf in Japan, but Max Factor reportedly rings up greater cosmetics sales in the Japanese market than in American department stores.

"They" is often really "us," since a sizable chunk of what U.S. Customs agents designate as "imports" arises not from ruthless foreign competitors taking advantage of America's open markets, but from American companies importing parts and components from their own cheaper-labor manufacturing sites abroad.

Yet it is important to bear in mind that governments are not being globalized as fast as markets are. We dream about a postindustrial world economy, but the prosaic reality is that the Japanese Diet and the U.S. Congress are still disproportionately dominated by representatives of the *preindustrial* interests of farmers, not to mention the lion's share of politicians in both countries whose careers are closely connected to the narrow outlook of traditional smokestack industries and labor unions. A share of stock in IBM may find a single world price whether it is traded in London, Tokyo, or New York. But unemployment rates, interest rates, tax policy, productivity, and profits don't seem to move with such national equanimity. The result is that even as the American and Japanese business worlds become more closely linked, the force of national self-interest is asserted with ugly consequences on both sides.

The epidemic of "Japan-bashing" exemplifies this tendency. But no matter how "unfair" Japan has been, the fault for America's problems cannot lie there. To believe that it does is to accept our own doom. The more we bash, the more the new Japan of the 1990s will bash right back—using those levers of control over our economy we have surrendered. Any real solution to the profound troubles gnawing at the United States must begin with changes we ourselves make.

In the years before Ronald Reagan, Americans worried that our economic system appeared to be growing fat and out of shape. Jimmy Carter even told us we suffered a "national malaise." But no one wanted to hear this, let alone take the radical measures necessary to nurse the economy back to health. In Reagan we found the doctor with the advice we preferred to hear: eat more, exercise less, and let the free market take care of everything.

It would be unfair to put full blame on the Reagan presidency for launching the country down the slippery slope of economic decline. Past administrations, together with forces of history more powerful than any president, had already set that process in motion. What the Reagan era did was dramatically accelerate the pace of decline while masking its dire consequences in a reign of heady unreality.

American politics in the 1980s resembled the classic fable "The Emperor's New Clothes." The president who was supposed to balance the budget allowed America to become the greatest debtor nation in history. The president who invoked rhetoric of "strength" allowed the economy to become more vulnerable to foreign pressure than it has ever been. The president whose tenure was supposed to represent a return to the basic values of the American heartland instead set in motion a frenzy of speculation, paper parasitism, and high living for the few at the expense of the many and of the future. The president known as the "Great Communicator" hollered barely audible reassurances about the faltering economy over the noise of helicopter propellers on the White House lawn.

Instead of addressing the economic challenges at hand, the president simply "borrowed a trillion dollars from the Japanese and threw a party," as New York Senator Daniel Patrick Moynihan dryly observed.[14] The "quick fixes" used by the Reagan White House to produce the economic expansion of 1983–88 have thus bequeathed a staggering bill that must now be paid.

By wrapping America in the myth that greatness could be achieved by doing more of what we had done in the past rather than undergoing any reevaluation or change, precious time was lost to the cause of stemming the American decline. And precious time was gained by our Japanese rivals.

There is still time, although we are quickly losing it, to prevent the U.S. economy from spinning into an irreversible downward spiral. There are also many ways to cope more intelligently with Japan's inevitable rise. This book, while it makes suggestions, does not contain fully elaborated answers. It is written more as a report—a report from the front lines of a war that has not yet been declared. It is my hope that by focusing attention on the high stakes in the conflict, the discussion in this volume can contribute to the urgent dialogue we must have on these questions and help prevent the worst-case scenarios from coming to pass.

1

Japan as Banker to the World

Japan is fast becoming the leading economic power in the world.... There have been other occasions when leadership has passed from one nation to another...but there has been no transfer of economic power as rapid as the one now taking place.

—George Soros, principal adviser of the Quantum Fund[1]

Live Lobster Sashimi

Masaaki Kurokawa is not exactly a household name in the United States, but he is one of the most important financial executives in the world. He works for Nomura Securities—a company whose own name was barely known on Wall Street just a few years ago. Today Nomura is not only Japan's largest securities company, it is the largest in the world. It dwarfs all those companies whose names are so much more familiar in the West. "In a takeover financed with stock," *Fortune* recently remarked, "Nomura could swallow Merrill Lynch like a bit of predinner *sashimi.*" [2]

Kurokawa is chairman of Nomura Securities International, the New York–based subsidiary of the giant Japanese firm. He is the quintessential "triad man"—a frequent flyer along the London-New York-Tokyo financial axis that captivates the imagination of Japanese financial houses like a three-fronted war. Before his posting to New York, he served as chairman of Nomura's London operation. Wherever Kurokawa lives, he makes monthly pilgrimages to Tokyo to participate in the shaping of worldwide strategy.

If Japanese businessmen sometimes appear to Westerners to be cut of the same blue-suited piece, Masaaki Kurokawa is a clear exception. Tall and powerfully built, he exudes an aura that is at once charismatic and mysterious. Some view him with trepidation: "Nomura is a cult, and Kurokawa is its Jim Jones," says an executive of a rival Japanese firm. Others are reverential: "Not too many people on Wall Street can match his thinking power," notes an American who works for him.

Nomura's international operations were the theater of an internal power struggle not long ago. According to company insiders, Kurokawa sought to bring an end to the regime of Yoshio ("Terry") Terasawa, his predecessor for many years at the helm of the American subsidiary. Among other issues, Kurokawa charged Terasawa with allowing Nomura to become "too Americanized."

The two men are like polar-opposite Gemini twins. Both in their fifties, they came up together through the same path, getting some of their education in the United States (Kurokawa at Wisconsin, Terasawa at Wharton) and devoting their entire careers to Nomura. When they started, Japan was still trying to recover from wartime devastation. Activity on the Tokyo Stock Exchange was negligible, and brokerage firms had little influence. But three decades later Kurokawa and Terasawa sat together near the top of Nomura's organizational pyramid with $50 billion worth of the company's market capitalization underneath them.

That Terry Terasawa had "Americanized" his operation in New York was indisputable. He was well liked by Nomura's American staff and had become the single best-known spokesman for Japanese finance in the English-speaking world. He not only understood the American realities, he appreciated them. On returning to Tokyo, he even complained of experiencing a certain sadness at attending a meeting of new Nomura recruits and seeing "the same face" wearing "the same clothes" everywhere. "In New York," Terasawa recalled, "I could not attend a meeting of this size without seeing blacks, whites, and Orientals, and a good balance of men and women. America's mix of people is exciting because it represents a mix of ideas we don't have in Japan."

Faced with the assignment of making Nomura a real force on Wall Street, Terasawa proposed using some of the company's $4 billion cash on hand to buy a top-tier American investment bank with the needed expertise and talent. He wanted to give local American executives real decision-making power and advocated recruiting a CEO from an American brokerage firm, even if it meant paying him a $2 million salary—more than ten times what Nomura's president in Tokyo is paid.

Masaaki Kurokawa disagreed. The key to Nomura's success, he reportedly insisted, lay in continuing to do things the way Nomura had always done them—to build principally from within and to rely on tried-and-true Japanese management methods. To allow Nomura's American operation to be run by a bunch of "butter-breath" foreigners with no loyalty to Tokyo would be a strategic mistake. Kurokawa didn't oppose American staff in principle—it would be impossible to do business without hundreds of them—but real power should remain with those on the Tokyo track.

Kurokawa won the struggle. As a result, he not only took over Terasawa's job but moved into line ahead of him as a likely candidate to return to Tokyo as president of the entire company sometime in the 1990s. Terasawa was shunted aside to do ceremonial duties on behalf of Nomura and, perhaps eventually, to be loaned out to the World Bank. Some American staff members resigned over the change in New York's corporate direction. But their resignations mattered little to those who held the Kurokawa line. The good thing about the lack of American corporate loyalty was that when somebody left, another could always be found to replace him.

The struggle was symbolic of wider issues. Should Japanese financial institutions continue to follow their American role models? Or had the time come for the Japanese to take the lead? Does "internationalization" mean changing Japanese ways to be more like the rest of the world? Or does it mean asserting Japan's leadership more aggressively in foreign countries? Terasawa's argument amounted to "Since we are in Rome, we should do as the Romans do." Kurokawa's retort could be synopsized as "Since Rome is falling and we are gaining strength, it's better to do things our way." Back at headquarters, Kurokawa's view accurately reflected the mainstream of thought.

Shortly after emerging victorious in this debate, Kurokawa entertained American guests in a restaurant at the top of one of the several buildings owned by Nomura in Tokyo. This one was in the Shinjuku district, fifty stories above the city's swirling neon and never-ending sprawl. His voice was deep and resonant. The drama of what he had to say was reaching its crescendo.

"We Japanese will have to come up with much bolder ideas to play our role properly in the world," he asserted, pausing to watch as his guests attempted to eat the live lobster sashimi in front of them. Kurokawa said he had a plan for how Japan could help the United States solve its trade deficit: the already mighty yen, which was then trading around 140 to the dollar, should be strengthened further until it reached 100 to the dollar. This, he said, would make Japan incapable of earning a profit on export products. The United States would no longer see its domestic industries threatened by Japanese imports.

Next, a single joint currency would be created, "dollar on one side, yen on the other." This way Japan could invest freely in the United States without worrying that American fiscal profligacy would weaken the dollar and thereby lower the value of investment portfolios. And what would Japan get in return?

"California," he said. The name of the state hung in the air for a moment; the still living lobster's antennae twitched.

Kurokawa resumed. California would be turned into a joint U.S.-Japan economic community to be shared by both countries. "No visas needed for Japanese to come and go," he said with a wave of his hand. Japan would export several million workers and build new factories to take advantage of "cheap" California real estate. (Kurokawa meant no offense to Californians who think their real estate is expensive; he was only comparing costs. A two-thousand-square-foot condominium in Tokyo had just sold that week for $12.4 million; a piece of land the size of two open pages in this book was going for $20,000.)

The rise of the yen had also turned American labor into "cheap labor" for Japanese employers. Like most Japanese, Kurokawa disdained the current state of U.S. workmanship, but he believed it was possible, with the proper Japanese methods, to retrain American workers. By manufacturing on American soil, Japanese-owned companies would be woven into the basic fabric of American life, lowering the risk of protectionist legislation that might someday close off the U.S. market. Kurokawa explained that if his experiment worked out well, it could be expanded to other areas of the West Coast.

All this was "just an idea," Kurokawa hastened to add. Just food for thought, not an actual agenda item. But he emphasized that in his opinion a radical change of some type was necessary to maintain order in the U.S.-Japan relationship. Although some Americans might feel threatened by the thought of a Japanese financier proposing to turn California into a common market, the irony is that in Kuro-kawa's long-range strategic view, such a measure would help *reduce* the threat Americans might otherwise feel if events simply continue along their present course.

Kurokawa is not the first Japanese to come up with an agenda of "bold ideas." In January of 1959 *The Wall Street Journal* reported that Toyota's bold visionaries were taking "a big gamble" with their plan to export more than seven hundred of their cars, then known as "Toyopets," to the United States. The *Journal* quoted a Toyota official who said, "By 1960, Americans are expected to import 500,000 cars annually. Why shouldn't we get part of this market?"[3]

Based on the history of U.S.-Japan economic relations since the arrival of the Toyopets, it would be unwise to continue underestimating either Japanese ambitions or abilities.

The World's Leading Creditor

That Nomura could make the transition from a firm virtually unknown on Wall Street five years ago to one whose executives brainstorm about ideas as far-reaching as a joint U.S.-Japan currency or a Californian common market is a product of Japan's new role as the world's leading creditor nation.

A creditor nation is one whose investments abroad exceed the size of foreign investments in its own economy. A debtor nation is one that owes foreigners more than the sum of its own assets abroad. Creditor nations obviously have a lot of leverage over those to whom they lend their money; debtor nations often become subservient to the interests of their creditors.

Japan replaced the United States as the world's leading creditor in 1986. The scope of recent Japanese capital outflows has been likened to the period in the 1950s and 1960s when the United States bought up much of Western European industry, but Japanese acquisitions over the last few years have actually far outstripped the American expansion of those days. In fact, Japan's net external assets already surpass by 20 percent the American record established over a thirty-seven-year period.

Every single working day, Japanese individuals and corporations generate over a billion dollars' worth of savings. This excess cash rushes into domestic bank accounts, stocks, insurance premiums, and real estate speculation, but even these institutions can't hold it all. Like water seeking its own level, a large amount of it *must* flow abroad. In 1981 Japanese traded foreign securities worth a total of $15 billion for the year. In 1986 the figure was $2.6 trillion—growth by a factor of 175 in five years' time. A newly popular Japanese saying summarizes the situation: "It took Britain one hundred years and the United States fifty years to become the richest country in the world, but it only took Japan five."

Japan's ascendancy to world leadership on the positive side of the ledger has been mirrored by America's fall into debt. A creditor nation since 1914, the United States became a net debtor for the first time in the 1980s. Its red ink ran quickly past Brazil, Mexico, and Argentina all the way to the position of world's leading debtor. By the year 2000, Japanese net external assets may reach +$1,000,000,000,000 (positive one trillion dollars). The figure for the United States could be −$1,000,000,000,000 (negative one trillion dollars).

To begin to grasp what this historic role reversal means, a short review of some of the ways Japan's financial influence is currently manifesting itself is in order:

- The United States has come to depend on Japanese investors to directly finance as much as 30 percent of the American government's budget deficit. Throughout 1985–87, the leading Japanese securities firms were almost always among the largest buyers of long-term U.S. Treasury bonds at auction. Several Japanese-owned firms are primary dealers in securities issued by the U.S. government. Without Japanese participation, it is safe to say the Treasury would have an extremely difficult time financing American debt.
- All ten of the world's ten largest banks (ranked by deposits) are today Japanese. Only one American bank—Citicorp—even makes the somewhat more broadly defined list of the world's top ten bank holding companies. Thirty years ago not a single Japanese bank was counted in the world's top fifty; as recently as 1980 only one Japanese bank ranked in the American-led top ten.
- The "Big Four" Japanese securities companies—Nomura, Daiwa, Nikko, and Yamaichi—are four of the largest securities firms in the world today. In terms of market capitalization, Nomura is currently more than twenty times the size of Merrill Lynch, the largest Amer-

ican brokerage house. Nomura's pretax profits in 1987—$4.1 billion—were about the same as the profits of the entire U.S.
securities industry.

- If U.S. subsidiaries of Japanese-owned companies (Nissan, Honda,
  Sony, and the like) were ranked in the *Fortune* 500, they would
  already account for thirty of the biggest U.S. industrial corporations. The Japanese-owned sector is growing 400 percent faster
  than the rest of the U.S. economy on the strength of direct investments approaching $10 billion for 1987 and an estimated $15 billion for 1988.
- A quarter-million Americans already work for Japanese employers
  in the United States. Economists expect that number to rise to a
  million in the 1990s.
- The total value of all stocks listed on the Tokyo Stock Exchange
  surpassed the total value of all stocks listed on the New York Stock
  Exchange early in 1987. Tokyo's lead has continued to widen since.
  A single Japanese company—Nippon Telegraph & Telephone
  (NTT)—is worth more than IBM, AT&T, General Motors, General
  Electric, and Exxon *combined*.
- The Osaka Stock Exchange, which even Asia-conscious American
  financial professionals know precious little about, is now bigger
  than the American Stock Exchange in market value and is the fourth
  largest stock exchange in the world.
- Chicago's Board of Trade recently launched nighttime hours to accommodate Japanese interested in U.S. bond futures. Now Tokyo
  traders can move the market during *their* daytime hours, while most
  American traders sleep. The Japanese were responsible for a record
  run-up in seat prices on both the Chicago Board of Trade and the
  Mercantile Exchange. The Merc has invited a leading Japanese financier to join its board of governors.
- Japanese banks control nearly 10 percent of the U.S. retail banking
  assets—up from next to nothing a decade ago. Assets of Japanese
  banks in the United States are so great that they now rival the
  combined assets of Citicorp and J. P. Morgan.
- In trend-setting California, five of the top ten banks are now Japanese. Bank of America, the world's most successful retail bank in
  the 1970s, was rescued from impending collapse by a Japanese
  consortium. When Los Angeles–based Union Bank was put up for
  sale, two American banks, Chase and Citicorp, expressed interest

in buying it but were prevented from doing so by interstate banking regulations. Instead, Union Bank was bought by California First, which is mostly owned by Bank of Tokyo.

- Japanese financial service companies have not only penetrated but actually *monopolized* several areas of domestic U.S. finance, such as the letter of credit business guaranteeing municipal bond underwritings. American banks, generally speaking, no longer maintain the credit ratings necessary to enter this business, now thoroughly dominated by Japanese banks.

- Japanese companies, with lower overhead and longer time horizons, are gaining prominence in important areas of domestic finance abandoned as unprofitable by Americans. When Salomon Brothers shut down its pioneering municipal bond department and laid off eight hundred people in 1987, Nomura's U.S. subsidiary simultaneously launched a new foray into American public finance.

- Some of the most hallowed names on Wall Street are being acquired in whole or in part by Japanese companies. Sumitomo Bank now owns a significant minority interest in Goldman Sachs, which had been a private investment banking partnership for over a century; Nippon Life holds a similar share of Shearson Lehman Hutton; Yasuda Mutual Life owns an even bigger share of Paine Webber.

- Japanese investors bought about $18 billion worth of prime U.S. real estate over the last three years. Among the notables in New York: the Tiffany, Mobil, Exxon, and ABC buildings, 666 Fifth Avenue, and a chunk of the Citicorp tower; in southern California, Arco Plaza, La Costa Spa Resort, and one-third of all downtown L.A. office buildings; in Washington, D.C., the U.S. News & World Report Building; in Las Vegas, the Dunes Hotel. Continuing to buy such high-visibility flagships, Japanese investors are now moving into office and commercial real estate in cities such as Atlanta, Boston, Indianapolis, Cleveland, and Charlotte.

- In Hawaii, Japanese investors own more than 75 percent of the equity in the twenty hotels along the Waikiki beachfront—just a small part of their $6.5 billion Hawaiian realty portfolio. "Although the U.S. flag still flies there, Hawaii looks to be well on the way to becoming an economic colony of Japan," observed *Forbes* recently.[4]

- Japanese companies now dominate the financing of U.S. commercial real estate projects over $100 million. Expanding heavily in construction, Japanese business interests can now buy U.S. properties, finance their development, and perform the construction work without recourse to American partners.

- Although hostile takeovers are rare in Japan, a few cash-rich Japanese companies have begun to play corporate raider in the United States. Dainippon, for example, went after Reichhold Chemical and finally got it in a protracted fight.

- While American venture capitalists have pulled back from high technology, Japanese financiers have filled the vacuum. One in fifteen new funding dollars for young high-tech companies now comes from Japanese sources, who see involvement with these innovative entrepreneurs as a "window" on the latest American advances. "If you look at recent risky high-tech start-ups, you see that money is easier to come by from outside the U.S. than inside," says Warren Wheeler, president of Gain Electronics in New Jersey. Japan's Mitsui invested more than $20 million in his venture into high-performance gallium arsenide chips.

- The flow of investment is not limited to such areas of traditional expertise as manufacturing. Sony recently acquired CBS Records, the largest record company in the United States, for $2 billion. This is a harbinger of Japanese investment in the service sector of the American economy, which is so often judged to be the area of greatest future growth.

- Japanese collectors are now the principal force in the international art market. They have not only set eye-popping individual records (such as the purchase of Vincent van Gogh's *Sunflowers* at a London auction for nearly $40 million), but at a typical Christie's auction recently, they swept up five of the ten most expensive pieces and accounted for half of the evening's total sale.

- Although the central focus of Japanese investment activity has been the United States, the same trends can be seen worldwide. In 1985 not a single Japanese firm ranked among the top ten lead managers of London-based Eurobond offerings. Two years later Nomura claimed the top spot; the rest of the Japanese Big Four finished among the top ten.

- With a one-third market share of Britain's international banking transactions, Japanese financial institutions have been accused of "overpresence" and urged to curtail their activities. From London's Big Bang to Toronto's "little bang," from the Paris Bourse to the

Frankfurt Börse, the Japanese are often cited as the prime movers in sudden market changes.

OPEC of the Eighties

Those who wish to make light of the strategic significance of Japanese capital surpluses argue that Japan is merely the "OPEC of the eighties." By this they mean Japan's role as a capital-surplus nation is only a temporary phenomenon produced by certain unique macroeconomic circumstances that have already begun to change. Those who hold this view believe Japanese surpluses will dissipate in due course, and U.S.-Japan financial relations will be restored to a state of balance.

But even if Japan's destiny is limited to mimicking OPEC's history of temporarily collecting and recycling much of the world's disposable cash, the implications will be far-reaching nonetheless. Although OPEC today is a shadow of its former self, the power it wielded in its prime shouldn't be forgotten. Not only did the wealth of its members hold the key to war and peace throughout a vast and turbulent region of the world, its policies churned the economy of every single industrialized nation. Many of the basic themes of U.S. economic decline can be traced back to how American business responded to the challenge of rapid inflation of energy prices in the 1970s. This is particularly true of the deindustrialization and disinvestment in manufacturing that took place during that time. Smokestack industries that could not adapt to sharply higher energy costs closed down, never to reopen. Merger mania was born when traditional companies suddenly decided to shed basic businesses and find something less sensitive to oil prices. The inflationary cycle took prime lending rates over 20 percent, making it appear foolish to borrow money to rebuild productive capacity. Mistaken valuations bankers placed on Third World energy assets opened the door to loans that now hang like a Damoclean sword over global economic stability.

In Japan, meanwhile, the rise of oil prices in the 1970s turned out to be a blessing in the disguise of terrible austerity. The "oil shocks" reined in the rising expectations of Japanese workers, enabling Japan to maintain low-cost labor advantages over Western countries well into the 1980s. It was skyrocketing oil bills, moreover, that led Japanese economic planners to dramatically intensify their development of export industries. Among other new markets they found was the fuel-efficiency niche left wide open by the U.S. auto industry.

These were just a few of the repercussions of OPEC's brief moment in the sun. This history bears mention only to recall the kind of dislocation set in motion by the sudden concentration of wealth in OPEC countries. Even if Japan's role is limited "only" to being another OPEC, similarly drastic consequences may arise, especially since Japan has already accumulated greater total foreign assets than OPEC enjoyed at its peak.

But what if OPEC's balance sheet had not just reflected holdings of a single raw material subject to world supply and demand, but instead had been the product of a diversified range of economic undertakings connected to the arteries of the international economy at a hundred different critical junctures?

What if OPEC had been a single, compact, unified nation, with the world's most efficient factories, most advanced production technology, second largest GNP, and second largest consumer marketplace? What if OPEC had been able to develop a consensus around a common long-term economic plan? What if some of OPEC's richest members had not destroyed their wealth in internecine revolutions and wars? What if instead of fearing the volatility of stock markets and the Koranic injunction against usury, OPEC had created the world's biggest stock market in Mecca and developed the world's best-capitalized financial institutions with hundreds of global subsidiaries? What if, instead of allowing its wealth to be managed by others, OPEC had dispatched thousands of its own best and brightest to become expert at global finance and to oversee an active, well-coordinated plan for investment of its assets?

Comparing Japan with OPEC is a useful analogy, *if* one takes into account Japan's vastly better set of circumstances for the maintenance and enhancement of its wealth.

Zaitek and the Symbol Economy

Money has always "made the world go 'round," but never more so than today. Japan has become the leading creditor nation not just at any random time in history, but at a time when a single world financial supermarket and a single world economy are being forged. Assets everywhere are being "equitized" and put up for sale. Entities once considered too strategic to be subjected to market forces—national

telephone companies, airlines, and energy monopolies, for example—are being spun off by governments to private investors. Even
socialist countries have joined the equity revolution, creating fledg-
ling stock markets.

These are the "days of lasers in the jungle," when people swap
fixed-rate dollar debt for floating-rate yen in an electronic flash. Anyone at a computer keyboard can trade Swiss francs and D-marks, pork
bellies, gold bullion, options on stock indexes, equities in Silicon
Valley or Sydney, Eurobonds or Eurodollars, pools of debt backed by
mortgages, or credit card bills.

We are witnessing the growth of what Peter Drucker calls the
"symbol economy."[5] Capital, credit, and currency flood across
borders in such a deluge that they replace the "real economy" of
goods and services. The transborder flow of funds is now thirty times
larger than merchandise trade. The symbol economy has become the
force driving all other economic activity. It is the common language
preventing world business from turning into a Tower of Babel. It is
the benchmark that gives definition to the future, whether that future
is measured in units of thirty days or thirty years.

The Roaring Eighties in American business gave us a taste of the
symbol economy in action. The wave of mergers and acquisitions,
LBOs, junk bonds, recapitalizations, and new techniques of corporate
cash management yielded a situation in which Wall Street became the
tail wagging the dog of American industry. Suddenly, smart young
investment bankers sitting at computer terminals contemplating the
green phosphor of Lotus 1–2–3 became more important than the
CEOs, workers, and products of the distant company whose vital
statistics were stored in the spreadsheet. Little-known investors took
over famous corporations. The mere threat that a company might be
"put in play" was enough to cause it to jettison conservative fiscal
policies for debt-laden restructuring schemes.

American financiers designed the symbol economy, extended its
modus operandi to the rest of the world, and made tens of billions of
dollars in doing so. But it is the Japanese who will reap maximum use
of the new opportunities Americans have created. Japan is now in the
enviable position of being able to simultaneously play both Lee Iacocca and Carl Icahn on the world scene. On the Iacocca side, the
Japanese show no sign of weakening their commitment to the "real
economy" of manufacturing and traditional trade. On the Icahn side,
Japan is becoming the leader of the incipient symbol economy by

virtue of having the greatest capital resources to export. With high savings, a persistent trade surplus, and low interest rates, Japan is the "low-cost producer" of capital resources. Conversely, the United States with low savings, a structural trade deficit, and high interest rates is the "high-cost producer." Everyone knows who wins over time when high-cost and low-cost producers compete.

A new word has been coined to describe Japan's particular use of the symbol economy—*zaitek*. Made up of the Japanese character for finance, *zai,* and the English-sounding phoneme "tek," the word in its original connotation meant making money the new-fashioned way— through electronic wheeling and dealing from the desktop. Traditionally, Japanese corporations shunned active management of their cash assets and disdained investment profits as less honorable than profits earned from basic industrial operations. But when Washington began forcing up the yen, many Japanese companies had little choice but to turn to *zaitek* techniques to make up for the profit squeeze they faced on the operating side. Early in 1987 fully 50 percent of the profits of Tokyo Stock Exchange–listed companies were derived from investments rather than operations.

The most publicized *zaitek* stratagems involved big corporations issuing bonds with low interest rates, either because the company had a AAA credit rating (as many cash-rich Japanese giants do) or because the bonds had equity warrants attached. In the rampage of Tokyo's Nikkei index during 1986–87, some companies like Mitsubishi Corporation were able to issue warrant bonds that essentially carried no interest because bond buyers expected to achieve their return—and usually did—through conversions into significantly appreciated stock. Having gathered billions of dollars' worth of such low- or no-interest funds, *zaitek* practitioners then turned around and invested the proceeds in higher-yielding instruments, ranging from U.S. Treasuries to junk bonds. Sometimes the profits were fat (swapping funds raised from a 1 percent warrant bond into an 8.5 percent U.S. Treasury bond), and sometimes they were dangerously thin (swapping funds from a Eurobond offering at 8.3 percent into a loan on the domestic market to a less creditworthy company at 8.5 percent).

The regulatory authorities in Japan took a dim view of the risks involved in some of Japan's biggest industrial companies and trading houses functioning essentially as banks (and freewheeling merchant banks at that). A few notable casualties of excessive speculation did occur, such as a $193 million bond-trading loss at Tateho Chemical Industries, which sent a momentary panic through the marketplace. But the normally stringent Japanese regulators took no steps to halt *zaitek*. They understood that the essence of these activities had to do with Japanese corporations learning to manage their vast assets and to take advantage of the new global opportunities before them.

If Japan enjoys a potent offensive advantage in global finance by being able to raise money domestically at low cost and invest it abroad at high yield, it simultaneously employs the industrial world's best financial defense as well. While Japanese money has poured into the bloodstream of other countries, Tokyo's own capital markets remain substantially closed to foreigners by culture if not by regulation. Japan has liberalized a great deal of its financial structure, and some American and other foreign firms are experiencing success in penetrating the system. But foreigners remain "flies on the Japanese elephant's ass," to quote an earthy American investment banker who spent a dozen years trying to crack the Tokyo financial market. To this day, for example, foreigners are barred from owning shares in NTT—the most important stock traded on the Tokyo exchange. At a period in time when Japanese firms regularly buy 30–50 percent of long-term American Treasury bonds, the Ministry of Finance (MoF) has only reluctantly agreed to allow foreigners a bit more than the traditional 0.07 percent participation in the syndicate that distributes the heavily traded ten-year Japanese government bonds.

In keeping with the needs of a debtor nation, the United States must open its doors ever wider to foreign participation in the economy. Japan, as a creditor nation, has the luxury of choosing when and how to allow foreigners access to its markets. So far it has chosen to keep the key controls firmly in Japanese hands, despite enormous pressure for faster and broader liberalization from the U.S. government and American financial firms.

A Pax Nipponica?

It is no mere accident of history that the world's leading creditor nation generally proves to be the world's most influential nation as well. The ability to export capital provides an extraordinarily efficient lever for controlling events around the globe. This trend can be seen in its primitive form going back at least as far as the Spanish and Dutch empires. It is more relevant after the birth of modern finance, when Britain's role as leading creditor (and the pound sterling's role as key currency) lay at the very foundation of the empire and of the period of nineteenth-century history known as "Pax Britannica."

In the twentieth century, a nearly one-to-one correspondence exists between America's role as creditor and its level of influence on the global scene. As soon as the United States became a creditor nation in 1914, it immediately found good reason to raise an army and involve itself in a European war. After World War II, when the United States took over Britain's former role as leading creditor, the dollar became the key currency, and a "Pax Americana" ensued. Since the mid-1980s, as the United States has become a debtor nation, the dollar's influence has waned, and America can no longer lead the world as forcefully as it once did.

Obviously this history cannot be reliably reduced into a mechanical formula, "Leading Creditor = Leading Global Power." Too many other forces are at work, and it is often hard to tell the causes from the effects. But history does emphasize a close correlation between the country that dominates world finance and the country that most influences the world in other ways—industrially, technologically, and politically. The experience of England is particularly instructive because it shows that a country need not have a large land area or extensive natural resources to build a global economic empire.

But can Japan recapitulate the pattern of Pax Britannica and Pax Americana with a "Pax Nipponica"?

As students of history know, the "Pax"—both Britannica and Americana—was a peace born of war. Both prior eras of global hegemony relied not only on financial leadership, but on many other kinds of power, the most visible being military. Japan today is not widely considered to be a military power, since its American-imposed postwar constitution specifically prohibits it from such a role, and the one percent of GNP that constitutes its defense budget is the lowest such allocation of any major economy. The gross disparity between Japan's strength as an economic power and its weakness as a military power would at first blush seem to render the idea of Pax Nipponica impossible.

Yet a compelling case for Pax Nipponica can be made, depending on exactly how the concept is defined and bearing in mind that since no two periods of world history are alike, no two styles of world leadership need be similar to achieve the same effects. Just as the United States managed to lead the world without Britain's extensive system of physical colonies, Japan may find it possible to lead the world without an American-style global military machine.

If one assumes that (1) the risk of global war is low because of the nuclear balance of terror, (2) the likelihood of a Soviet or Chinese threat to Japan is minimal as a result of internal changes in those countries, and (3) in the era of high-tech warfare, Japan is perfectly capable of building adequate conventional defense systems at reasonable cost, then development of a grand military strategy becomes largely irrelevant to the exercise of Japanese influence on a world scale.

Under those assumptions Japan could avoid the pitfalls of heavy military spending and continue using its surplus capital to reinvest in its own global economic leadership. Meanwhile the superpowers would continue to bankrupt their own economies through the arms race and thus diminish their global influence.

Ezra Vogel, the Harvard scholar whose book *Japan as Number One* shocked many American businessmen just by its title when it appeared in 1979, envisions a certain kind of Pax Nipponica arising from such conditions. He predicts that the already vast competitive strengths of Japanese industry and trade could become so awesome that future world development would necessitate a system of self-imposed Japanese restraints. Japan's ability to dictate the terms of such solutions—rather than armies, navies, or missiles—could become the basis of a "limited" Pax Nipponica, Vogel argues.[6]

Despite Japan's pacifist bent—and despite the degree of economic success the country has achieved precisely because of its undercommitment to the military sector—it is not altogether clear that Japan will continue to avoid the quest for martial power. Short of imagining a Japan that becomes militarily expansionistic once again—a possibility that should not be entirely discounted, given the noisy right-wing demonstrators who frequently fill Tokyo's streets in support of rearmament—any change in the assumptions about the balance of forces cited above could cause Tokyo to radically shift its defense policy.

The issues affecting Japan's potential remilitarization are examined in greater detail in chapter 11. But they deserve to be put on the table briefly here, since they are usually glossed over on the theory that the military component of the U.S.-Japan relationship has been permanently fixed. Military power is supposed to be the one area of clear-cut American strength and explicit Japanese weakness. The unstated assumption behind the blithe attitude exhibited by much of America's power elite in the face of Japan's growing economic strength is that Japan cannot pose a real threat to American interests as long as its own security is dependent on a defense treaty with the United States.

Yet Japan's wealth will inevitably alter even this seemingly institutionalized relationship. It has already begun to do so. The commitment of one percent of Japan's GNP to national defense seemed like a token sum when the limit was first set. Yet today one percent of Japan's huge GNP places it in a dead heat with Britain as the world's third biggest military spender. What's more, as Washington tries to reduce the chasm between the far-reaching nature of current American military commitments and dwindling economic resources to finance them, Japan, like other American allies, is being encouraged to "burden-share." Burden-sharing, in fact, is becoming politically urgent. Congressmen angered by Japan's trade policies find it increasingly unconscionable to approve U.S. military budgets that include billions of dollars for Japan's defense. The yen is so strong that the American servicemen stationed in Japan can't afford to make ends meet with their dollar-based salaries.

American politicians seem to be gravitating toward the demand that Japan increase defense spending to 3 percent. But if that were to happen—if the Japanese were to start spending around $100 billion a year on defense in the 1990s—the geopolitical repercussions would be stunning. With such a small territory to defend and with the likelihood that the Japanese could achieve more "bang for the buck" in their weapons systems than either Washington or Moscow, the ramp-up to independent military power could be far more rapid than is widely assumed. Certainly Japan will try to profit as long as possible from its undercommitment to the military sector, even as the U.S. economy continues to be bled by overcommitment. But ultimately it seems unlikely that the Japanese will attempt to build the first modern empire unable to protect and advance its interests with armed force.

The military issue is not the only one determining whether or not there will be a Pax Nipponica. The consensus of contemporary economists and political scientists holds that the world is moving away from the long-standing bipolarity of American and Soviet spheres of interest. A multipolar arrangement is already beginning to take shape in which a greater variety of countries and regional blocs share power. According to this view, neither Japan nor any other country is likely to again achieve the degree of single-nation dominance experienced at the height of Pax Americana.

The reforms of Deng Xiaoping and Mikhail Gorbachev, each in their own way, make it possible to imagine that over time the Chinese and Soviet economies will become centers of real influence in global manufacturing, trade, and finance—in addition to the powerful military and political positions they already command.

West Germany is much like Japan in the sense that it has welded productivity, technological excellence, a high savings rate, and a strong currency into a tower of economic strength. Other European economies, borrowing a few leaves from the Japanese books on protectionism and industrial policy, are experiencing success in restoring a measure of their world competitiveness. Since the "Big Bang" of 1986, London has played the role of Europe's international financial center, adding a bit of luster to Britain's faded glory. The EEC's plan to further integrate financial and other markets in 1992 and to expand usage of the European Currency Unit could finally yield the long-sought promise of a unified Europe whose economy is stronger and more vigorous than today's America.

In Asia, meanwhile, the "little dragons" (Korea, Taiwan, Singapore, and Hong Kong) are successfully following Japan's path to the high-growth miracle, as are newly industrializing countries (NICs) elsewhere. The next time the world faces shortages of oil, we will all be reminded of the power still residing under the deserts and in the jungles of oil-producing countries.

Amid all these new centers of power, the United States, of course, is certainly not to be forgotten. No matter how much America's traditional industrial base erodes, the arrival of the information age presents new possibilities for certain vibrant regions (Silicon Valley, Route 128, for example) and certain advanced sectors of American business to exert their share of global leadership very far into the future. While the United States may suffer a partial "Britainization" as it declines, it might be spared Britain's steep, fast fall from the pinnacle, especially if new policies come to the fore. "Even when it has declined to the position of occupying no more than its natural share of the world's wealth and power . . . the United States will still be a very significant power in a multipolar world, simply because of its size," predicts historian Paul Kennedy.[7]

Yet while the world of tomorrow is likely to have a multiplicity of power centers, one should not rush to conclude that such diffusion prevents a single nation from exerting a predominant influence— especially when that nation is Japan. Precisely because power will be more differentiated than it has been in the past, Japan need not monopolize it to exert extraordinary influence. Reporters covering the 1988 economic summit in Toronto—Ronald Reagan's farewell party with the rest of the industrial world's leaders—already observed the Japanese delegation "acting like the Americans used to" at such meetings. Being just one rank above the rest of the world's leading economies may be a suitably subtle Japanese way of asserting itself. It could also be a very cost-beneficial one, enabling Japan to enjoy most of the benefits of world economic leadership without being obliged to pay for the rest of the world's security or development.

In the end, the crystallization of Pax Nipponica may have much to do with Japan's relationships to other Asian countries. Lately it has become fashionable to speak of the twenty-first century as the "Pacific Century." And for good reason. Many east Asian countries—not only Japan—have been at the top of the world's economic growth charts for the last two decades. Nearly 2,500 years after the death of Confucius, his influence is still deeply felt in this part of the world, encouraging such virtues as hard work; productivity; education; consensus building; national unity; the willingness to sacrifice for family, company, and country; long-term planning; high-quality civil service; and a preference for saving rather than consuming and for prosperity rather than politics. Mastering the complexities inherent in character writing and the abacus, among other factors, seems to predispose the children of these cultures to an affinity for mathematics, engineering, and other valuable technical skills.

Clearly, most of the countries of the Pacific Rim are well suited for the challenges of the period ahead and are likely to make spectacular economic strides. The shift of world business, technology, and trade to the Pacific region is already such an obvious pattern that both Ronald Reagan and Mikhail Gorbachev have tried to gain admission to the conceptual definition of the "Pacific Century" by emphasizing the fact that their countries too have Pacific coasts and vital Pacific interests.

But there is also a sense in which the "Pacific Century" is more properly viewed as a euphemism for the "Japanese Century." The popular image of the "little dragons" hot on Japan's heels is not quite accurate. Singapore and Hong Kong, while exceedingly successful, are both city-states where domestic output is less than in Japan's third largest city, Osaka. Taiwan and South Korea, while very important as trading states, are a long way from approximating the scope and diversity of Japanese industry. Both are highly militarized economies facing large unanswered political questions about their future. As for the biggest potential dragon of all, China, even her most optimistic planners believe two more decades of uninterrupted peace and continued reform are needed to obtain the level of economic development typical of Japan around 1980.

That some of these countries will outcompete Japan in producing lower-cost industrial goods for export is inevitable and is already happening. But it is happening in no small part because Japanese industry is moving offshore to these locations—investing, building factories, and transferring some low-end technology. While the Asian NICs may gain export markets at Japan's expense in VCRs, computer chips, and low-priced cars, the Japanese ultimately win more than they lose by developing the rest of the Pacific region into a haven for investment, low-cost sourcing of components, and markets for their own high-end products.

The appropriate analogy here is the American relationship to Western Europe in the 1950s and 1960s. The domination of Atlantic markets by American multinational corporations and the immense political leverage obtained in Europe was integrally bound up with the rise of the United States to global supremacy. Even though individual European economies were themselves among the world's strongest, European leaders from Gaullists to socialists frequently decried their exploitation at American hands.

Today, from Thailand to China, complaints of Japanese exploitation of local economies are heard with increasing frequency. The prospect of the "Pacific Century" serving largely as veneer and context to what will actually be a "Japanese Century" (at least until China matures) is quite real.

Debtor's Burdens and the Argentina Syndrome

Most Americans have never known a world in which our nation was not preeminent. Our language is the international language, our dollar is the international currency, our economy is the fulcrum on which the world economy balances, our news is news everywhere, our popular culture is the global standard, and our armed forces provide the free world's security umbrella.

Are we ready for life in a world where we are no longer the richest and the most powerful? We have adapted once to coexisting with another superpower, but that adaptation only came after a "cold war" skirting the brink of world destruction. Even today, coexistence with the Soviets requires a million men and women in uniform and the expenditure of 7 percent of our GNP by the Pentagon. Furthermore we are aided psychologically in coming to terms with the reality of another superpower by our definition of it as an "evil empire" capable of competing with us only in the realm of brute force, not in higher human pursuits of economy, technology, living standards, or life-styles. How will we feel living in a world where the Japanese, pledged at least in name to the same broad tenets of capitalism and democracy as we, *are* able to outperform us in many of those higher human pursuits?

A small, prosaic example provides an illustration of the changes that lie ahead for Americans living in a more Nipponized world. Today we take it for granted that our dollar is the world's key currency. What few of us realize is that our standard of living is markedly higher simply by virtue of the fact that we live in a dollar-based world economy. Morgan Stanley managing director Lewis Bernard has come up with this analogy: If world finance were a basketball game, losing the currency edge would be the equivalent of losing the home court advantage.[8] Basketball fans know that the home court advantage is often the difference between winning and losing when otherwise equal teams are matched. When the world goes off the dollar standard, we will be shocked by the increased costs of doing business abroad, higher fees for issuing debt, and the volatility of oil prices and other international commodities that are now conveniently quoted in our own currency. In short, American living standards will decline as foreigners force us to do business in *their* currencies.

To make that sort of prosaic example a bit more provocative, let us bear in mind that although we legitimately pride ourselves on a high degree of democracy in the United States, it is no secret that we are also a society that encompasses a large number of rich and a large number of poor. Putting an average figure on the percentage by which our living standards must decline to overcome our deficits and down-size our economy in line with its declining position is a relatively straightforward mathematical calculation. MIT economist Lester Thurow quoted that figure at 8 percent in 1987. But statistics never cut evenly across the board.

In the last years of Reaganomics, for example, the United States experienced a decline in real wages that amounted to only a fraction of a percentage point. But that fraction was innocuous only as an *average*. Life at the extremities that combined to achieve the average was another story altogether. At one pole, the rich got much richer. At the other, factory wages dropped precipitously, the dream of buying a home moved out of reach of many in the middle class, and hundreds of thousands of people actually became homeless—something that had once been thought impossible in America.

If that happened while the national average was falling less than one percent, we would be wise to consider the dangers to the American way of life if Thurow is right. What will happen to race relations, labor peace, and the desperation of the underclass beneath the weight of an 8 percent decline? And what happens if Washington continues to ignore the heart of the problem, the deficits balloon, and the cuts in living standards necessitated in the 1990s begin to add up to 10 or 15 percent?

Growing our way out of the disastrous indebtedness incurred in the last decade will be as difficult as Sisyphus trying to push his rock to the top of the hill. Even if current efforts to reduce the U.S. budget deficit enjoy better than expected results, the government may owe foreigners, principally the Japanese, half a trillion dollars by the year 2000. We will be sending foreign investors $50 billion annually—and perhaps much more—just to pay the interest on that debt, not to mention what will be owed by U.S. corporations, local governments, and private citizens, who are also now borrowing aggressively from abroad. Today's U.S. Congress is plunged into virtual paralysis trying to comply with small deficit reductions mandated by the Gramm-Rudman Act. By the year 2000, one would assume most of the "fat" in the budget would be long gone. How deep will Congress have to slice the bone—Social Security, for example—or how much will it have to raise taxes, to repay our debts to foreigners?

Even the 1987 outlay of $23.5 billion in foreign interest payments was analyzed by budget experts as "crowding out" allocations for domestic programs. To put that sum in perspective, it was "triple the amount requested for federal housing programs, 50 percent greater than the administration's federal education budget, more than double the request for Navy shipbuilding, and more than the total requested for cancer research, running the national parks, airline safety, trade promotion and the Environmental Protection Agency *combined.*" [9] Against that current backdrop, the possibility of foreign debt turning future American workers into a generation of indentured servants becomes frighteningly believable.

As American debt deepens, we will continue to lose what leverage we still have in our negotiations over trade and other issues with the Japanese. It is difficult to "pressure" the people we are relying upon to finance our deficit. To put it bluntly, "You don't argue much with your banker, especially if he is also your landlord and employer."[10] Even today American debts are directly reducing Washington's ability to lead its own allies. REAGAN GOES TO VENICE HURT BY U.S. POSITION AS TOP WORLD DEBTOR, headlined the *The Wall Street Journal* just before the 1987 economic summit. A senior government official confided that the United States wanted to urge various actions on its allies but couldn't press too far, quite simply because "we owe them."[11]

The burden of being a debtor nation will depress the value of the U.S. dollar against other currencies for a long time to come. Cyclic improvements will take place, and speculators will occasionally jump back into dollars, driving up their value as they do so. But the long-term trend of the dollar is downward. The business plans of Honda, Sony, and several other Japanese companies already assume the dollar will fall below 120 yen. Some Japanese firms have drawn up reports on how to stay profitable with a yen as strong as 100 to the dollar. MoF brainstormers have addressed the question of seizing the moment when the magic "100" number is reached to dispense with the zeros and redenominate Japanese currency at 1 yen = 1 dollar.

Cheap dollars—and the fact that we keep sending them across the Pacific to pay off our debts—will also mean that the Japanese can continue buying larger sectors of U.S. industry, real estate, and equities for fewer yen. "For all practical purposes, America today is the Filene's Basement for the Japanese," noted Emmanuel Goldman of Montgomery Securities in the wake of a series of acquisitions by Japan's Kirin breweries that made it one of the largest Coca-Cola bottlers in the United States.[12]

In buying American companies, the Japanese *are* helping to provide jobs for U.S. workers as well as hope for industrial revival in blighted areas of the country. But that's not all. Bringing with them economies of scale, new production technology, low-cost capital, strategic time horizons, and new, more efficient approaches to managing human resources, the Japanese are demonstrating that after some initial culture shock, they can often outcompete American industry on its home ground. Very few American companies are building new factories that could bring thousands of jobs to a certain town or state —but dozens of Japanese companies are doing just that. Those realities will, over time, confer increasing political power on the Japanese.

Ohio's Governor Richard Celeste, for example, is visibly more interested in the new Honda plant in his state than in the old General Motors plants. Even though employment at Honda represents only one-tenth of GM's seventy-thousand-strong work force in Ohio, the politically important fact is that Honda is providing new jobs while GM is laying off. "Honda is state of the art," the governor says. "It's going to be a challenge to everyone, no matter whether they call themselves American or Japanese, to match them."[13] Governors like Celeste and legislators from states with large new Japanese factories have, for obvious reasons, been in the forefront of arguing against protectionist trade bills in Washington.

Generally speaking, Japanese-owned factories practice greater respect for ordinary assembly-line workers than the American industrial standard. The Japanese ability to get workers more involved in the manufacturing process is widely credited with improving quality and productivity at U.S. factories like NUMMI (the Fremont, California, joint venture between Toyota and General Motors) and Bridgestone's La Vergne, Tennessee, plant acquired from Firestone in 1983. At La Vergne, workers say the change of management has been like "going from hell to heaven."[14]

But not always without a price. Mirroring the influences of Japanese society, Japanese-owned enterprises are generally good places for Americans to be workers but difficult places to be managers. American executives accustomed to wielding decision-making power find that ultimately, real power always rests with the Japanese. Two former top executives at an NEC factory in California have filed a suit that essentially alleges discrimination against them as Americans. Women have also found Japanese employers to be extremely reluctant to promote them to managerial positions, triggering a number of legal actions alleging sex discrimination.[15]

At the moment, these trends are countercurrents to benefits derived from increased Japanese participation in the U.S. economy. But they are also ominous premonitions. Americans have very little experience at being second fiddle anywhere in the world, let alone in their own home. If the U.S. economy as a whole declines much further, the resulting sense of power and destiny lost to the Japanese could become incendiary.

The raw nerve of the prospect is already inflamed in places where Japanese investment presence is greatest. Honolulu lawyer and community leader Wallace Fujiyama declares, "Some of these Japanese speculators are raping this state." Hawaii's prime residential areas are becoming Japanese only; many resort facilities catering to the Japanese are simply too expensive for either mainland American tourists or locals. In what must be the first statement of its kind ever made by the mayor of an American city, Frank Fasi vowed, "We're not going to let them carve out a piece of Honolulu and make it a suburb of Tokyo."[16] Indeed, with Japanese real estate purchases climbing to 27 percent of all transactions in the exclusive Kahala area and 40 percent in Waikiki—and with characters like Tokyo billionaire Genshiro Kawamoto cruising Honolulu in a black limousine, stopping for a few minutes here and there to buy one of the 113 homes he acquired on a recent $32 million binge[17]—Fasi has begun giving serious consideration to legislation that would restrict Japanese purchases of residential real estate.

Despite the aggressiveness with which Japanese companies have moved manufacturing operations to the United States, Tokyo economic planners still expect to continue running large trade surpluses for another decade. The combination of continued U.S. trade deficits, wider use of the yen as an international currency, and growing American government budget deficits is likely to reinforce a structurally strong yen and weak dollar.

At some point soon the Japanese suppliers of America's desperately needed capital transfusions will insist on being paid back in yen, just as American banks today insist on being repaid in U.S. dollars when they lend money to foreign countries whose own currencies are unstable. Leaders of the Japanese financial community, like the Industrial Bank of Japan's Yoh Kurosawa, have already pressed Washington to issue a yen-denominated Treasury bond. The Reagan administration, to its credit, resisted. Eventually the pressure—and the temptation of attracting Japanese investors back to the U.S. debt market at lower interest rates in the next inflationary spiral—will be too great to resist.

If and when the Treasury begins to offer yen-based debt, Americans will learn firsthand about the treadmill of the "Argentina syndrome." American workers will be *forced* to work harder, produce more, and live less well in order to obtain the yen needed to pay off foreign debts. Only when the economic pain of that situation materializes will we realize the great economic advantage we enjoyed without even understanding it: the ability to borrow money from foreigners in our own currency.

Inflicting that pain on Americans is already a conscious goal of an increasingly influential section of the Japanese business community. Declares Takashi Hosomi, former chairman of the Overseas Economic Cooperation Fund of Japan: "The basic rule for debtor nations is to pay their borrowings back in real terms and *feel the pain* of accumulating debts irresponsibly. In order to restore this basic rule, it is necessary for other countries to help create a system to compel the debtor nations to make borrowings in currencies other than their own." More bluntly, he says, "What is now strongly required of the United States is to issue 'Reagan bonds' (i.e., yen-denominated U.S. debt instruments), and Japan, as the largest creditor nation, should urge that country to take the plunge."[18]

In that dangerous debtor's prison of tomorrow, an emboldened Japan will hold America's feet to the fire to get paid what it is owed and to reap the rewards of its investments. American politicians will no longer think about "punishing" Japan for offenses to our standards of fair trade. Instead they will have their work cut out for them to avoid being "punished" themselves by Japanese bankers imposing International Monetary Fund–style austerity measures on us, just as American bankers now do in the Third World. Some Japanese experts are already predicting such an outcome. "The United States will have to follow a set of austerity measures similar, in some sense, to those imposed by the IMF on the debt-ridden countries," forecasts a Nomura Research Institute report.[19]

If such a scenario unfolds, a broad spectrum of Americans will learn very quickly what it means that Japan is now the world's most powerful creditor nation and the United States its biggest debtor.

2

Sunrise, Sunset:
The Talk of the Town in Tokyo

While the Emperor who signed the surrender in cowed
Tokyo's rubble in 1945 is still alive, his Japan has become the
world's most efficient manufacturer and by far its largest
source of internationally investible cash. A country that has
become top manufacturer and top banker in 40 surprising
years is bound eventually to start moulding its era, instead of
sitting idly on its money.

—*The Economist*[1]

Yen Shock and the Shock of the New

The dollar was testing yet another record low to the yen. An American investment banker arrived in Tokyo having lost his luggage in
transit. Far from naive about money or about Japan, he was well
aware of the strength of the yen in a general way. From his office in
California he routinely did business with Japanese investors and kept
daily tabs on the dollar in *The Wall Street Journal*. But this was his
first trip to Tokyo in a while. After trying at a local department store
to replace the most necessary items he had lost, he returned to his
hotel empty-handed. "Three hundred dollars for a shirt?" he inquired
incredulously as he recounted his experience with yen shock. It is one
thing to read about the macroeconomics of the rising yen. It is quite
another to feel the encroaching realities of a yen-based world in person.

"Now I know what Third World immigrants feel like when they
come to the United States," the American remarked ruefully. "I can't
afford anything in this country."

A visit to Tokyo is in a sense a visit to the future. For Americans it is a challenging, disturbing, and even frightening encounter. It begins with "yen shock"—$200 for a taxi from Narita Airport to the hotel; $7 for coffee, $800 for dinner and drinks with three business associates at a first-class Japanese establishment. For those planning to stay any length of time, things get much worse: $7,000–$15,000 a month for a three-to-four-bedroom apartment comfortable for an American executive and his family; $125 per square foot for rental office space, with a year's rent as a noninterest-bearing security deposit.

But the high costs are only superficial indicators of what is truly daunting about Tokyo today. More Americans are doing business there than ever before, but they are frequently unhappy about the results. "They've got us by the balls," said one machine tool executive after he had endured a week of negotiations in Tokyo. "A year ago, they just sort of smiled and seemed content that we all acknowledged the situation. This year, they're squeezing." Putting a somewhat brighter face on the same sentiment, an American lawyer observed, "When I walk around Tokyo, I can't help feeling our future is pretty bleak. Japan's future is absolutely awesome."

Today's Tokyo is a city coming alive with a cultural electricity and cosmopolitanism it has never before known. It is a whirlwind of new Pacific possibilities in fashion, design, dance, and architecture; a kaleidoscope of gadgets, gizmos, new media, and new technologies. It is the vortex of the planet's convulsions into the postindustrial age—a brave new world with its own unique ideas about life, work, family, and community.

The sheer weight of money is finally cracking through the isolation that once enveloped Tokyo, metamorphosing it into a truly global city—the ultimate meeting ground of East and West. Americans who speak Japanese are routinely swooped up by high-paying financial firms desperate for bilingual, bicultural talent. About 10 percent of the tax revenues in Tokyo's exclusive Minato Ward are now paid by foreign nationals—a staggering statistic for a city where a resident *gaijin* (foreigner) was a rarity just a decade ago.

"We're experiencing an exciting moment that doesn't come often in the history of a city," says Fumihiko Maki, one of Japan's boldly innovative architects. A former Harvard professor, Maki understands the difference of mood between constructing a building in North

America and in Japan. "Tokyo is ascendant; flourishing. We have the money, the opportunity, and the tradition. The zeitgeist tells us, 'This is the time to create something new.'"

Maki is among the dozens of future-oriented thinkers helping to redesign Tokyo in preparation for the next century. Vast new housing complexes and decentralized government, scientific, and cultural institutions are in the works. Magnetically levitated high-speed commuter trains, which may get even faster by using superconductor technology, are in trial development. If experiments go according to plan, these trains will allow the city's work force to live one hundred miles away and still commute to central Tokyo in thirty minutes. Japan will soon become the first country to bring ISDN (Integrated Services Digital Network) on-line—the set of standards that promises to pull together today's babel of disparate communications technologies (telephone, computer data, fax, microwave, video, and satellite transmissions) into a single, integrated, useful whole.

While Americans worry about the decaying U.S. infrastructure, built decades ago, the Japanese erect a spectacular new $9 billion string of bridges and viaducts to span their Inland Sea, plow $11 billion into upgrading the port of Yokohama, and commit $20 billion more to new airports, highways, and high-speed rail systems. Man-made islands are planned crammed with information-age utilities and Buck Rogers–style living environments. Architect Kisho Kurokawa is pushing for a forty-year undertaking to build an artificial island city in Tokyo Bay that could eventually provide homes and offices for six million people. Kurokawa refers to the plan's $2 *trillion* price tag as one that could be "easily financed privately," although he thinks government involvement would be preferable.[2]

Not too many years ago, Japanese electronics wizards designed their most innovative products for export. Now, increasing affluence in the domestic market has caused them to design first for Japanese tastes. In Tokyo's Akihabara District, a twenty-first-century bazaar of electronic goods, one finds such devices as an electric fan driven by a computer chip replicating the ebbs and flows of famous winds in various Japanese country retreats, a deodorizer that emits its scent only when a sweating person enters the room, and the professional sound-reproduction capabilities of digital audio tape (DAT) systems, still unavailable in the United States. Every office has a fax, as do many homes; cellular telephones sprout in company cars; and even computer-aided dashboard navigation screens have moved into the retail market. Billboard-sized televisions, flat-screen and high-resolution TVs are pouring out of Sony and Matsushita factories, raising the prospect that Americans will soon have to replace every TV they now own just to pick up the television signals of the future.

From the commercialization of outer space (where Japanese industry plans to be doing some specialized manufacturing by 2001) to exploration of "biochips" linking electronic circuitry with recombinant DNA technology, Japanese scientists unabashedly say they are pursuing "original research that will serve as the nucleus of the 21st century's science and technology."[3]

The year 2000 has a magic pull. Companies and government organizations are busy drafting plans for how they will function in the next century. Nowhere is this more evident than in the financial services field. Banks and brokerage houses speak confidently of skyscrapers, satellites, teletopias, and infoports that will free them from the confines of the Marunouchi-Otemachi-Nihonbashi corridor where they now dwell. The dull, low-rise, jury-rigged assemblage of buildings that passes for today's financial district will be turned into a model of gleaming efficiency. The Nomura Research Institute predicts that well before the turn of the millennium, Tokyo's share of world financial business will eclipse New York's current share. "We must start preparing the infrastructure now," says a Nomura spokesman. "We must be able to lead history, rather than try to catch up to it."

If financial executives put things in sweeping historical terms, fashion designers are more conscious of the current moment. Kenzo, Japan's best-known designer, had to go to Paris twenty years ago to find a following. But on a visit to Tokyo recently, he declared, "There's so much passion here now! So much enthusiasm! So much electricity!" Asked why the change, he replied, "The money! The money! It's because all the money is here now."

While the eyes of Tokyo are focused on the future, a part of the city's consciousness is also in the throes of an obsession with 1950s Americana. Japanese college students cruise the narrow streets of Roppongi in gigantic tail-finned convertible Cadillacs and T-birds they've imported. The wild teenaged dancers who pour into Harajuku on weekends perform ritualized group versions of fifties' dances missing no authentic detail. Packs of Camels are rolled up in their white T-shirt sleeves, and greasy kid's stuff slicks down their hair. James

Dean is their god. Disneyland, the quintessential American fantasy of the 1950s, is more successful in Tokyo than in Anaheim.

The real 1950s in Japan were, of course, nothing to be nostalgic about. Everyone old enough to remember those days recalls rampant hunger, cold, and suffering in a land defeated and destroyed. Part of the nostalgia craze can therefore be read as a collective wish-fulfillment dream for a youth Japan never had. But another part is no dream. The Japanese sense their present and their future as very much like the American fifties—a time of boundless expansion, overwhelming national optimism, and swashbuckling self-confidence. The "Japanese way" has proven itself to be just as ideal as the "American Way" was to Americans of thirty years ago. For proof, the Japanese need look no further than their bank accounts.

Conspicuous Consumption

Visitors willing to step outside their own national bias for a moment can see the writing on history's wall in Tokyo's teeming-yet-antiseptic streets, in the cohesive "can-do" way its people move, and in the attention to service and detail paid by its workers. It is visible in the drenching downpour of prosperity that has decorated the entire city in Louis Vuitton, Hermès, and Chanel and in the Ginza shop windows where historic American properties are offered for sale at multimillion-dollar prices deemed "bargains" by Japanese buyers. No thinking American who looks and listens can fail to perceive a Japanese society that is becoming more prosperous, productive, and confident than our own. This Tokyo is one with an inchoate sense of itself as the world capital of the twenty-first century.

Before 1986 the visitor would not have received this impression— at least not so overwhelmingly and not without probing. But in 1986 something snapped in the tightly wound strings that balance the Japanese national mood, and a new Japanese self-image bubbled up to the surface as a result. That spring the Japanese government published statistics showing Japan had become the world's leading creditor and the United States its biggest debtor. These facts didn't necessarily cause the shift in public attitudes. They did, however, ratify it.

Economic statistics have a life of their own in Japan. In the 1960s government planners called for double-digit annual growth in GNP. The country pulled out the stops to work toward that goal—watching, worrying, and constantly sacrificing for the sake of achieving it. Next, the race was on to pass West Germany in total output. The campaign was viewed like an economic Olympics, complete with regular progress reports in the press on how the one-hundred-million-plus members of the Japanese national team were doing against the Germans and ecstatic celebrations when the gold medal was finally won.

By the mid-1980s the Japanese people were well aware that they were alone at the top of the economic world with the United States. At first they settled in for a long race to catch up to Americans who were quite far ahead. But all of a sudden, under the weight of Reaganomics, the United States began tumbling down the hill toward them. When the finance ministers of the world's five leading economies met at the Plaza Hotel in New York City in September of 1985 and agreed collectively to push the dollar down, the yen was thrust into a high-flying orbit, carrying the Japanese economy with it. It was as if the U.S.-Japan economic contest had entered *Double Jeopardy,* where, as the show's announcer used to say, "everything doubles, and the scores could really change."

From early 1985 on, Tokyo's citizenry marveled as the yen grew stronger and stronger, doubling against the dollar over the next two years. Throughout central Tokyo, in office corridors and on huge public billboards, the shrinking number of yen it took to buy one dollar was displayed moment by moment along with the time and temperature. The Japanese were apprehensive about what *endaka* (strong yen) would mean for the exporting industries long considered primary engines of the nation's growth. But that didn't stop taxi drivers, shop clerks, and waiters from taking delight in what they understood the numbers to mean: the once feeble yen was climbing to record heights because the rest of the world had growing confidence in Japan and slackening confidence in America.

A stream of serendipitous news reinforced the widening public perception that Japan had arrived ahead of schedule on top of the world:

- Nippon Telegraph & Telephone was suddenly the most valuable corporation on the face of the earth with its much coveted shares worth $20,000 apiece.
- The Tokyo Stock Exchange, which in the late 1970s was only one-fifth the size of the New York Stock Exchange in market capitalization, shot past New York and continued flying.

- A skyrocketing real estate market turned the California-sized Japanese archipelago into a stretch of real estate more valuable than the entire American land mass.
- The richest man in the world was now Japanese, and Japan even had more billionaires than America did.

These tidbits were devoured by a Japanese public eager to bask in their nation's collective success. The *Forbes* survey on Japanese billionaires was front-page news in Tokyo before the magazine hit the streets in New York with its startling report that Yoshiaki Tsutsumi of Seibu Railway had unseated Sam Walton of Wal-Mart Stores as the world's wealthiest private citizen.[4]

In direct relation to this stream of reports, the Japanese mind-set began to undergo a profound change. Plain living turned to conspicuous consumption almost overnight. Humility turned to arrogance, while the historic phobic insularity of the Japanese was transformed into a swaggering internationalism.

No event better typified the transition than Yasuda Fire & Marine's $40 million purchases at a Christie's auction in London of Vincent van Gogh's painting *Sunflowers*. Yasuda, Japan's second largest insurance carrier, paid three times more than had ever been paid for any painting in the history of art. But for a company bulging at the seams with yen-based profits, everything in the dollar-based art world was a bargain. Even at $40 million, *Sunflowers* made an excellent one-hundredth anniversary present from the company to itself.

While the incident was most notable as a case study in nouveaux riches gone amok, Yasuda's bid had a subliminal text as well. *Sunflowers* closely resembled another van Gogh floral image, which had been destroyed in the American bombing of Japan. In buying this painting and bringing it back to Japan, Yasuda demonstrated that the country's new wealth made it possible to reverse at least some of the verdicts of history.

Yasuda was not alone in its rampant spending for status. A Japanese group headquartered in Nagoya acquired Australian billionaire Alan Bond's America's Cup yachts. Asked how the Japanese syndicate could reasonably be expected to build a championship capability from scratch less than four years before the next cup, Hideto Eguchi, president of Yamaha, declared simply, "We have no financial problems." His consortium will sink $80 million into the venture and enjoys access to a Cray supercomputer and hydrodynamics test facilities at a state-of-the-art Japanese laboratory. Dennis Conner, skipper of defending champion *Stars & Stripes,* doesn't disagree with Eguchi's assessment: "Money translates into the bottom line. When you have an $80 million budget for one program, you're going to be competitive."[5]

Other Japanese showed their new international panache by buying the Duchess of Windsor's jewels, the world's most expensive postage stamp, and the world's most expensive Ming porcelain. Even Japanese baseball, traditionally a dumping ground for washed-up American players, became suddenly aggressive in its quest for the best. The Tokyo Giants offered New York Yankee pitcher Dave Righetti $10 million to jump across the Pacific. Righetti didn't go, but teammate Bill Gullikson did—accepting a $3.3 million contract that was twice the best offer made him by the Yankees.

Japan's wealth was perhaps best summarized by Kenichi Ohmae, the managing director of McKinsey & Co.'s Tokyo office and author of many thoughtful books about Japan and the world: "Our capital surplus is like a vast dam breaking. Japan cannot begin to hold it all. We've been racing to find buckets to catch the overflow. U.S. Treasury bonds, equities, buildings on Fifth Avenue, a van Gogh painting, or even a golf club membership have become buckets. If someone says Deutschemark bonds are a good bucket, we rush there. If someone else says New Zealand is undervalued, we rush there. Japanese capital now threatens to flood the world."

Most of Japan's wealth is corporate wealth, and it will be a long time before this excess of cash percolates far enough through the system to allow the average Japanese citizen to consume the way Americans do. Most Japanese still live in housing that would be considered substandard in the West. Even when people who thought of themselves as "middle class" (88 percent of Japanese describe themselves as such) woke up to discover the real estate boom had made their "rabbit hutch" homes worth hundreds of thousands of dollars, they still didn't "feel" wealthy. One young professional who bought a two-hundred-square-foot apartment in Tokyo for $50,000 saw it jump in value to $350,000 in two years' time. "If I sell it, I will have nowhere to live," he said, "and if I stay there, we are still a family of three living in two hundred square feet."

But for those with spare parcels of old family lands to sell, as for many households willing to borrow against the inflated equity in their homes to invest in the booming stock market, becoming an instant millionaire wasn't hard. Brokerage houses opened counters in department stores, where big boards flashed the latest quotes to crowds of shoppers who ended up going home with stocks as well as socks. The traditional door-to-door retail sales of equities turned housewives who managed the family's savings into global investors. For such people wealth was created on a scale rarely seen in modern history. As a result Japan began to see personal consumption it had never before known.

Memberships in golf clubs began to be traded on an over-the-counter exchange, with prices reaching up to $3.5 million for the best locations. A disco thought nothing of spending $10 million on interior decor; youthful *shinjinrui* (literally "new human race," the poetic Japanese equivalent of yuppies) vied for the chance to pay scalpers $500 to see the American pop star Madonna. Tea salons in Tokyo department stores took to serving Japanese tea speckled with flecks of real gold; for soft drinks, ice cubes imported from Antarctic icebergs became de rigueur.

Proving that they could enjoy foreign imports (usually European rather than American), the Japanese began soaking up BMWs at a fifteen-thousand-per-year rate, as well as Ferraris and Porsches. They also found themselves home to nearly half the Louis Vuitton boutiques in the world. A random check of the Tokyo subways showed an average of $10,000 worth of Vuitton paraphernalia visible in every rush-hour car. Dunhill's suddenly found itself doing a third of its worldwide business in Japan, including brisk sales of Dunhill-labeled socks designed specifically for delivering an understated yet clear message in a country where people frequently take off their shoes in public. Gucci's goods, the final word in name-brand consumption, became available at three hundred Japanese outlets. From Häagen-Dazs ice cream to Wolfgang Puck's California-style Spago restaurant; from the designers of New York's Soho to Paris's Place de la Victoire, the best of what the outside world had to offer streamed into Tokyo for sampling by Japan's newly affluent. A popular game show on Japanese television (akin to *The Price Is Right*) said it all with its title: *How Much for the Whole World?*

The long insular Japanese also embarked on a fit of unrestrained jet-setting. Office girls headed for long weekends of duty-free shopping in Hong Kong. High school graduates took class trips to China or Saipan. Even with airfare, these destinations were cheaper than going to a nearby Japanese lake or mountain. Beaches in Australia and New Zealand were promoted by Tokyo tour operators as "the Japanese Coast." "Fly and buy" tours were arranged for those who wanted to bring home title to a piece of foreign property as a souvenir. From Hawaii's beaches to Vermont's bed and breakfast inns, Japanese tourists poured into the United States, delighted to discover how "cheap" everything was.

In New York, where Japanese tourists became the city's largest foreign group, twice daily buses took them for a tour highlighting Manhattan skyscrapers like Exxon and Mobil now owned by Japanese investors. "Welcome to the next Japanese city," the guide intoned as he began his tour.[6]

Affluence, Arrogance, and America-Bashing

It wasn't just the odd Japanese tour guide in New York who made facetious comments tinged with hints of the Japanese desire for empire. Los Angeles became widely known as "the 24th Ward" (Tokyo has twenty-three wards); Hawaii as "the 48th Prefecture" (Japan has forty-seven prefectures). An adviser to Prime Minister Yasuhiro Nakasone reportedly suggested buying Hawaii outright as a way of balancing American trade deficits with Japan. In a completely serious TV interview, a businessman boasted about how Japan would turn Australia into its mining concession and the United States into its grain silo in the twenty-first century.

Such ideas were symptomatic of what Japanese government officials themselves took to calling the "arrogance problem." Convinced of the superiority of their way of doing things—and bolstered by economic facts that seemed to prove their position—some Japanese no longer hesitated to proclaim their triumph out loud. Opinion polls reported a dramatic upturn in the number of Japanese who no longer believed they had anything to learn from the West. The number of Japanese saying they felt "friendly" toward the United States sank to a postwar low.

Nor did prominent Japanese intellectuals conceal their contempt for the United States. "Americans must accept an absolute decline in their standard of living in order to relieve their nation's economic woes, for which they mistakenly blame the Japanese," wrote Masahiko Ishizuka, editor of the English-language *Japan Economic Journal*. America, he prescribed, must stop "believing itself free to force others to change at whim, must now remove itself from its catatonia [and] admit its mistakes."[7] Ishizuka made clear the implications of American decline for Japan: "As long as Japan lacks its own grand strategy —in terms of defense, economics, and other matters—for the survival of its own nation and the whole world, it will continue to be pushed around by the U.S."[8]

Long-standing reverence for the United States was rapidly turning into serious criticism and even blatant America-bashing. What one commentator called America's "nagging and whimpering" about trade matters only worsened the problem. Not only had the United States become a weak economy incapable of balancing its books, all it seemed able to do was blame Japan.

Equality in relationships is a concept that runs against the grain of the neatly ordered, intricate hierarchies of Japanese culture. It is a simple matter for the Japanese to accept being inferior to someone else. It is equally simple to be that person's superior. These are not subjective judgments but objective ones determined by criteria like age, education, and rank. An inferior speaks and acts in one manner, while his superior employs a totally different behavior and language. Cases of true equality are rare and hard to manage because they fall outside the rules.

So it is with Japan's relationships with foreign countries. For most of the postwar period, Japan was extremist in its view of itself as subservient to the strong, successful, and victorious United States. This is not to say the Japanese ever abandoned their national pride. They merely *accepted* a temporary position in the world as an inferior to the United States. The great Japanese success in export industries began to break down Japan's inferiority complex. The financial role reversal shattered it.

Just as it seemed perfectly natural to the Japanese to adopt an inferior position when facts showed the United States to be richer, it became logical to adopt a superior position once those same facts showed Japan to be number one. Mimicking the "arrogance of power" at the high tide of the American economy in the 1950s and 1960s, Japanese power was developing its own arrogance; the "ugly Japanese" was replacing the "ugly American."

The arrogance issue was of such concern to the Foreign Ministry that its senior bureaucrats took to issuing public warnings about it. The 1987 "Blue Book" (the ministry's annual report on Japan's role in the world) noted that the winds of history were shifting, and Japan was becoming a great global power while the United States declined.

But the report expressed deep concern that "arrogance" could alienate Japan from the rest of the world, as could the neonationalism euphemistically described as the "trend to look back to prewar days with nostalgic feeling."[9]

The warnings, however, had little impact. The Foreign Ministry, almost by definition, is one of Tokyo's least influential institutions since it is seen as tainted by its overabundance of contacts with foreigners. Its message about arrogance, moreover, struck a note of cognitive dissonance with the visible realities of Japanese success. We are not being arrogant, many Japanese thought. We are only being realistic.

Consider, for example, the casual discourse of Ichiro Yamanouchi, one of NTT's top executives in North America, just before NTT's stock offering made it the world's largest corporation. Over lunch one day, Yamanouchi mentioned that he really wanted to bring some American products back to Japan as gifts for friends and business associates. This would be his own personal gesture to help alleviate the trade deficit. But he couldn't find anything made in the United States that could measure up to the scrutiny of a quality-conscious Japanese. At long last he had found one perfect item: Vermont maple syrup, a high-quality product suitable to the Japanese taste—in this case, Japan's national sweet tooth.

Without the least self-consciousness that an American listener might find it an overstatement to imply that maple syrup was America's only exportable product, Yamanouchi continued on to talk about how America could get more competitive in trade. The United States should market its national parks more aggressively as tourist attractions. Nature-loving Japan had nothing to compare with Yosemite or Yellowstone. Bringing more tourists across the Pacific would bring more Japanese dollars back to the economy.

Finally, he said, NTT had learned so much from AT&T years ago. But it was disappointing that AT&T wouldn't listen to *his* advice, now that NTT had become the world's biggest telephone company. AT&T should stop trying so hard to sell their telephone switching systems and other advanced technology in Japan, since the Japanese have the capability to make all these things themselves. But he had an idea about what AT&T *could* export successfully. At AT&T headquarters in New Jersey he'd seen displays of sweatshirts and baseball caps made by company employees for sale as charity fund-raisers. These products, he said, would be a big hit in Japan.

Yamanouchi, an extraordinarily polite man, was certainly not *trying* to be offensive. He was simply expressing the image of the United States he'd developed as his country catapulted ahead of it. Some Japanese had begun to see America the way some Americans see exotic countries in the Third World: beautiful game parks, delicious indigenous agricultural products, and workers capable of turning out sports clothing at low cost.

The image of the United States as a country whose main asset was its large land mass was increasingly enshrined in official Japanese government policies. Urged to come up with innovative ideas on expanding two-way trade, think-tankers at MITI (Ministry of International Trade and Industry) announced a plan to build "silver communities" abroad. The idea was to export Japan's exploding "silver" population (those over sixty-five) to a series of Japanese-style leisure worlds in countries that met three criteria: good medical care, political stability, and a high concentration of Japanese restaurants. The meager yen-based pensions of silver-haired Japanese who retired in the United States would convert into so many dollars, they'd live out their days like kings. By pumping their pension funds through the American economy, the retirees would be improving America's current account deficit.

MITI's high-handedness could be seen in the fact that this plan, which targeted the United States, Canada, Australia, and New Zealand, was announced without ever consulting any of the countries involved. Nor did MITI consider that providing homes for hundreds of thousands of elderly Japanese might not be the way foreign countries would prefer to expand trade with Japan. MITI's assumption was that beggars couldn't be choosers. Like Americans who retire to the sunny climes of Cuernavaca in Mexico, MITI believed the money would be so helpful to the local economy, no one would mind the imposition on national dignity.

With a similar paternalism, the Japanese press singled out for praise American businessmen who discovered export niches in products one would expect a colony to produce for its metropolitan motherland, like Boston fishermen who caught fresh Atlantic tuna for shipment to Tokyo restaurants or a Minnesota company that cut down American forests to make chopsticks for the Japanese market.

In the same vein, the Japanese praised the American states that had opened representative offices in Tokyo (thirty-six states had such offices at last count) and were vying madly with each other to attract Japanese factories to their locations. The scene bore an uncanny resemblance to feudal times when local lords from across the kingdom came to court to sit for weeks at a time, awaiting an audience to beseech the shogun for a favor. Kentucky Governor Martha Layne Collins was undoubtedly the champion: her seven visits to Tokyo finally netted a decision by Toyota to locate an $800 million plant in her state. (By way of tribute to Toyota's shoguns, Collins arranged to buy the land for them at a cost of $12.5 million and agreed to spend another $115 million improving the site, building access roads, and training workers.[10])

The American way of doing business, which had once appealed to some Japanese entrepreneurs, was fading. "When I first encountered American offices, I loved them," said a young Japanese laser engineer. "I thought to myself, 'Executives need privacy; private offices are the right way to get business done.' But now I realize that the Japanese way, with everyone working together in one big room, even the boss, is really best."

AIDS, considered an "American disease" long after the first Japanese had died from it, was seen by businessmen as the ultimate symbol of America in decline. They joked about the danger of getting the dread disease by breathing the air or drinking the water on a U.S. business trip. While laughing at the irony of "macho" Americans allowing their society to be ruined by what they perceived as a homosexual plague, the same businessmen invested heavily in every pharmaceutical company listed on the Tokyo Stock Exchange that was developing AIDS products for the American market.

One of the most disturbing jokes making the rounds of Tokyo bars went like this:

Q: "How will Japan win the next war?"
A: "We'll get together with the Germans again, but this time we'll leave the Italians out of it."

In these and a thousand other ways both small and large, Tokyo's talk of the town in 1986 and afterward grew ever more focused on the speed that the sun was setting on the American empire and rising on Japan.

Reprise of the Master Race

Basking in the sun of wealth and success, Japanese supremacist ideas experienced their first real renaissance since the war. The perennially popular genre of literature known as *Nihonjin-ron*—books that attempt to explain why the Japanese are such a unique people—took a more pronounced turn toward answering the question not just of why the Japanese are different, but of why they are superior. A typical best-seller was *The Japanese Brain*. This work purported to demonstrate that "Japanese brains" develop differently from those of other races.[11] As one Japan watcher put it, "The basic message non-Japanese now seem to be hearing from Japan is, 'The reason we are number one is that we Japanese are biologically and culturally unique in ways no one else can ever emulate.'"[12]

In the Diet, a faction of eighteen members of the ruling Liberal Democratic party (LDP) demanded that the government stop "groveling" in front of foreign powers. By this they meant Japan should stop trying to accommodate American interests on trade matters and cease responding to political pressure from other Asian countries to keep new textbooks out of Japanese schools. The textbooks contained a whitewashed version of World War II and Japan's role in it. Defending them, Education Minister Masayuki Fujio insisted Japan had done "nothing to be ashamed of." He reiterated the old logic of the Imperial Army that Japan had committed no atrocities in China and that Korea was responsible for its own occupation because it invited Japan to annex it.

"The core of our education should be to make our children Japanese again," said Fujio, articulating an idea with immense populist appeal.[13] Ultimately Fujio was forced out of the cabinet over his remarks. But the fact that an important government official had at last said out loud what many people thought was more significant than his political demise.

Inexplicably, and almost from nowhere, a wave of anti-Semitism swept through the country. Masami Uno's best-seller argued that Japan was victimized by "an international Jewish conspiracy." Former Diet member Eisaburo Saito penned *The Secret of Jewish Power to Control the World*. Between them the two books sold almost two million copies. In 1986–87, nearly one hundred titles about Jews flooded Japanese bookstores. Some argued that American Jews—alleged to control the U.S. business world—were conspiring to drive the yen up, causing unemployment in Japan.

Swastikas appeared in the Ginza with messages accusing "Jewish multinational companies" of being behind rising land costs in Tokyo. When American reporters picked up on this perplexing trend, some Japanese even saw a Jewish conspiracy behind the coverage of Japan's talk of a Jewish conspiracy. At a *New York Times* dinner for foreign journalists after the paper reported on the trend, a Japanese correspondent demanded to know "how many Jewish editors are employed at *The New York Times*" and why the paper covered "so many Jewish stories."[14]

Despite flowering rhetoric about "internationalization," many Japanese worried about allowing foreigners too much access to Japan. Of 1.6 million crimes committed annually, foreigners now account for 0.1 percent. This tiny fraction was seen as having a "big effect on Tokyo's security," according to the director of a newly formed police unit dedicated to fighting foreign crime. *Mainichi Shimbun* declared it was "necessary to be cautious against foreigners in the age of internationalization."[15]

Of all the troubling words emanating from Japan that season, the most important came from Prime Minister Nakasone himself. Important because Nakasone was not an obscure fanatic or peripheral intellectual, but the strongest, most effective Japanese leader of modern times. He was billed as America's good friend. He had so much in common with Ronald Reagan that their dialogue was dubbed the "Ron-Yasu connection." He was seen as the West's best hope for convincing Japan to open its markets and render its society more pluralistic.

But there was another side to Nakasone, which he revealed in a single sentence heard around the world in September of 1986, just before he was due to take his vision of Japan's new role to the rostrums of the United Nations and the U.S. Congress. In a talk to LDP members, Nakasone made the declaration that he believed *America's intellectual level was lower than Japan's because American society had too many blacks, Mexicans, and Puerto Ricans.*[16]

The comment was a reflection of the widely shared Japanese view that dark-skinned peoples, whether in America, Africa, or elsewhere in the Third World, simply *are* inferior. Nakasone's remark ignited a howl of protest in the United States, but most Japanese found nothing to disagree with in it.

When thirty-five members of the congressional black and Hispanic caucuses demanded an apology, Nakasone agreed to give them one. But like other instances when Japan has bowed to American pressure, the remedy was worse than the original problem. In "apologizing," Nakasone offered not sorrow but pity. He said he would "explain all"—and he did. What he really meant, he said, was that Japan succeeds where America fails because Japan is a "monoracial society," whereas the United States is weighed down by the presence of "multiple nationalities." He wasn't denigrating black and Hispanic Americans, he argued, he was merely taking note of the fact that racially pure Japanese society functions more efficiently than racially mixed America.[17]

Americans who paused to reflect on the incident felt a shudder run down their spines. There was more to Nakasone's comments than garden-variety racism—there were echoes of *master racism*. The more he apologized, the more his line of reasoning sounded uncomfortably like the rhetoric of World War II.

The timing of Nakasone's endorsement of a "monoracial" society was significant. The United States and Japan were locked in heated rhetoric of trade war, Japan had just become the world's leading creditor, and Nakasone had just finished hosting the Tokyo Economic Summit. He had repeatedly pledged to the heads of the other industrial democracies that his country would henceforth share the burdens of world leadership. Was this a foreshadowing of the type of "leadership" he had in mind?

Nakasone's comment was anything but an accidental slip of the tongue. What he said was what he really believed. And although Americans reacted first to its racist content, few could deny a maddening kernel of truth to it. The Japanese educational system *does* function better than the American system in many respects. Adult illiteracy in the United States is estimated at 8 percent, while in Japan the figure is the world's lowest—only 1 percent. About 70 percent of Americans finish high school versus 95 percent of Japanese. American high school seniors score twelfth in the world in math ability, while Japanese score second. Over the last generation Japan's mean IQ score rose to 111 compared with the U.S. norm of 100.[18]

As the world heads deeper into the information age and the U.S.-Japan competition begins to focus on "brain-intensive" industries, Japan, with 7 percent higher literacy, 25 percent better high school completion rates, demonstrably better math skills, and eleven more

IQ points, is going to turn its educational advantage to economic benefit. Nakasone wrongly attributed this situation to an ethnic imperative. He was right, however, in the notion that the homogeneity of his society makes the Japanese educational system more workable than the American system, which is trying to cope with an explosion of conflicting demands brought on by the world's most heterogeneous society. The truth he highlighted was that if pluralist-minded Americans want to remain competitive with homogeneous Japan, resting on pluralism's moral laurels won't do. Americans must find ways to prove we can educate our many different constituencies to be as intellectually competitive in the future as the Japanese will be. So far we seem to be losing this battle not because of ethnicity, but because of national priorities.

In the same speech, Nakasone spoke in even more provocative—if less noticed—terms about the need to save the world by propagating Japan's superior philosophy abroad. The whole speech, taken in context, was seen by some observers as representative of a mushrooming revival of "Yamatoism"—the doctrine of the purity of the Japanese soul derived from the Yamato clan, which unified Japan fifteen hundred years ago.

During World War II, Yamatoism functioned as a Japanese equivalent of Hitler's Aryan supremacy. It provided well-developed justifications for spreading the Japanese empire across Asia. In his book *War Without Mercy,* John Dower documents the rapidity and rabidity with which racism spread on both sides of the Pacific as the United States and Japan were thrust into war. Yamatoism, as depicted by Dower, was no less virulent a racist doctrine than Hitlerism, although considerably more sophisticated.

"To view those who are in essence unequal as if they were equal is in itself inequitable," declared the wartime Japanese report cited by Dower, "Global Policy with the Yamato Race as Nucleus." The report reasoned, "To treat those who are unequal unequally is to realize equality."

Outlining the strategy for Japan's triumph in the Pacific, the report made it clear that the Japanese were to "assume the dominant financial and economic roles formerly played by the European and American colonial powers." The war would continue "until Anglo-American imperialistic democracy has been completely vanquished and a new world order erected in its place." After the war's end, twelve million Japanese would be dispatched to other parts of Asia to oversee the development of the "Greater East Asia Co-Prosperity Sphere." The Japanese would thus obtain their version of the German notion of lebensraum—the "broader living sphere of the Yamato race."[19]

Forty years later, it was more than coincidence to find Nakasone funding a national "Japanology Institute" whose mission was to delve into issues defining the uniqueness of the Japanese race. During his tenure, Nakasone often argued for a "postwar settlement of accounts," by which he meant Japan should close the era of self-deprecation and develop a strong national identity again. For inspiration as to the content of Japan's new identity, Nakasone conversed regularly with a group of ultranationalist scholars known as the "Kyoto School." Among their circle, some preached an overt brand of Yamato supremacy and called for a drive to purify Japanese culture by ridding it of Western influences. The significance of Nakasone's colloquy with the Kyoto School, noted Japan expert Ian Buruma, was comparable to the West German chancellor deciding to hold an ongoing dialogue with a circle of Munich intellectuals inspired by the ideas of Nazi theoreticians like Julius Streicher and Alfred Rosenberg.[20]

The link between Japanese nationalism and militarization is nowhere near as inextricable as it was in the 1930s. But there is more than a casual connection. In the face of powerful domestic and international opposition, Nakasone became the first postwar Japanese prime minister to accede to right-wing pressure to visit the Yasukuni Shrine, an emotionally charged memorial to those who died for the empire, including many so-called class-A war criminals responsible for Japanese atrocities. Most leading politicians (including today's prime minister, Noboru Takeshita) have since made their own visits.

Neither Nakasone nor Takeshita, nor any other senior leader of the LDP, is consciously advocating a renewal of Japan's wartime policies. But in assuming its role as a great international power for the first time since World War II, the new Japan has not rooted out the philosophy that led to such disaster in the past. The real significance of Nakasone's remarks is this: The drive for empire is alive and well in Japan, and so too are the intellectual premises necessary to support and implement it.

3

GUT WARNING:
THE GREAT JAPANESE SQUEEZE
PLAY IN AMERICAN BONDS

> We are obviously in danger of losing control over our own
> economic destiny.
> —Paul Volcker, at the end of his tenure
> as chairman of the Federal ReserveBoard.[1]

The Hoarding of the February 2016s

The first time Wall Street glimpsed the power Japanese investors had gained in the American financial marketplace was in 1986. And the quake was half over before most of the financial community even realized what was happening.

It began toward the end of April. Up and down the Street, high-salaried bond traders watched their computer terminals in stunned disbelief. Somebody was doing something weird to the biggest, most liquid, and best-guaranteed financial market in the world: the bonds that represent the debt of the United States government.

Bond departments at Wall Street's major firms had a lot to lose. Traders were riding the crest of a discovery that they could play the arbitrage game just like their colleagues on the stock side. And one of their standard arbitrage gambits involved the quarterly auctions of U.S. Treasury bonds, particularly the benchmark thirty-year variety known as the "long bond."

Over the years, long bonds have been extremely attractive investment vehicles for cash-rich institutions like pension funds and insurance companies. Even with America's massive debts, the financial

77

world still believes there is no better guarantee than the one offered by the historic stability of the U.S. government. Presumably even in a cataclysmic panic Washington would continue to honor obligations to holders of its own debt. At least that's what the vast majority of global investors have believed up until now, based on Washington's unblemished record of debt repayment throughout the twists and turns of twentieth century economic history.[2]

Treasury bond interest rates are also considered the world's most competitively determined. This is because they are sold in a full auction system with dealers bidding on how many bonds they will buy at what interest rates. Because U.S. government debt is so large but its credit is so good, the market is huge, global, and constant. The owner of a long bond can sell to a buyer in the secondary market often in a matter of minutes and usually without precipitating a major price movement.

The long bond's unique characteristics make it one of the most widely watched barometers of interest rates. Its movements are reflected in trading patterns for the shorter-term bills and bonds issued by the government. Together these instruments directly influence the prime rate, mortgage and car loan rates, CD yields, and the other financial reference points that ultimately have a powerful impact on the daily lives of most people.

Since the end of 1984 the most enthusiastic buyers of these bonds have been Japanese. As Japan's trade surplus climbed to staggering figures, Japanese banks, insurance companies, and industrial corporations had little time to rationally plan how best to invest the proceeds. Like a scene from the "Sorcerer's Apprentice," they raced to find foreign markets large enough to absorb the extraordinary overflow of dollars piling up in Japan. "Our philosophy toward Treasury bonds during those days was very simple," recalls Masahiro Dozen, chief of the bond department at the Tokyo headquarters of Daiwa Securities. "It could be summed up as 'Buy! Buy! Buy!'"

And buy they did. The "Big Four" Japanese securities firms—Nomura, Daiwa, Nikko, and Yamaichi—routinely bought a third to a half of all new long bonds during this period. At one 1986 auction Japanese investors bought 80 percent of the issue. In business terms Japan had become the lead banker to the Reagan administration and the chief financier of the exploding U.S. budget deficit. To put it in street language, Washington had grown addicted to foreign capital. America had become a desperate junkie, and Japan was its pusher.

The White House seemed perfectly comfortable with the situation. Ready availability of Japanese buyers for U.S. bonds enabled interest rates to continue falling during 1985–86. Lower interest rates, in turn, allowed millions of Americans to release pent-up home-buying desires and permitted business and industry a chance to expand without the double-digit borrowing costs that had paralyzed the economy in the prior decade. Falling interest rates also fueled what was then a rampaging bull market on Wall Street as investors abandoned conservative money market funds and CDs in favor of the ecstatic New York Stock Exchange ticker.

Japan's willingness to lend its trade surplus back to the United States (rather than investing it at home or in other countries) was a critical ingredient allowing Ronald Reagan to expand military spending, expand the budget deficit, and stimulate the economy—all while slicing taxes. The sleight of hand most Americans failed to notice while Reagan performed this illusion was that once every three months, when the Treasury had to be refunded, it was foreigners who were paying the bill. If Japanese investors hadn't bought $90 billion worth of U.S. government debt in 1986, the U.S. budget deficit would have intruded painfully on American life in forms ranging from sharply higher mortgage rates to higher taxes and deeper, more socially divisive cuts in government programs.

At the beginning, bond traders found nothing particularly disturbing about a Treasury market driven by Japanese investors. They merely followed their instincts and adjusted their sights in the direction of Tokyo. "Every morning, the question is: What are the Japanese doing?" a top specialist observed of life in First Boston's bond department.[3] A lot of money could be made by knowing the answer to that question.

One thing traders noticed the Japanese doing was selling off previously acquired long bonds just before a new Treasury auction in order to buy new bonds. The theory behind this pattern was that being long-term planners, the Japanese wanted their portfolios invested as far into the future as possible, even just three months farther. Thus, as the May 1986 Treasury auction approached, Wall Street bond dealers fully expected Japanese investors to continue the pattern they had established: selling off chunks of their holdings in long bonds maturing in February of the year 2016 to replace them with newly available bonds maturing in May 2016.

Bond "arbs" had learned how to play this pattern. In April they began a reprise of what most believed would be an axiomatic profit. They shorted the February 2016 bond—meaning they sold bonds they didn't yet own. They expected that by the time they needed to actually deliver the bonds, they'd have no problem obtaining a fractionally cheaper supply from Japanese investors eager to sell before buying the new issue. Even though the price differential between selling a bond short today and buying it back next week might be only a few hundredths of a percent, those decimal places are life and death in the trading room. Dealers who handle volumes in the billions on a daily basis know how to get very rich very quick on seemingly infinitesimal percentages.

This time, though, their strategy went haywire. Instead of falling, the price of the old bonds began *rising*. Traders went into a frenzied scramble trying to buy back the bonds they'd "shorted." This motion drove prices up still further. When bids are met, the word "HIT" flashes on the trader's computer screen, just as in a video game. But nothing was hitting.

The big squeeze was on, and much of Wall Street was caught in the vise. Somewhere, the February 2016 U.S. Treasury bond was being hoarded. Somewhere, owners of that bond were refusing to sell it even for a substantial premium over its technical market value.

That somewhere, Wall Street eventually figured out, was Tokyo. The Japanese, whom most bond traders had taken for being conservative, predictable, and inexperienced in U.S. financial markets, were enacting what appeared to be a brilliant, daring strategy no American professional had foreseen. "The Japanese did to us on the long bond what they did to us at Pearl Harbor," fumed a top trader. Another compared the wild price distortions to the Hunt brothers' attempt to corner the world silver market.[4]

The bloodletting got worse as the days wore on. Aggregate losses on Wall Street reached $350 million. Senior traders making high six-figure salaries found their jobs suddenly on the line as management committees began to realize the extent of the damage. "Get a hold of those bonds somewhere!" the word went out. "Do it now, or you're finished!" But for all their Street smarts, nothing the New York dealers tried could break the back of the squeeze.

When salvation finally came, it came from Tokyo. Like a white knight on horseback, Nomura Securities stepped in from Japan to make $500 million worth of the hoarded American bonds available to

American dealers. Once those bonds started flowing through the system, the costly crisis receded.

When it was all over and Wall Street had finished emptying its pockets, there was still confusion about what had happened and why. If it had been an orchestrated attempt to corner the market à la the Hunt brothers, why had Nomura stepped in so gallantly just when the squeeze was working best? If cornering the market wasn't their intention, just what were the Japanese trying to prove?

One theory held that the Japanese—Nomura, in particular—had conspired to hoard the bonds in order to teach their American counterparts a lesson. "They felt they were given bad service and rotten prices by the U.S. dealers," one New York banker reported. "Nomura wanted them to know they wouldn't put up with it."[5]

Another line of reasoning viewed the squeeze as a power play carried out by some or all of the Big Four Japanese houses then applying to enter the exclusive club of "primary dealers"—a group of approximately forty securities firms accorded the right to do business directly with the Federal Reserve Bank of New York. Primary dealership increases bond-trading profits modestly by cutting down on middlemen. It also carries a great deal of prestige. Ever since a wave of scandal-laden bankruptcies shook the bond business in the early 1980s, many blue-chip buyers insist on trading exclusively through primary dealers.

Japanese firms, steeped in the cultural desire for honor and enmeshed in the implementation of a business strategy aimed at acceptance in the American marketplace, wanted very badly to become primary dealers. The volume of their business justified elevation to such status. But rival American securities firms afraid of losing market share wanted the Japanese blackballed. More visceral was the opposition of politicians who believed the bargaining chip of primary dealership should not be given away until Tokyo agreed to open its financial markets to wider American participation.

Thus the bond squeeze may have been mounted by Japanese houses intent on demonstrating they were too powerful to be denied their rightful place. If true, the tactic worked well: six months later the Federal Reserve Bank welcomed the two biggest Japanese firms, Nomura and Daiwa, as primary dealers.

Yet the full explanation of the squeeze may rely on a phenomenon at once more prosaic and more profound: Americans do not understand the Japanese financial system. According to sources at Nomura, the cause of the uproar was no grand design, but rather the logical result of Japanese tax law. The squeeze took place at a moment when American interest rates were in free fall. The February bond auction had produced a yield of 9¼ percent, while May's yield had dropped to 7¼ percent. Such a massive rate differential in such a short period of time created a tax problem preventing large Japanese institutional investors from playing out their usual strategy of selling off old bonds to buy new ones.

The older 9¼ percent bonds had suddenly become very valuable because they carried a coupon radically higher than current market rates. Japanese corporations selling the 9¼ percent bond would have incurred a huge capital gain. That may have sounded good to Americans who then enjoyed preferential treatment of capital gains under the former U.S. tax law. But in Japan such gains on the corporation's books aren't always pleasant news. Unlike recurring income from the bond yield itself, a capital gain, in many cases, could not be disbursed as untaxed dividends to shareholders. This time around it made more sense to keep the bond, avoid the tax, and continue reaping the high yield.

"If traders took the time and trouble to learn about the Japanese tax law, they would have seen this coming and avoided screwing themselves," says an American at a Japanese house.

If indeed Japanese tax law explained the squeeze—and it is far from clear that it did—then the problem was more insidious than it looked. An evil-intentioned Tokyo trying to carry out a "Pearl Harbor"–style attack on American markets presents a straightforward, alarming challenge. An investment community that doesn't yet understand the degree to which America's finances are now subject to foreign controls—and therefore continues to rely one-sidedly on American thinking—is capable of sleeping through the apocalypse and waking only after it's too late.

The 1986 bond squeeze was a seminal event. Congressman Schumer, from his position on the House Banking Committee, posed some barbed questions about the implications of the squeeze to the Federal Reserve Bank's E. Gerald Corrigan. The gist of the response was that the Japanese had done nothing illegal.

One wouldn't have expected Corrigan to say otherwise. His bank's mandate is to raise funds for the U.S. government at the lowest possible cost. Strong Japanese participation in American bond markets supports that goal. He was not about to look the Japanese gift horse in the mouth.

Those who missed their chance to learn the lesson of the warning provided by the May 1986 bond squeeze got a second, and much more revealing, chance exactly one year later.

All Quiet on the Tokyo Front

It was 12:25 P.M. on May 7, 1987, at the offices of Nomura Securities in a skyscraper high above New York's Maiden Lane. Robin Koskinen, a short dynamo of bond-trading savvy, tugged nervously at his suspenders. His piercing green eyes scanned the government bond department he'd helped build for Nomura's New York subsidiary.

Two years earlier the entire department consisted of Koskinen and a secretary. Now it numbered fifty-five people, trading more than $2.5 billion worth of U.S. bonds daily. This firm, whose chief customer base lay twelve thousand miles away, had arguably gained greater ability than any American firm to influence the interest rate that the United States government would pay for the next thirty years on the May 2017 Treasury bond about to be auctioned.

A clock above Koskinen's head indicated it was 1:25 A.M. in Tokyo. Back at headquarters in Nihonbashi (Tokyo's version of Wall Street) Nomura's key people were awake, camped out for the vigil as they always were on Treasury auction nights. Normally, open telephone lines would be burning up now as Tokyo forwarded last minute orders to New York in an atmosphere bordering on pandemonium. But this time an eerie silence prevailed.

Koskinen caucused with John Niehenke, a former U.S. Treasury official now putting his experience to work for Nomura as manager of fixed-income securities. Niehenke was the all-American type Japanese companies love to hire: tall, blond, and blue-eyed. He was fresh from a strategic job with the U.S. government, a favorite talent pool for headhunters on retainer to Japanese interests.[6] Niehenke polled his three Japanese-speaking managers of New York–Tokyo communications and then reported back to Koskinen.

Koskinen returned from his meeting at the center of the trading floor with Niehenke like a manager stalling for time to warm up a relief pitcher. Finally he said out loud what had become obvious: "It's quiet. Interest from Japan is light. *Very* light."

A sharp-minded intellectual who understands world history as well as Treasury yield curves, Koskinen appeared somewhat uncomfortable. He'd taken a job with a Japanese company because he'd sensed that was where the future in financial services lay. In theory his views on America's decline and Japan's rise were sanguine. "Go back through history," he observed. "Those in power always want to believe that something in their national character makes them great. But the fact is, no nation can maintain anything but short-term global domination. America rose to world leadership while Britain fell; Japan is rising while America is falling. In the long view of history it really isn't very surprising."

On this particular day, however, the thought of Japan holding a knife to the American jugular didn't seem like any cause for celebration either.

In thirty-five minutes the Federal Reserve Bank a few blocks away would close the sealed bidding process on $9.25 billion worth of bonds. America's rising debt (the result of spending more than it produced) combined with Japan's growing wealth (the result of choosing to save, rather than consume, a significant portion of what it produced) had come together on auction days over the last two years like the confluence of two great rivers irrigating the world economy. Today, however, there was fear of drought.

All over town every bond trader was asking every informed source for an opinion on whether or not the Japanese would show up for the day's auction. Like Koskinen, sources close to the Japanese were reporting back to American interlocutors that the Japanese would certainly not buy as heavily today as they had at prior auctions. The bond market had turned very nervous as a result.

To understand what was happening, the political context is critical. And that context can only be understood by examining the winds of the U.S.-Japan trade war that had then begun to blow.

Of Chips, Tariffs, and Bonds

The U.S.-Japan relationship was fraying badly in the spring of 1987. Feverish "Japan bashing" emanated from Capitol Hill. Blaming Japan for the trade deficit, politicians such as Congressman Richard Gephardt of Missouri unlocked the secret to getting Americans emotionally involved in economic issues that until then had usually triggered the proverbial "my eyes glaze over" response. "The Yellow Peril is widely viewed as the issue that could retake the White House in 1988," reported *Barron's*.[7] While it turned out not to be true, it was an apt summation of a leading trend of thought within the Democratic party.

Nor were the Democrats alone. Congressmen from both parties were endorsing the most protectionist trade legislation since the disastrous Smoot-Hawley tariff, which helped thrust the world economy into the Depression of the 1930s. The simplicity of blaming Japan for the unabated hemorrhaging of American "competitiveness" enjoyed an irresistible bipartisan appeal that seemed to triumph over the irrationality of that position.

Those bashing the hardest didn't stop long enough to explain why the United States was running a staggering trade deficit with nearly *all* its trading partners, not just the Japanese. If Japan's markets were as hermetically sealed as the bashers claimed, how could the Japanese import nearly $30 billion worth of American products annually— more than any other country besides Canada? Clearly, fundamental problems other than Japanese "unfairness" lay at the heart of lost American competitiveness, but the unfairness issue provided a much more expedient political focus.[8]

Two years into the Reagan administration's attack on the dollar, the Japanese yen had appreciated a shocking 80 percent against the greenback—with no noticeable effect on the trade deficit, the very problem a weak dollar was supposed to solve. The yen   once viewed by Americans as some kind of "funny money" with too many zeros to be mentally fathomable—rose to what was then a postwar record 137 to the dollar, putting it nearly on a par with one American cent. It was anything but funny money now.

After a few diminutions in the U.S. deficit, which the White House had attempted to use as "proof" that its ill-conceived dollar policy was working, the February statistics released in mid-April ballooned once again, showing a $15 billion trade gap for the month, one of the worst in history. The stock market plunged in reaction—a foreshadowing of what would come later in the year when lack of progress on the trade and budget deficits would be cited as critical factors in the "Black Monday" panic of October 19 that saw the Dow Jones Industrial Average plummet 508 points in one day.

Time echoed the national sentiment on its cover—TRADE WARS: THE U.S. GETS TOUGH WITH JAPAN—which depicted a hefty Sumo wrestler dwarfing Uncle Sam. Uncle Sam, however, was rolling up his sleeves in preparation for fisticuffs. California's Senator Pete Wilson declared, "We are already at war with Japan."[9]

The Reagan administration remained outwardly committed to "free trade" and opposed to what it viewed as Democratic party–inspired protectionism. The president continuously announced he would veto any protectionist legislation arriving on his desk. But his advisers believed it vital that the administration take a highly visible action against Japan to keep the Democrats from running too far with the issue. In pursuit of this strategy, Commerce Secretary Malcolm Baldrige, Defense Secretary Weinberger, and top officials of the CIA moved concertedly on behalf of the administration to block Japanese electronics giant Fujitsu from a planned $200 million buyout of California chipmaker Fairchild Semiconductor.

There have been Japanese acquisitions of U.S. companies that a more strategy-conscious American government might have acted to prevent. But Fairchild wasn't one of them. Although the company was depicted as a supplier of advanced components to the U.S. military in danger of slipping into treacherous foreign hands, the reality was otherwise.

Actually Fairchild was already "foreign-owned"—acquired years earlier by Schlumberger, a largely French company. But its technology had stagnated, resulting in layoffs of twenty thousand out of thirty thousand employees and losses totaling $1.5 billion. A reporter who regularly covered Silicon Valley inquired, "If the U.S. government was so concerned about the strategic value of Fairchild . . . where has it been for the last seven years?"[10] Rather than American technology falling into Japanese hands, the "technology flow in the agreement would have been a net positive from Japan to Fairchild," making the company a "stronger provider of military components," according to its president, Donald Brooks.[11]

Japanese public opinion did not take kindly to being told Fairchild was off limits. "First Americans attack us for stealing American jobs by exporting computer chips made in Japan," observed a Japanese foreign ministry official after Fujitsu was forced to withdraw from the deal. "Then, when a Japanese company wants to invest its own capital to preserve American jobs in America, you attack us even harder.

This is hypocrisy. You tell us you are for free trade, but you try to stop a business deal because the buyer is Japanese. This makes us very angry in a very emotional way."

Putting the kibosh on the Fujitsu-Fairchild deal, however, was only a warm-up for the Reagan administration's main event—the decision to slap tariffs on Japanese products in retaliation for violations of the 1986 U.S.-Japan Semiconductor Agreement. The tariffs were to be a bone thrown to a Congress vociferously complaining that the administration was too soft on Japan. In a rare display of bipartisan unity, the Senate passed a unanimous resolution calling for action on Japanese semiconductor dumping.

Thus, on the heels of the devastating trade deficit figures released in mid-April, President Reagan, the ideological sine qua non of free trade, summoned up his angriest Hollywood vitriol to denounce Japan's unfair practices and to demand retribution. Singling out violations of the U.S.-Japan Semiconductor Agreement, Reagan imposed a 100 percent tariff on the import of certain Japanese laptop computers, color TV sets, and power tools—products that accounted for $300 million worth of 1986 imports. The Reagan tariffs were billed as America's toughest retaliatory measures taken against Japan since World War II.

Although the tariffs certainly had symbolic value, they were doomed from the start as a policy lever in solving trade problems or reducing trade friction. Even the Reagan administration must have known this, because nine days after imposing the tariffs the White House was already hinting they would soon be removed. Six weeks into this supposedly "get tough" action, Reagan lifted the color TV tariff, even though not a single substantive change had taken place in U.S.-Japan trade relations.[12]

Nor was there likely to be any change on the two particular points of the semiconductor agreement the Japanese were charged with violating. One was failing to allow American chipmakers sufficient access to Japan's domestic market—a historic and complex problem of both culture and technology that no one believed could be rapidly solved—least of all in the midst of a worldwide glut in semiconductor capacity. Even American negotiators who fought to include this clause in the agreement saw it as a symbolic commitment, not a tool for immediate remedy of the situation.

On the second, and more important, issue—"dumping" computer

chips at below manufacturing cost—the Japanese had in fact taken action to curb the most abusive dumping by their chip exporters in the American market. But dumping was continuing in other Asian countries, creating a "gray market" where Americans could still get Japanese chips at below-market prices.

Those who believed Japanese manufacturers would refrain from dumping simply because their government had signed an agreement sorely misunderstood Japanese business culture. Americans regard dumping as morally abominable. But dumping is not such a bad practice in Japan. In fact, it accomplishes two great industrial goals: it keeps employees employed in times of overcapacity, enhancing company loyalty for the profitable times to come, and it builds market share by driving out competition.

In the Japanese business mind, dumping is competitive, not anticompetitive. It is samurai logic: let's both start cutting our prices. The one who can withstand the deepest cuts must have the greatest strength and deserves to win. Since Japanese chipmakers tend to be subdivisions of deep-pocketed electronics giants while American chipmakers tend to be stand-alone companies specializing in semiconductors, it's no surprise which side withstands losses better. When the bloody price-cutting wars were over, the three biggest chipmakers in the world were suddenly Japanese. This, in an industry that a decade earlier had not only been American-dominated, but had been touted as a pillar of the twenty-first-century U.S. economy.

Given the Japanese propensity for dumping, it still takes two to dump: a seller as well as a buyer. American companies reliant on Japanese suppliers for the world's cheapest, highest-quality chips aggressively connived with gray market dumping. Reports abounded in California of businessmen flying to Asia with a few hundred thousand dollars stuffed in a suitcase and returning on the next flight with the same suitcase crammed with DRAM chips.

The reality the Reagan administration sought to escape was that Japan had already won the "chip wars"—at least in the high-volume commodity chip sectors covered by the semiconductor agreement. Most of the once world-leading U.S. manufacturers—companies like Intel, Motorola, and National Semiconductor—had long since formally bowed out of the commodity memory-chip race. Setting higher prices alone could not revive an American industry that had almost ceased to exist.[13] Richard Shaffer, publisher of the *Technologic Com-*

puter Letter, observed, "To save the memory business, we would have had to impose sanctions five years ago."[14] When Japanese dumping of commodity chips finally did abate in the gray market, the reason had more to do with increased worldwide demand buoying prices than with American pressure. Demand grew so intense, in fact, that massive chip shortages occurred in 1988. Exasperated, many of the American computer industry's leading executives denounced the semiconductor accord and Washington's enforcement of it as causes of shrinking supplies.

As substance, the Reagan tariffs of April 1987 were clearly unworkable. But did they succeed in sending a symbolic message? The answer is yes, but the message didn't produce the response Washington wanted. Japan did not become convinced, as the Reagan people had hoped, that America was now "getting tough" and that Tokyo would now have to take greater initiative to reduce the trade deficit and play by America's version of free and fair trade.

Instead Japan grew angrier and more exasperated with the United States. Tokyo's trade negotiators no longer smiled and bowed. For the first time in postwar trade history, they provoked and taunted the American side. This change of style could best be seen in the persona of Makoto Kuroda, vice-minister of MITI, who emerged as point man for the Japanese side of the trade story. A squat, heavyset man, Kuroda spoke fluent English, ran intellectual circles around his Americans counterparts, wore Pierre Cardin ties to express his willingness to import high-quality foreign items, and reveled in speaking his mind.

"You Americans are so impetuous. You are like little children. Try to grow up," Kuroda declared on one occasion.[15] This bull-in-the-trade-negotiations-shop also announced he would not dignify the tariffs with the term "sanctions." The proper way to speak of them, he said, was as "silly American actions in violation of international trade agreements."

The truth was that by 1987 the Nakasone government had made important strides toward opening Japanese markets, reducing tariffs, curbing the most excessively unfair Japanese business practices, and giving play to the form, if not always the substance, of what the United States seemed to want. Now, just when Japan was doing what its leaders believed was their utmost to accommodate American needs within the constraints of their culture and time horizons, Washington's free-trader president slapped Japan with the most antagonistic, pro-tectionist measures since the two countries were deadly enemies half a century ago.

Kuroda saw the situation clearly. Reagan, he said, was attacking Japan in order to win the battle of public opinion at home. But what Reagan didn't understand was that Japan was no longer America's whipping boy. "If America continues to put unreasonable pressure on Japan," he warned, "it could provoke a very extreme reaction."

For many Japanese, the Reagan tariffs were the last straw. A body of public sentiment began to crystallize around several neonationalist ideas. Among these was the notion that Japan had endured enough pressure and public humiliation from the United States. That America had reached its peak of greatness and was now in a period of decline. That the decline of America was characterized by an irrational lashing of Japan for the sin of being successful where America was failing. That while the Japanese were once willing to listen to criticism about unfair trade practices and attempt to rectify them, it was now clear that Washington's rhetoric was a veneer to excuse America's refusal to rebuild itself through hard work and self-sacrifice. That America, once teacher and role model, was substituting protectionism and self-interest for its lofty commitments to internationalism and free trade, betraying in the process those Japanese who'd once been inspired by the American example. That it was time to find the right way—something subtle and suitably Japanese—to express Japan's frustration. That it was time to retaliate.

"Japan's Weapon Is Money"

Clayton Yeutter, the chief U.S. trade negotiator, was engaged in wishful thinking when he declared, the day the tariffs went into effect, "Japan has far too much at stake in this relationship to seriously entertain thoughts of retaliation."[16]

True, Japan did not abrogate the semiconductor agreement, as some officials hinted it might if tariffs were imposed. Nor did it add any new tariffs on American products or take any other openly retaliatory measures that might escalate the trade war. Whether or not Japanese authorities experimented with trying to provoke a U.S. computer chip shortage is not clear. Reports circulated that MITI was going to such great lengths to invoke the letter of the semiconductor agreement that it was effectively "choking off the supply of chips to hurt American computer makers."[17]

At some point the idea began to mature in the minds of Japan's elite that the most effective way to get the Reagan administration to back down would be to boycott the May auction of Treasury bonds. It would be a silent kind of retaliation, since the purchase of these bonds is theoretically decided by private sector investors, not the Japanese government. It would be an invisible, hard-to-prove act of retaliation, because the U.S. government, in its tragic affection for a bygone world order, keeps no definitive statistics on who buys and owns its bonds.[18]

Staying away from Treasury bonds would also be a measure entirely justifiable in its microeconomic fundamentals. The decline of the dollar had wiped out an estimated $13 billion worth of American bond holdings by Japanese insurance companies alone. With the dollar still in free fall, no Japanese investor could be blamed if he shied away from the auction—and many might do just that in any event. American experts were already predicting a shift by Japanese investors to other global currencies to avoid continued exposure to dollar risk. Robert Brusca, chief U.S. economist for Nikko Securities, confirmed this trend, noting, "Since the beginning of the year, nearly every single investment the Japanese have made in U.S. bonds has turned to fertilizer, and that's not the sort of thing that leads your investment to grow."[19]

In Tokyo a secret meeting of the Tanaka faction was convened. The biggest power bloc within the LDP, this faction includes some of Japan's more nationalist, anti-American voices. According to Japanese press reports, the dialogue went like this:

"We don't need to buy any more U.S. government bonds," asserted Masaharu Gotoda, the chief cabinet secretary ominously nicknamed the "violent secretary." Then he added, "We have been condemned enough by the U.S. We would be complete fools to proceed with the purchase."

Gotoda was seconded by Hajime Tamura, MITI's chief:

"He's right. Japan's weapon is money. We should let the U.S. know what would happen if Japan refused to buy U.S. government bonds."[20]

Throughout late April and early May, the bond market zigzagged on news about what the Japanese would do at the upcoming auction.

Wall Street largely discounted reports of a Japanese investment strike, preferring to believe that America still had the upper hand. "The Japanese have no other place to put their money," ran the popular explanation. "No other market in the world can absorb so much cash. Besides, U.S. Treasuries have yields 5 percent higher than Japanese government bonds. No professional investor can pass up that kind of premium."

It may have been a comforting way to deny Japan's real role in the American economy, but it was a sorely flawed line of reasoning on every point. True, the U.S. bond market represents 57 percent of the world total, but that still leaves 43 percent of the world available—enough to house Japanese capital flows at least on a short-term basis, even without resorting to equity markets and other parking places for excess cash.

The idea of a Japanese investor unable to resist the temptation of a 5 percent yield spread is a naive American way of looking at the world. Only now in the late 1980s is the idea of investing for maximum return becoming a popular current of thought in Nihonbashi. The history of the Tokyo Stock Exchange is one of investment for the sake of cementing business relationships and extending interlocking business networks, not a search for return on investment (ROI). The history of the Tokyo government bond market is a history of financial institutions loaning money back to the government at low rates in return for the government's benevolent protection. To a large Japanese institution whose fund managers have no fear of losing their job if another institution shows better year-end performance, 5 percent is nothing to get terribly excited about—especially when Japanese economists were predicting declines in the dollar's value that would vitiate much of the yield spread between American and Japanese government bonds anyway.

Those who doubted Japan's willpower to resist the Treasury auction began to change their minds after a Sumitomo Life Insurance executive announced that his company—normally a big buyer—would not participate. Rumors swirled through Tokyo's financial press of a full-scale boycott by institutional investors. The rumors sent bond prices plunging and interest rates soaring. "The escalation of trade problems between the U.S. and Japan poses new doubts about the potential for a continuation of Japanese capital flows to this country," noted Nomura's chief New York economist.[21]

Interest-rate-sensitive markets didn't wait to find out whether the rumors were true. Even a small reduction of Japanese capital inflows would have a formidable impact. Mortgage rates, which had been declining almost without interruption for two years, suddenly stopped dead in their tracks, turned around, and shot up by two full percentage points before April was over. "Chaos," "stampede," and "turmoil" were the words used to describe what was happening to shoppers for the American dream house during those volatile weeks. Enormous jumps took place "in the blink of an eye," said the president of a mortgage banking company. "I've never seen anything like it in my fourteen years."[22]

Just how important a force had Japan become in the daily life of the American economy? *Forbes* offered a fitting illustration: the spike in interest rates caused by the Japanese withdrawal from the Treasury market was directly responsible for a slowdown in home buying in Peoria.[23]

Worried about the consequences of a Japanese flight from the American market, Federal Reserve Chairman Paul Volcker convened a secret emergency telephone meeting of his policy-making committee. He received their support for a hike in short-term interest rates with the goal of firming the dollar to make American bonds more attractive to the disappearing Japanese. "Fed policy is now increasingly influenced and even dictated by the needs of our foreign creditors," the Mellon Bank's top economist explained.[24]

Treasury auctions usually take place over a three-day period. The first two days are devoted to short-term T-bills and notes, while the final day is reserved for the drama of the thirty-year long bond. In this case, Japanese investors spent the first two days acting as bearish as possible. "Interest from Japan was virtually nonexistent," *The Wall Street Journal* told its readers.[25] A dire *New York Times* report appeared under the headline BONDS DIVE AS JAPANESE HOLD BACK; TENSION BUILDS.[26]

In the psychology that had come to dominate Wall Street, American investors were waiting for the Japanese to show their hand before making up their minds about their own level of confidence in the American bond market. "Suppose the U.S. Treasury held a bond auction and nobody came?"[27] wondered *Newsweek* in a blackly humorous vein that illustrated how the auction had vaulted out of the domain of bond watchers and into the mass media—even when competing for space that week with far juicier news stories such as Gary Hart's fling with model Donna Rice and the death of ex–CIA chief William Casey.

The stakes mounted as long bond auction day dawned. The lower the demand from Japan, the higher the yield would have to be to sell the bonds. Each percentage point in higher yield would cost the U.S. Treasury roughly $3 billion over the next thirty years. A jump of a single point would also cost consumers and businesses untold billions in higher interest rates. The Japanese were in a position to teach Americans a most expensive lesson.

What happened next remains enigmatic. Even though powerful figures within the Japanese government had initiated talk of using the auction as a political weapon, Nakasone's cabinet now shifted its stance. Reports leaked out that MoF was using its influence with financial institutions to make sure they took their usual positions in the auction. American Treasury officials were quietly assured Tokyo would prevent a boycott.

To the degree official attitudes shifted, the change was probably the work of Finance Minister Kiichi Miyazawa, a brilliant economist and one of Japan's most internationally minded politicians. Miyazawa believed the world economy was too precariously perched to withstand bond market brinksmanship. Those "anti-Americans" in the Tanaka faction might not understand their own strength. Too massive a Japanese retreat from U.S. bonds could actually induce a recession in the American economy with severe international repercussions chilling world demand for Japanese products and ultimately undermining Japan's domestic economy.

The existing climate of fear in the U.S. bond market had made Japan's point clearly enough to those in the Reagan administration capable of understanding it, thus removing the necessity of pressing it much further. Japan, it turned out, could have more impact on the United States by inducing fear of retaliation than the United States could have on Japan by carrying out actual acts of retaliation. It was all very Zen.

The Clock Strikes One

About 12:45 P.M. in New York on auction day, activity began to pick up perceptibly on Nomura's trading floor. A few sizable orders came in at the last minute. Robin Koskinen, John Niehenke, and other top

American and Japanese executives huddled again to finalize No-mura's bid, which would be called in to their representative standing by at the Federal Reserve Bank ninety seconds before the close of bidding. Hand-scrawled calculations on yellow legal pads—an amaz-ing anomaly in this computer-intensive business—were passed back and forth among the top traders. One last check with Tokyo. A little wave of electricity vibrated through the room. Traders got to their feet. The bid was called in. A collective exhalation of relief went up.

At the end of the day, Nomura had bought about a billion dollars' worth of bonds—the firm's lightest participation in a Treasury auc-tion in more than a year, but a heavyweight participation by anyone else's standards. Directly across the lower end of Manhattan Island, Daiwa had taken down a similarly large—although smaller than usual—chunk of the auction. There, the ever-polite Bill Brachfeld, a lanky, oxford blue–shirted veteran of twenty-one years trading bonds at Salomon, looked at the auction's result—an average yield of 8¾ percent. It was more than a point higher than the last auction just three months ago and represented a dramatic swing in a dangerous direction for interest rates. By itself the hike wouldn't necessarily shut down the U.S. economic boom, but it would certainly cast a shadow over it.

"The problem," Brachfeld said, weary from the tumult of the long day, "isn't the Japanese." Excusing himself for lapsing into profanity, he continued. "The problem is that we're a goddamned debtor nation, and when you're a goddamned debtor nation, you're at the mercy of your goddamned creditors."

When it was all over, estimates of Japanese investor participation ranged from a quarter to a third of the issue—not the strongest show of enthusiasm for the American bond market the Japanese had ever made, but not bad under the circumstances. Japan hadn't inflicted the damage it could have with a full-scale boycott. This time it had only extracted a severe penalty from the U.S. government in the form of sharply higher interest rates. Those higher rates would protect the value of the bonds for Japanese investors when the dollar slid further. But that was only a by-product of two far more important victories on the bond market battlefield of May 7.

The first was that Japan obtained a tacit truce in the brewing trade war with Washington without further meaningful action on the Japa-nese side—and in spite of a record U.S. trade deficit of nearly $18 billion for the month of July and another record again in October.

Even the Washington hysteria touched off in June, when it was learned that a Toshiba subsidiary had illegally sold sensitive submarine-quieting technology to the Soviets, passed surprisingly quickly. Toshiba Machine's flagrant violation of COCOM export procedures cost the United States far more in the military technology race with the Soviet Union than any amount of Japanese chip dumping. But after a few weeks of inflamed rhetoric, which included the highly publicized Toshiba smashing action by Capitol Hill law makers, the brouhaha subsided. Throughout the rest of 1987 a chastened Reagan administration took no further punitive action against Japan on the trade front. The only presidential action on trade was to rescind more of the April tariffs.

The second and more far-reaching result of May's events was that public perception of the United States as a debtor country reliant on foreign capital made a quantum leap. Although U.S. economic growth would continue in a statistical sense for many more months, May's auction-fueled interest rate hike represented the end of the economic pendulum's travels in one direction and the beginning of its return swing. Even those most bullish on Reaganomics began to turn bearish, sensing something terribly wrong with an American economy riding on the twin rails of budget and trade deficits while propped up by foreign investors. To those who took the time to think about it, May's events demonstrated exactly what the Japanese wanted Americans to understand: push Japan too far, and the Japanese could pull out the props.

The fear that this near death experience engendered for the U.S. economy, bottled up through months of inaction by the Reagan administration, finally found its catharsis in the form of the October 1987 stock market panic. Influential segments of the American business community, if not the White House leadership, had begun to recognize the nightmare inherent in foreigners holding the mortgage on the Reaganomic dream house.

Part II

CREDITORS AND DEBTORS, SURPLUSES AND DEFICITS

4

Zaitek! From Toyotas to T-Bills, Japan's Amazing Transition from Exporting Goods to Exporting Capital

At the beginning of my career, we were still under occupation and had practically no foreign exchange. Japanese mills needed to buy American cotton, but the Americans told us no commercial bank was creditable enough to borrow the $40 million needed. The Bank of Japan, our central bank, was in this case the only bank creditworthy enough to borrow money from the Export-Import Bank in the U.S.

The negotiations were difficult. I commuted to the Exim Bank in Washington so often that thirty-five years later, I still remember their address: 811 Vermont Avenue. Eventually, we got the loan. The text of the agreement was in English, and the currency was U.S. dollars.

At the end of my career, our foreign exchange reserve was increasing sharply. We wanted to use a part of our wealth for the benefit of the world. We decided to make what was then the biggest single loan to the World Bank—100 billion yen. Mr. Brochas, general counsel for the World Bank, flew to Tokyo and signed the agreement written in Japanese, not a word of which he understood. The currency was, of course, Japanese yen.

—Shiro Inoue, former senior
executive, Bank of Japan

The Simplicity of Samuel Smiles

Yoshitoki Chino, the chairman of Daiwa Securities, was standing next to a huge Western-style painting by a Japanese artist that covered most of a wall at Daiwa's headquarters in Nihonbashi. The image depicted the rape of Europa—a beautiful, buxom, flaxen-haired nude being carried off on the back of a large brown bull. It was a startling choice of decoration for the boardroom of the most international-minded of Japanese brokerage houses.

Chino is the lone fluent English speaker among the chairmen and presidents of Japan's Big Four securities companies. His commitment to the international aspect of Japanese finance probably runs the deepest. "Fifteen years ago, the competition among Japanese securities companies was very intense in the domestic market," he recalled. "The other companies were fighting over market share in the tiniest corners of Japan. We examined the international arena and found a void of Japanese activity there. So we decided to fill it."

Once number four in Japan, Daiwa had become number two largely through its innovative activities abroad. These include pioneering the Asian Dollar Market in Singapore (now $200 billion in size) and the Euroyen Market in Europe (where yen bonds now account for a major share of all issues). Daiwa was also the first to introduce an American company to a Tokyo Stock Exchange listing, the first Japanese house to lead manage a U.S. dollar bond offering for an American company (General Telephone), and the first to add a former Western leader to its advisory board (Helmut Schmidt).

Daiwa has come a long way from its humble origins more than eighty years ago as the Fujimoto Bill Broker Co. Today it is second among world securities firms in market capitalization, trailing only Nomura, which is headquartered just a few blocks away. In a year when many American brokerage firms would be lucky to show a profit, Daiwa's net was over a billion dollars. Employing nine thousand people in 120 domestic and foreign offices, Daiwa is a member of every major world stock exchange. It is a primary dealer in U.S. Treasuries, and it has a hand in global activities ranging from raising funds for China's venture-capital arm to managing pension assets for the state of Oregon's employees.

Chino is a philosopher as well as a financial pioneer. Asked how

Japan had grown so rich so fast, he said he could explain most of the process with two simple ideas. Both made reference to British history, an area in which Chino was quite knowledgeable.[1]

The first idea was the devotion to hard work and self-reliance summarized by the saying, "God helps those who help themselves"—a rubric popularized in Samuel Smiles's nineteenth-century classic *Self-Help*. This book had an enormous impact on Japan immediately after the Meiji Revolution of 1868. The Meiji era was a time of great opening to foreign ideas. It marked the beginning of Japan's century-long drive to catch up to the West industrially, scientifically, and militarily. Translations of foreign books swept the country. But the most popular of all was *Self-Help,* a veritable bible of British Victorian ideas on economics. To a generation of Japanese whose goal was catching up to the British standard of success, Samuel Smiles offered a how-to manual. He emphasized the importance of thrift and duty and argued that nothing was impossible with hard work and self-reliance as the cornerstones of entrepreneurial undertakings. In Smiles the Japanese found an Industrial Age expression of traditional Asian virtues, and they enshrined it as gospel. The book sold a million copies to a total population that was then only about thirty million. Chino's own great-grandfather read it and became a true believer. Today's wealth, Chino said, was the product of an entire nation's collective hard work, self-reliance, and thrift.

Chino's second principle was "Don't make war"—something he believed Japan was fortunate not to have done for more than forty years. Referring again to the British experience, Chino pointed out that when Robert Walpole became prime minister, France was richer than England. But by emphasizing trade and industry and avoiding war for most of his twenty-one years in power while Europe was mired in conflict, Walpole's England surpassed France economically. Japan, he said, had enjoyed peace for twice as long as Walpole's tenure. "If you don't destroy your economy in war, and don't waste productive resources on building armaments, a hardworking nation will become rich."

Despite the simplicity of Chino's "two ideas," they go a long way toward explaining Japan's competitive economic edge.

Americans pride themselves on a hardworking spirit, but Japanese log two hundred hours a year more on the job. Only recently have Japanese companies begun to think of Saturday as a day off. The

U.S. supports a large unemployed population that has averaged 5–10 percent of the work force during the 1980s, compared with Japanese unemployment rates of 2–3 percent. While Social Security and other entitlement programs make up a large slice of the U.S. budget, it is only in the last few years that Japan has begun to allocate any substantial portion of its national resources to these sorts of budgetary commitments. Even today most Japanese are expected to save enough during their working years to be self-reliant in old age. Holding fast to Samuel Smiles–type principles that have long since slipped away from Anglo-American culture, the Japanese simply work longer and harder than Americans do.

Douglas MacArthur was well aware of the competitive advantage inherent in the Japanese approach to work. In 1951 he warned that Japanese veneration of work could eventually propel Japan forward against an America consumed with the desire for less work and more luxury.[2] It was a prophetic observation. Even though leisure-time industries are now booming, the Japanese still do not begin to draw the sharp distinction between work and the rest of their lives that Americans do. In many respects work is still viewed as the purpose of life itself.

Imagine what the U.S. economic snapshot might look like today if Americans worked as many hours as the Japanese, and if large sections of the U.S. welfare state were unnecessary because of nearly full employment. *Now add to that picture the 6 percent differential in GNP between the American and Japanese defense budgets redeployed for the purpose of rebuilding the U.S. industrial base.* Under such circumstances, it is doubtful the United States would suffer a "competitiveness" problem.

Such a course is not an immediately viable policy alternative for Americans at this moment in time. History prevents unilateral abandonment of either our military commitments or our social programs. It is imperative, however, that we recognize Japan's lighter burden in these regards as a major competitive advantage. The reason the playing field in the U.S.-Japan economic rivalry isn't level has less to do with Japanese "unfairness" than with the basic facts of life suggested by Mr. Chino.

To propose solving American economic problems by clubbing Japan over the head until it is willing to save less, consume more, and work less hard—to force it, in other words, onto a level playing field by injecting it with the same social ills the United States faces—is a travesty on America's own sense of values. Yet that is exactly what many in Washington are doing when they call on Tokyo to "expand" an already expansive Japanese economy, lower already microscopic Japanese interest rates, and tax the Japanese citizenry into spending rather than saving. Such an approach will never work. Too many wise men like Chino know all too well from whence Japan's wealth comes, and they aren't about to pull out the foundations unless they find an alternate source.

The Miracle in the Rabbit Hutch

Japan's leading export to the United States is no longer automobiles or electronic goods, it is capital. Throughout this decade Japan has exported back to the United States the capital surplus it accumulated by trading with Americans, using these billions to purchase bonds, extend long-term loans, buy equities, and make myriad direct investments.

In the past, the Japanese focused on making their money the "old-fashioned way"—working hard, saving hard, and trading hard. Like a nation of 125 million Horatio Algers, they have amassed a fortune by following that path. With that fortune they now roam the globe, buying up the best of everything and hiring the rest of the world to work for them. It's an old story Americans know well, having done exactly the same thing in the past.

Many good books have been written about how the Japanese achieved their great economic success, and it would be superfluous to dwell on that subject at length here. But we need to review a few basic features of the Japanese economy to understand Japan's growing role as world banker and investor. This select tour will show that Japan's prodigious strength as a generator of surplus capital is rooted in the carefully designed structure of the Japanese economy itself. What most people in the West have always thought of as an industrial miracle was more or less *destined* to mature into a financial miracle by virtue of the way Japan chose to industrialize. The conclusion that emerges from this way of looking at Japan's postwar growth is that its ability to export capital on a large scale has become a structural feature of its system. Rather than being a short-lived phenomenon, the outflow of Japanese capital still has a very long way to go along the trajectory of its likely historical curve.

The evidence that Japan at some point would become the world's

leading capital exporter has been visible for a long time, particularly
to those who made the effort to look. Nearly twenty years ago Herman Kahn alluded to such a possibility in his book *The Emerging
Japanese Superstate*. He and his colleague Thomas Pepper came back
to the idea with a more specific prediction in 1978: "By the end of the
century, Japan is almost certain to become . . . the world's largest capital exporter, with an annual net capital outflow in the tens of billions
of dollars."[3]

That this result occurred in the 1980s rather than the 1990s is a
product of a fortuitous run of international events—particularly the
advent of Reaganomics in the United States—which dovetailed perfectly with prescient Japanese policies. We will examine some of this
recent history further on. But let us return first to the underpinnings of
the Japanese economic miracle. To Chino's ideas about work and
peace, three corollaries should be added:

1. *Japan does better what the West was already doing well.*[4] In
ancient times the Japanese imported their language and culture from
China and Korea; in modern times they imported business and technical know-how from the West. There is some validity to the Western
notion that the Japanese are "superadapters" rather than creators, but
this popular idea should be handled with extreme caution. American
business theory erroneously deifies "creativity" while assigning a pe-
jorative connotation to "adaptivity." In reality successful adaptations
can be just as important as original creations. The American experience itself underlines this theme: Henry Ford invented very little that
had to do with the automobile; Steve Jobs invented none of the basic
technology inside the Apple computer. What both entrepreneurs did
was exactly what the Japanese do so well—adapt, mass-produce, and
market a better package based on what others have already created.

From the transistor to the computer chip, from lasers to biotechnology, the Japanese approach to this issue is now a well-traveled road:
they reverse-engineer, license, and occasionally even steal American
technical breakthroughs. Then they adapt them, improve the production process, raise the quality, lower the cost, and eventually put the
inventors out of business. Although this approach won't carry Japan
too much further, since its industries have already caught up to the
Western state of the art in most respects, it has been a highly cost-effective way of pursuing industrial development until now.

In an analogous way, the Japanese have absorbed Western operational principles. The now famous Japanese penchant for quality control, for example, was inspired by the work of W. Edwards Deming, an American business thinker who became a national hero in Japan while remaining virtually unknown in his native country. Other elements of much vaunted "Japanese management theory" (the "hands-on" approach, attention to customer service, and so forth) also come right out of the American model the Japanese studied in the 1950s, even though these ideas now have to be reimported from Japan into American corporate life.

2. Japan's success is also attributable to something the West has mostly not done very well: *Japan balances the healthy, cleansing efficiencies of the free market with the larger and longer-term needs of society requiring national planning and a cooperative consensus.*

Although Japanese industry is perceived in the West as functioning like a series of giant conspiratorial cartels, the domestic market is actually an intensely competitive proving ground. Few industries in the world know the ferociousness of competition that typifies domestic Japanese automobile and electronics production. Profit margins are routinely shaved to the bone, and companies engage in all-out war to add features and streamline manufacturing. When the survivors come to the United States, Americans perceive them as newcomers. In reality, however, they are skilled, experienced giants, preselected for success by the violent Darwinian jungle of their home market.

Even as the Japanese economy relies on such efficiencies of the free market, it also utilizes a heavy dose of economic planning and government industrial policy emanating from the twin power centers of MITI and MoF.[5] Japan's great national undertakings, such as the "full employment plan" launched in 1956 and the "income doubling plan" set in motion by Prime Minister Hayato Ikeda in 1960, proved to be textbook studies in successful macroeconomic management by government. Current efforts to carry out a planned, balanced stimulation of the domestic economy appear headed for similar success. The choice of which industries to develop for export, which areas of R&D to encourage, when to establish tariffs, and when to remove them are all products of highly deliberate planning. MITI, MoF, and other government institutions exercise far more control over the economy than can be deduced from afar, because much of what they do isn't legislated or written down anywhere. Instead their influence takes the form of what is politely termed "administrative guidance" and "moral suasion." These pleasant-sounding phrases are often the government's chief tools in making sure that Japanese companies temper their search for profits and returns on investment with the national interest.

Direct government intervention in the Japanese economy is now waning as Tokyo unfolds an array of liberalization measures. But unlike American-style deregulation, the process of change itself has thus far been slow and well ordered. The motion toward a less planned economy is itself the subject of intense planning.

If Japan does better what the West does well, it also does better what the socialist East has always promised but never yet achieved. "Japan is really the world's best example of socialism," a Nomura investment banker once observed. "The Russians and the Chinese should come to Tokyo to find out how to mix a planned economy with a market economy."

3. Finally we come to the area of Japan's success most shaped by its unique cultural experiences. This is the fact that *Japan has the ability to rally broad national support for its economic goals, including public acceptance of personal or corporate sacrifice to achieve them*. America and other Western countries have generally exhibited this strength only in wartime. The Japanese have been able to evoke it for sustained periods of peacetime development.

Alone in modern history, Japan for the two decades prior to 1986 could manufacture state-of-the-art products to be sold on world markets at relatively high prices, while paying its workers wages typical of a less developed country. At times, of course, the trade unions attempted to secure a bigger piece of the miraculous pie. But by and large Japan succeeded in depressing the revolution of rising expectations throughout the great growth years of the 1960s and 1970s with appeals for patriotism, austerity, and national sacrifice. Eventually wages were raised and standards of living improved—but long after workers had earned them through their increases in productivity.

Alone among today's industrial democracies, Japan retains the right to openly demand sacrifice from its people. When Japan enters a downturn, its employers seek and usually gain labor's cooperation in accepting lower pay until the crisis is over. Keeping wages artificially low, Japan was able to consistently gain global market share for its exporters over a twenty-year period. The cult of market share worked: even now that Japan has become a high-wage country, its exporters are hanging on to their markets much more tenaciously than American economists generally expected.

To oversimplify a bit, the difference between what Japanese workers of the 1960s and 1970s should have been paid (commensurate with Western standards) and what they were paid accumulated on the books of Japanese corporations as cash. That trend was magnified even further in the early 1980s because of the dollar's strength. With Americans bingeing on imports and paying strong dollars for goods produced by Japanese workers paid in weak yen, those dollars piled up inexorably on balance sheets. As Kazuo Nukazawa, the chief economist for the Keidanren (Japan's powerful federation of economic organizations) notes, "Traditional industrial companies like Toyota and Matsushita are known in Japan today as the 'Toyota Bank' and the 'Matsushita Bank.'"

Japan's ability to mobilize its people is doubtless connected to its cultural and geographic reality. Just as Americans see openness and optimism in our national character rooted in the drive west to settle new frontiers, Japanese believe their insularity and closed culture derive from three centuries of autarky they experienced before Commodore Perry's "Black Ships" arrived in 1853 to forcibly pry open the country.

"We are a small, crowded island with few natural resources that has only been open to the outside world for a short period of time," foreigners are told over and over again in Japan. It is a catch-all used to explain everything different about Japan from the United States—why the Japanese still think of themselves as poor even though they are rich; why adults are workaholics and children studyholics; why Japan puts the interests of the group ahead of the individual, the future ahead of the present, exporting ahead of importing, and saving ahead of consuming.

Virtually every Japanese learns to think this way at an early age. With the world's densest population, one cannot physically act or move without thinking of the group. The shared belief system embodied in such ideas as "we Japanese," "Japan against the world," and "sacrifice for the good of the nation" is a material force absorbed osmotically by every schoolchild who must learn to survive the Tokyo subway's crushing crowds at rush hour.

Japanese culture is also endowed with long-term time horizons. Just as Japanese corporations are free to pursue distant goals without American-style quarter-to-quarter pressure, Japanese prime ministers and economic planners are under no compulsion to deliver the goods immediately. Japan is, for all intents and purposes, a one-party state. The LDP has been in power continuously since the mid-1950s. Although organized factional quarrels are rife within the party, its economic policy has been far more consistent than that permitted by the swinging American political pendulum. In Japan policies are generally pursued until they bear fruit, while changes are made slowly to spare dislocation. Most of all, Japan can dare to embark on the grand visions of the type that no longer exist in the West, except in the fairy tales of presidential campaign rhetoric.

The Japanese economy is certainly not immune to serious problems. Its strengths are strengths chiefly in relation to American weaknesses, not in an absolute sense. As the government relaxes its role and the economy adjusts to its maturity and global position, some traditional Japanese virtues may diminish or disappear from its operations. The hypothesis that Japan is more capable than the United States of coping with the demands of systemic change will be put to a severe test in the coming years. But it is also important that we not assume a weakness in the Japanese system simply because it would be a weakness in ours.

The American press, for example, has expended considerable energy pitying the poor Japanese "salary man" who works too hard and consumes too little of Japan's new wealth. This seems to be an obvious flaw in the Japanese scheme of things. More than a few foreigners in Japan actually relish such realities as a way of maintaining their sanity in the otherwise all-consuming sea of Japanese success that surrounds them.

"Applying for a securities license was a nightmare, like something out of Kafka," the head of one foreign brokerage firm in Tokyo confides. "I can't count the number of times I had to go up to the Ministry of Finance and grovel before some petty bureaucrat over whether or not we could pass through the golden door of the Tokyo Stock Market. The only way I survived the ordeal was to remind myself that when it was over, I'd be living like a king back at home, and this guy would still be living in a rabbit hutch."

Given a choice, anyone would rather live like a king than in the prevalent Japanese housing unit derisively designated as a "rabbit hutch" by a European Economic Community official some years ago. But is the fact that the dedicated, well-educated, highly skilled MoF man lives in such a humble dwelling a weakness of national economic strategy? Arguably, the social contract behind his willingness to do so (even if he complains about it more today than ever before) represents one of the greatest sources of strength in the Japanese system.

The truth is that Japan promises its citizens less, and expects more from them in return, than any other developed nation. For a quarter of a century the Japanese economy has grown far faster than the American economy. But over that entire time the Japanese have also been expected to save more of what their economy produces than Americans save of theirs. Those are two very powerful multipliers. In the early days, when Japanese industry needed to reinvest heavily for future growth, that equation translated into what appeared only as incremental increases in accumulation of capital. Now, with Japan's internal needs diminishing and the same equation still in force, the enormous savings locked up by history inside the Japanese economy explodes in geometric progression.

As a matter of policy, the Japanese government in the postwar period extended no tax incentives to encourage home ownership—or any other type of consumer debt for that matter. In fact, the government restricted the growth of mortgage-related financial products and made it difficult for people to buy homes without first saving up considerable cash down payments. As a result the portion of personal income going into savings shot up, freeing capital reserves for allocation to the development of new industries. (These measures were, of course, diametrically opposed to postwar U.S. policy, which encouraged homeowners to take out mortgages by providing generous tax incentives.)

Housing conditions are one of the great sacrifices the Japanese people have made for their economic miracle. Often living with three generations of their family in a unit less than half the size of the average American home, they surrendered more than living space. In such confined quarters they were physically constrained from owning or consuming material possessions, even long after Japan had fully recovered from its lengthy campaign of postwar austerity.

The important thing to understand here is that the rabbit hutches were not a random accident of the real estate market, but a *choice*

Japan made; part of the price of a larger economic strategy.

Today that choice is being rewarded. Japanese industry no longer needs the capital infusions it did early on. Balance sheets of industrial companies are so cash heavy that they can afford to lend low-interest money to their employees to build homes. Thus, even though real estate prices in and around Tokyo have skyrocketed, interest rates are low enough to permit the greatest housing boom in the country's history. Construction starts are running at an annual pace of almost two million units, meaning that more homes are now being constructed in absolute numbers than in the twice-as-populous United States. While most are still small, they are bigger than before. The era of the multi-generational family sharing a home is drawing to a close. American-style townhouses are being built in the suburbs; glossy condominiums with the latest life-style features are going up in the cities. Ironically this housing boom is taking place at a time when young Americans are finding it increasingly difficult to become homeowners.

The Japanese have saved their money and deferred consumption; Americans have consumed their money and gone into debt. Japan *underconsumes* the wealth it produces by a factor of almost 20 per-cent—leaving vast sums to accumulate and compound. America *overconsumes,* spending 3 percent more every year than the value of what it produces, thus compounding every type of public and private indebtedness.

At a certain point the numbers start to do funny things. While on the housing subject, let us consider a relevant analogy. The United States economy today is in the position of the man who takes out an adjustable-rate mortgage on a $250,000 house. Interest rates go up, he sweats to make his payments, and, if he survives the ordeal, he winds up paying the bank back almost $1 million by the time he's through.

Japan, on the other hand, is like the man who has already saved up $1 million, even though he had to live in a rabbit hutch while he was doing it. Now he too buys a $250,000 home, but he pays cash for it and deposits the remaining $750,000 in the bank, where it earns high interest. When interest rates go up, his savings are fattened. With these windfalls he adds improvements to his house and begins to invest in real estate elsewhere.

It is the race between the tortoise and the hare; the fable of the hedonistic grasshopper and the hardworking bee. We all know who wins such contests. It is easy for Westerners to look down their noses at life in the cramped quarters of Japanese rabbit hutches. But as it turns out, they deserve more respect. They stand at the very foundation of the Japanese miracle.

A Nation of Savers

The architects of the postwar Japanese economy did not specifically set out to make their country the world's financial leader. But in hindsight the basic choice they made about Japan's industrial recovery inevitably set that process in motion.

Out of the rubble of World War II, three obvious reconstruction alternatives presented themselves. Japan could rebuild by inviting in foreign (that is, American) direct investment; it could borrow heavily from abroad; or it could nationalize what remained of its industrial structure and pursue a centralized, state capitalist model. Most Western European countries relied on one or all of these mechanisms, along with the American-sponsored Marshall Plan, to rebuild their devastated economies.

Japan chose none of the above. In part, foreign capital was not easy to come by. The Americans provided substantial reconstruction aid, but there was no Marshall Plan for Japan. As late as the end of the 1960s, American financiers were still relatively skeptical about Japan's creditworthiness. Nobuya Hagura, president of Dai-Ichi Kangyo Bank (the largest bank in the world today with assets of more than a quarter-trillion dollars), remembers 1965–68, when he was posted to New York, as a time when "my biggest job was to try to borrow from the money center banks. It wasn't easy. I constantly had to try to convince them that Japan was a good risk."

Even if foreign capital had been more abundant, it is not clear Japan would have opted to rely on it. The Japanese did not want foreigners to gain undue influence over the economy, nor did they particularly want to share the wealth on that distant day in the future when they knew they would be prosperous once again. Until the 1980s Japan made itself one of the world's most inhospitable climates for outside capital, forcing foreign companies into joint ventures, subjecting them to a wide range of controls, and prohibiting them from repatriating profits. Under these circumstances even those American companies that had played a prominent role in prewar

Japan—like Ford and General Motors, which together had dominated the Japanese automobile market in the 1930s—never regained their foothold.

Instead of relying on foreign capital, postwar planners chose to adopt measures compelling Japan to generate its own capital surplus through savings and trade. That surplus, in turn, would be tapped as Japanese industry moved up the ladder of skill and technology toward competition with the world's industrial leaders. Even now that we know they succeeded, it still seems like an impossible dream. The audacity of this vision, as it migrated from exporting steel to exporting VCRs over a twenty-five-year period, is aptly described by Pulitzer Prize–winning historian Thomas McCraw in a compendium of Harvard scholarship, *America versus Japan:*

"Export steel to the United States, with its rich deposits of iron ore and coking coal, its immense steel mills around Gary, Pittsburgh, and Birmingham? Send Japanese-built cars to compete with the world-renowned products of General Motors, Ford, and Chrysler? . . . Export motorcycles into a world market dominated by long-established and powerful giants from the United States (Harley-Davidson), Germany (BMW), and Britain (Triumph)?

"Cameras? How could Japan possibly carve out a niche for itself in a world market dominated at the inexpensive end by Eastman Kodak and Polaroid, and at the high end by the advanced optics technology of Leica and other German producers? Watches? Again, Timex and similar companies already held a tight grip on the low end of the market. The upper end was occupied even more solidly by the Swiss, whom all would-be competitors had failed to dislodge over a period of several centuries. Export television sets, tape recorders, and VCRs to America, the very nation whose companies had invented them and which still held proprietary rights to the necessary technology?"[6]

To understand how the Japanese could dare to dream this impossible dream, it is necessary to dispense with the popular notion that the Japanese economic miracle is the exclusive product of the last forty years. Industrialization really began in the nineteenth century with the Meiji Revolution. By the 1930s Japan was one of the world's greatest industrial powers and a net creditor nation. Even then Britain condemned Japan's rising exports to India, while France was shocked to see Japanese traders appear right in their colonial backyard as competitors in the Maghreb. Even then the West perceived a Japanese economic conspiracy taking shape in the monopolistic structure of the huge industrial groupings known as *zaibatsus*—Mitsui, Mitsubishi, Sumitomo, and Yasuda. Then, too, Japan was not exactly inexperienced in building high-technology products—its armaments industry proved capable of churning out a high volume of advanced aircraft for the war.

Although much of Japan's physical plant was destroyed after World War II, its knowledge about industrial organization, manufacturing, trade, and finance was not. The very *zaibatsus* blamed for the rise of Japanese militarism were nominally broken up, but the same old names and faces resurfaced afterward in the form of loosely associated conglomerate groupings today known as *keiretsus*. Less than one percent of Japan's wartime business leaders were purged from their posts. In one respect the new environment was easier: Japanese business could focus single-mindedly on increasing production without having to bear the extraordinary burden of fueling a military economy.

Properly speaking, the Japanese economic miracle has been a century in the making, minus a severe interruption during the war. To think of it this way is not to minimize the stunning feat of human effort required to get Japan back on its feet and attain parity with the West in less than forty years' time. Rather, it only suggests that those who chose this course knew what they were doing. Japan's postwar recovery and growth was not a wild gamble, but a calculated, measured plan.

From today's vantage point, the most interesting part of that plan was the decision to generate internally the capital required to fund the nation's industrial rebirth. And to do that Japan needed first to build the mechanism that today stands as the greatest of its many engineering triumphs—a national savings machine unparalleled in economic history.

The Confucian cultural bent toward savings provided a good foundation for economic architects to assemble pro-savings policy structures. But in comparing the Japanese household savings rate, which has averaged over 15 percent of personal income in the 1980s, with the paltry American average of 6 percent during the same time period, or in examining Japan's 30 percent gross national savings rate (meaning all types of saving—personal, corporate, and government), which is twice as large as America's, the biggest part of the difference is *not* attributable primarily to Japanese culture. Before World War II, American and Japanese national savings rates were roughly equivalent. Americans, after all, also once believed that "a penny saved is a penny earned."

The difference in savings rates—and the resulting exponential difference in capital formation—is chiefly explained by Japanese policies consciously designed to promote savings. American postwar policies, meanwhile, have been consciously designed to promote consumption at the expense of savings.

GRASSHOPPERS AND BEES:
U.S. AND JAPANESE HOUSEHOLD SAVINGS RATES COMPARED

	U.S.	Japan
1980	7.3	17.9
1981	7.7	18.3
1982	7.0	16.5
1983	5.5	16.3
1984	6.5	16.0
1985	5.2	16.0
1986	4.0	16.5

We have already seen how Japanese housing policy bolstered the savings rate in the past. But other policies served the same end. Whereas the United States after the war entered the golden era of "buy now, pay later," Japan has still not moved too far away from an all-cash, "pay now" society. Checks are almost unknown. Credit cards only appeared recently, and many of them are really debit cards, charging the cardholders' bank account immediately. The discipline of spending hard cash rather than easy credit is a pillar supporting the savings rate.

Another pro-savings vehicle is the "bonus system," where workers get large lump-sum distributions of 25–50 percent of their salary in annual or semiannual payouts. Americans trying to save money out of weekly or monthly paychecks find themselves asking, "What's the point?" since the amount looks so small. Japanese workers, who live within the confines of a regular salary usually parsimoniously doled out by the woman of the house, find it much easier to put most of their impressive-looking bonus into the bank when they get it. Curtailing bonuses in a bad year is also one of the chief corporate mechanisms for obtaining tolerable sacrifices from employees, since what is being lost tends to be savings rather than living income.

Tax benefits have also made saving a way of life. In the United States the IRS *penalizes* Americans who save, by taxing the interest they earn. In Japan, however, individual savings accounts have been allowed to accumulate largely untaxed. Only now are measures coming into effect to tax savings interest. As a result of offering tax-free savings accounts at the windows of twenty-two thousand post office branches—and paying a slightly higher rate than similar accounts in private banks—the *maruyu,* Japan's postal savings system, is now the largest financial institution in the world outside of central banks (current assets $1 trillion). Although tax-free savings have always been limited by individual account ceilings, this problem was circumvented for years by savers opening multiple accounts. The normally statistics-happy Japanese threw up their hands and said there was simply no way to track who had how many *maruyu* accounts. A likely story!—whose real significance was that until recently, Tokyo favored a policy that amounted to nearly unlimited, untaxed household savings. No better example of the direct relationship between a high national savings rate and the funding of economic growth can be found than the Fiscal Investment and Loan Program (FILP), under which the government uses a portion of postal savings deposits each year on a discretionary basis to finance specifically targeted industries and projects.

Japanese tax reform is imminent. Between new taxes on savings and a growing emphasis on domestic consumption, savings rates may fall. But few expect a sharp decline. "There is talk about the younger generation working less hard than their parents and spending more," says a MoF official. "That they don't like to work as hard is obvious to us in the older generation. But statistics show that they are saving *more* than their parents."

Where Interest Rates Look Like Misprints

A high savings rate is only one of the finely tuned parts of the Japanese financial engine. The uses of those savings are dramatically enlarged because of the way MoF and the Bank of Japan (BoJ) manage to hold interest rates to a minimum. With certain cyclic exceptions, the government has been able to array such an arsenal of downward forces on interest rates that the figures prominently displayed in bank windows end up looking like misprints to Western eyes. An average yield for an ordinary household savings account of only 1.76 percent at commercial banks had no trouble attracting depositors in the winter of 1987–88.

In another unique clause of the Japanese social contract, the citizen is not only called upon to save the world's highest proportion of his earnings, he is also expected to accept the world's most microscopic yields in return. By paying depositors such low rates, banking institutions can afford to lend money to corporations and to the government at bargain rates.

CAPITAL AS COMMODITY: JAPAN IS THE LOW-COST PRODUCER
(Typical comparison of U.S. and Japanese interest rates in 1987)

	Prime Bank Lending Rate	Money Market	3-Month Bank Time Deposit	Long-term Gov't Bond	Corp. Bond
U.S.	8.75	7.00	7.62	8.18	8.98
JAPAN	3.38	3.38	1.76	4.24	4.91

The merits of an economy in which the cost of capital is consistently lower than comparable world levels are considerable:

• When industry can borrow money for expansion cheaply, the path to new investment is smoothed. Lower borrowing costs reduce the degree of risk Japanese companies undertake when they build new factories, invest in productivity tools, or enter new businesses. Americans, held hostage by "discounted cash flow" projections, often forgo new investments not because they aren't potentially profitable, but because financial executives can't prove they will be profitable *enough* to justify high borrowing costs. Japanese industry's cost-of-capital advantage has always been important. But today it has taken on a new dimension. Now the Japanese can borrow at low rates from their bankers in Tokyo and Osaka to expand their business inside the United States.

One of the classic explanations of Japan's postwar industrial competitiveness is that in rebuilding a bombed-out economy from scratch, the Japanese were able to introduce modern machinery, while American factories, unscarred by wartime destruction, chugged along with outmoded equipment. Decades later we may revisit that technology gap—but with both sides within American borders. As U.S. automakers try to maintain domestic market share against Toyota manufacturing in Kentucky, Nissan in Tennessee, and Honda in Ohio, they will be competing against companies that can finance the installation of the next generation of manufacturing technology at a distinct cost advantage.

- Like industry, the Japanese government itself can borrow funds cheaper than most others. Even though Tokyo's debt is comparable to Washington's as a percentage of GNP, the Japanese deficit is not causing a crisis in part because the cost of servicing it is so much lower. MoF finances Tokyo's deficit with long-term bonds yielding 5 percent, while the U.S. Treasury must offer 9 percent to attract investors to its long bonds. The implications of this differential are particularly sobering in contemplating the scientific and infrastructural challenges of the future, involving costly projects that can only be feasibly underwritten by national governments. The balance of technology will be radically altered if Japan funds space shuttles, superconductor commercialization, and biotechnological gene mapping with 5 percent money, while the United States borrows at twice the cost.

- As Japanese financial institutions expand worldwide, cost-of-capital advantages more than compensate for expertise they lack in the risky new areas of global finance they are entering for the first time. Borrowing low at home and lending high abroad, financial firms can buy plenty of time to learn the art of deal making and cover the cost of inexperience. Japanese securities houses are already being accused of "dumping" financial services by engaging in what are known as hara-kiri bids—underwriting bond offerings not just at thin profits, but at losses, subsidized of course by the home office. It is a very good way to attract some of the most important clients in the world.

Maintaining low cost of capital in Japan would have been impossible without rigid controls. Obviously, if foreign banks had been able to operate freely in the Tokyo market, or if Japanese companies had been free to invest their savings abroad at will, MoF and BoJ would have lost their ability to dictate interest rates. The Japanese financial world's interaction with foreign forces was therefore heavily proscribed until recently.

Only in the last few years have foreigners been able to play more than a peripheral role in Tokyo's financial marketplace, and only recently have the Japanese themselves been able to move any significant portion of their funds offshore. It wasn't until the early 1980s that Japanese insurance companies could invest any substantial assets abroad. After several rounds of liberalizations, they still must keep 70 percent of assets at home, although the 30 percent they invest abroad has placed them among the very biggest buyers of U.S. Treasury bonds and real estate.

In addition to keeping government control of interest rates and preventing the siren song of market forces from luring capital offshore, a rigid segmentation of financial institutions historically worked to keep Japan's flow of funds in a constant steady state. As part of the process of rebuilding the Japanese financial system after the war, article 65 emulated the American Glass-Steagall Act by erecting a wall between banks and securities companies. But the Japanese went much further. Banks were confined to specifically mandated areas that kept them well away from each other's turf. These categories include the giant "city banks" (most of which lead the list of the world's largest banks —Dai-Ichi Kangyo, Fuji, Sumitomo, Mitsubishi, Mitsui, and so on), long-term credit banks, trust banks, and regional banks. City banks could make loans, but only on a short-term basis; long-term credit banks could make long-term loans for corporate expansion but couldn't accept public deposits as city banks could. Only the Bank of Tokyo was allowed to engage in foreign exchange trading; only trust banks could manage pension funds; and so forth down a list of carefully drawn boundaries—almost all of which are now undergoing some form of liberalization.

On the securities side, similar efforts were made to maintain stability and control growth. The near bankruptcy of Yamaichi in the 1960s—and its subsequent rescue by BoJ—is considered such a cataclysmic event that it is still cited as a reason why tight controls on securities operations must be maintained. Brokerage commissions are still fixed at fat profit margins, much as they were in the United States until 1975, and are only now shifting to competitive rates. Foreign firms were barred from the Tokyo Stock Exchange until 1985. For that matter, the number of Japanese member firms is quite low—less than one hundred. The Big Four control nearly half the equity trading. They also indirectly control many of the smaller firms.

New financial products are added very slowly. The government bond market, for example, only came to life in the 1970s. Even now bond issues are in the hands of a tightly controlled syndicate. The OTC market, patterned after its American namesake as a tool for providing equity capital to smaller firms, is so restrictive in its listing procedures that only extremely well established small companies can qualify. It wasn't until 1987 that the first corporate commercial paper was issued. Even today Tokyo hesitates to explore equity trading practices considered standard elsewhere, such as index products. Until recently, those wanting to trade Nikkei index futures had to do so in Singapore, not Tokyo.

As with other aspects of Japanese life, the securities world is guided as much by unspoken, mutually-agreed-upon practices as by explicit regulation. Laws on "insider trading" are so vague as to be virtually meaningless. No one has ever been prosecuted for it, and no specific penalties for such an infraction really exist. Although that issue worries Tokyo regulators, there is general agreement that "it is better to have a system where the pressure of the professional community's standards curb excesses, rather than one where you first have to envision every possible abuse, and then draw up rules against it," as a Nikko executive observes.

Dividends on Japanese shares are typically less than one percent. Selling short was not practiced until recently, and even now remains an activity of dubious legality. As a result, individual investors buy shares almost exclusively for capital gains. Banks hold huge blocks of shares in companies to which they lend; cross shareholdings are also typical between companies that do business with each other. But these shares, which account for about half of Tokyo's huge equity total, are almost never traded. On the floor of the stock exchange itself, a complex system of price limits allows stock prices to fluctuate considerably, but not wildly. Despite rumors, rampant insider trading, and frenzied floor activity, these controls have worked to enforce what has essentially been a one-way direction of Japanese stock prices over the years: up. (See table on page 120.)

The segmented hierarchies and rigid controls of the Japanese financial world shortchanged the consumer of competitive interest rates, forced most major Japanese corporations into dependence on a single "primary banker," and retarded financial diversity in many ways. But the structure served the purpose of stability: bank failures in Japan are

TOKYO'S ONE-WAY STOCK MARKET: UP
Annual averages of the Tokyo Stock Price Index (TOPIX)

1950	11.5
1955	32.9
1960	97.3
1965	91.6
1970	163.3
1975	312.0
1980	474.0
1981	552.2
1982	548.2
1983	647.4
1984	815.4
1985	997.7
1986	1324.2
1987	1828.1

almost unknown, even though capital requirements and loan ratios are considered shockingly risky by Western standards. Indigenous capital supplies were able to grow undeterred by one of the worst problems of developing countries—capital "flight" to markets with higher returns. Small securities firms and small companies, as well as foreigners, may not like the Tokyo Stock Exchange setup. But the large houses, whose TSE activity has made them the biggest in the world; leading corporations, whose TSE-listed stock had quadrupled in yen value in the last decade; and investors looking at the swollen portfolios of the world's best-performing stock market can hardly complain.

Liberalization will change some of the historic truisms about the operations cited above. Obviously Japanese savers would prefer better interest rates, and as the scope of investment choices has begun to widen, they have shown little timidity in making a run for better returns—into newly accessible government bond funds, unit trusts, CD-type instruments, and foreign investments. Yet four years after Tokyo's liberalization began in earnest—in spite of huge shifts of funds into these higher-yielding sectors—Japan's discount rate was the lowest in its history and the lowest in the world. Even if all the reforms now on the drawing board are implemented, it is likely to be 1995 or later before Japanese interest rates become fully subject to global market forces.

A Nation of Traders

Augmenting a high savings rate and a controlled financial environment, the most explosive force contributing to Japanese capital surpluses in recent years has been the staggering surplus in Japan's balance of trade with the United States and the world.

From the very beginning of Japan's postwar growth, its planners envisioned an economy that would be "import-resilient and export-promoting." One senior official recalls that in the 1950s, "we knew it would be a long road to creating a trade surplus, since we had to import all our raw materials. But we also knew that if we imported only those things we absolutely needed, and supplied everything else ourselves, we would eventually create domestic industries that could compete internationally. In time, we knew we could create a surplus. That surplus could then be reinvested to generate a larger surplus."

Hard as it is to imagine today, Japan ran a trade deficit with the United States every year from 1955 to 1964. In 1957 the Ways and Means Committee of the U.S. Congress even issued a report on the U.S.-Japan trade "crisis," by which the committee members meant Japan's massive trade *deficits* with the United States. But 1964 was a watershed year. The Olympic flame burned over Tokyo, signaling Japan's return to the ranks of advanced economies. By 1965 Japan posted a small trade surplus. By 1972, when Japan recorded a global trade surplus of $5 billion, the country's total postwar trade account moved into the black. More money had now been taken in from the sale of exports than had been paid out since 1955 to acquire imports.

With a $5 billion trade surplus, public sentiment held that the time had come for Japan to "relax and enjoy life." The prior "cult of the GNP" was even denounced as having skewed society to an extreme, causing Japan to be perceived as a nation of "transistor salesmen," as Charles de Gaulle had scornfully called them. But just when dour planning pessimists were finally ready to relent, the first "oil shock" threw Japan into the kind of crisis on which its competitive edge thrives. From 1973 to 1975 the rising cost of Japan's biggest import —oil—forced the trade balance back into deficit. The economic miracle, concentrated as it was in heavy industry like steel and shipbuilding, was suddenly in grievous danger of crashing down under the weight of rising energy prices. Japan needed a new plan for the world of expensive energy.

MITI's leaders devised such a plan. Among its visionary hallmarks was the decision to encourage automakers to step up exports to an American market that was suddenly in desperate need of fuel-efficient cars. MITI also suggested initiatives to move Japanese industry into high-technology areas requiring less fossil fuel for manufacturing. Until now, Japan had sought only a modest trade surplus to reinvest in domestic growth. But the oil crisis outdated that part of the design. Henceforward Japan would need massive surpluses to keep pace with rising oil costs.

Jimmy Carter once likened the energy crisis in the United States to the "moral equivalent of war," but he could never get the American people to see it that way. The Japanese, on the other hand, always conscious of themselves as a "poor island nation with few natural resources," required little prodding to grasp the sacrifices required. They drastically reduced their energy consumption, accepted lower wages from employers whose fuel bills had trebled, and worked over-time to design new products that could expand exports and thus com-pensate for rising energy costs. As a result Japan recovered quickly. By 1978 it recorded a trade surplus of $10 billion with the United States alone and $18 billion with the world as a whole. Japan's global surplus was three times larger than the biggest one the United States had known at the height of its productive achievements in the 1950s.

No sooner did MITI again breathe a sigh of relief than the second "oil shock" struck in 1979–80. Again Japan adjusted quickly with the same sort of emergency measures as before. Despite a record trade deficit in 1980 of almost $11 billion, it restored a surplus in 1981. The adjustments made to the economy as a result of the two oil shocks set the stage for ignition and lift-off of what would become the Japanese financial miracle. Japanese industry was now revved up to be the most competitive force in world trade, not only in smokestack sectors, but across a broad spectrum that included emerging high-tech fields as well. For once, history's winds were now at Japan's back. A series of international events unfolded, allowing the Japanese to take maximum advantage of the position they had achieved in ways that exceeded their wildest dreams and astonished the rest of the world.

The first blessing was Reaganomics. If Reaganomics hadn't ex-isted, the Japanese would have loved to invent it. In all probability, however, they wouldn't have dared for fear it would be too obviously advantageous to Japan and too detrimental to America. The Reagan administration's early policies had the effect of stimulating domestic U.S. demand through supply-side tax cuts and rapidly rising government spending. This demand could not be met fully by U.S. industry, which had been cutting back, disinvesting, and otherwise "hollowing out" manufacturing capacity for years.

Japanese economists found it profoundly curious that an American president committed in name to conservative principles would carry out what was obviously an "unprecedented Keynesian-style demand stimulation,"[7] as economist Jiro Tokuyama called it. What was still more curious was the fact that the United States would launch such a stimulation—which pulled the whole world along with it—when its own industries were ill prepared to capitalize on the opportunity. Japan, on the other hand, was well positioned to provide everything needed by the superheated American economy: machine tools to help American industry ramp up for its part in the expansion, cars for millions of Americans releasing pent-up new car demand, household appliances for millions more buying new homes, computer chips for the Pentagon's new weapons systems, electronic innards for the flowering computer revolution, and the latest audiovisual paraphernalia for the growing yuppie population.

Japanese manufacturers knew they were antagonizing their American rivals with this onslaught of goods flooding the docks. But Ronald Reagan reassured them that he would veto any protectionist legislation that came to his desk! What's more, the American president chose to finance his neo-Keynesian expansion with the greatest mountain of debt ever undertaken by a national economy, providing Japan with the perfect temporary parking place for the cash piling up

AN EIGHTEENTH-CENTURY JAPANESE PHILOSOPHER ONCE SAID: "FOREIGN TRADE IS A WAR IN WHICH EACH PARTY SEEKS TO EXTRACT WEALTH FROM THE OTHER."[8]

	Japanese global trade surpluses:	U.S. global trade deficits:
1981	$ 8.7 billion	$- 28.0 billion
1982	6.9	- 36.4
1983	20.6	- 62.0
1984	33.6	-107.8
1985	46.1	-132.1
1986	82.7	-152.7
1987	96.5	-160.7

from its trade surplus. True, the Reagan years saw a strong U.S. economic recovery, but history is likely to remember instead how in a world economy that had become globalized, America lost its trading edge and forfeited it to Japan.

Reaganomics was a bonanza for Japan. But the run of Japanese luck didn't stop there. A second windfall arrived mid-decade, courtesy of OPEC and the collapse of world oil prices. Japanese businessmen, having survived two devastating oil shocks, had learned to build their corporate plans around the assumption that oil would continue to cost $40 a barrel. When oil skidded down below $13 a barrel and moved to a long period of stability in the $18 range, Japan was spared billions of dollars allocated for foreign oil purchases. The Japanese economy, always import adverse, suddenly didn't need to spend so much on its biggest single import item.

Japan would have been enriched quite enough by the combination of its extraordinarily high savings rate and its extraordinarily massive trade surplus. But, as we shall see in chapter 5, Ronald Reagan's final gift to Japan would be the 1985–87 attack on the dollar, which had the effect of taking every single yen Japan had amassed through forty years of savings and trade—and *doubling its value overnight*. One can best "see" the drama of this change during the Reagan years in the chart opposite, which tracks the net external assets of the United States and Japan.

In the hands of another country, the $300 billion trade surplus Japan accumulated from 1981 to 1987 might have triggered rampant inflation and domestic excess. But MoF and BoJ authorities exhibited a phobic fear of inflation, considering the inflation rate was at times barely more than one percent. New policies ensured that virtually all trade surplus–derived capital was steered outside Japan. Undesirable pressures on the domestic economy were thus diffused; strategic advantages were gained abroad.

Taken as a whole, the flow of $300 billion back into the economies from which it was taken is winning Tokyo new political friends to counterbalance the enemies antagonized by the impact of Japanese exports. Trade surplus investments are also having three other significant results:

• One part of the money is being used by industrial corporations to expand their manufacturing capabilities inside the United States and

FOR RICHER AND FOR POORER

(Net external assets: U.S. vs. Japan)

Billions
of
Dollars

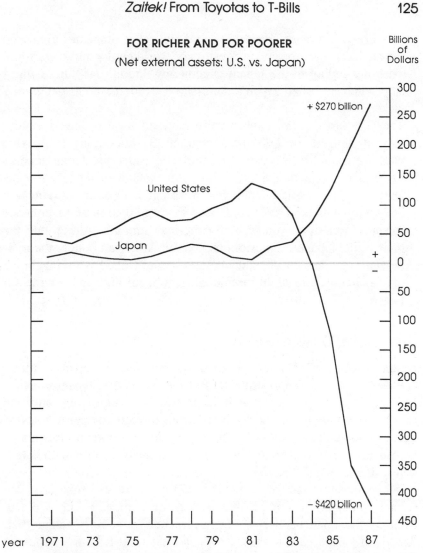

Chart shows America's precipitous decline from world's leading creditor to world's leading debtor, and Japan's astonishing rise. By the end of 1987, estimated net American external assets stood at − $420 billion, while Japan's were + $270 billion.

other developed markets, effectively creating an insurance policy for the day protectionist walls might be erected against the flow of goods at foreign docks, as well as rendering them super-competitive by virtue of their ability to switch production back and forth across the Pacific depending on costs, currencies, and other factors.
• A larger part of the surplus is being used by Japanese banks, secur-

ities firms, insurance companies, and real estate magnates to buy up the choicest, most promising sectors of world equity and real estate. They are adding to the Japanese economy through far-flung ownership interests what Japan's land-short, resource-poor geography lacks.

* The very largest sums, meanwhile, are still flowing into the recycling system of the U.S. bond market. By continuing to provide working capital to the deficit-ridden U.S. economy, Japan appears to be doing America a great favor. In actuality, Japan's role as lender of first resort encourages Washington to avoid solving the budgetary deficit. That avoidance, in turn, continues to enhance Japanese wealth and undermine American strength. Along with the high yields Japanese investors receive on American bonds, the relationship of financial dependence now being forged is giving Japan real, material, and highly exploitable political leverage for the future.

Upstream, Downstream

Neither MoF nor MITI will admit to having planned Japanese financial services as an export product. But the fact is that Japanese banks and securities firms, like their industrial predecessors, were nurtured in a domestic environment protected from foreign competition. Now that they have developed economies of scale and scope unimaginable in America, they are going overseas to compete directly with established world financial leaders.

While Japanese industrial giants like Toyota are still smaller in absolute size than a comparable American company like General Motors, the financial service firms are not only bigger than their American counterparts—they are *much* bigger. At least five Japanese banks have greater asset bases than Citicorp, the largest U.S. banking institution. Not only is Nomura the financial services company with the highest market capitalization and net income in the world, its share of global equity trading volume is twenty times greater than the leading American firm.

Two different trends intertwine here. With its prodigious savings capacity, voluminous trade surplus, and strictly controlled cost of capital, the Japanese economy is accumulating an increasingly dominant share of world capital resources at the upstream end of the world's

WHERE THE WORLD'S MONEY IS GOING

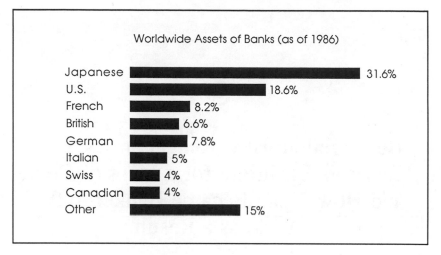

Worldwide Assets of Banks (as of 1986)

Japanese	31.6%
U.S.	18.6%
French	8.2%
British	6.6%
German	7.8%
Italian	5%
Swiss	4%
Canadian	4%
Other	15%

The World's 10 Largest Banks, 1982 vs. 1986

1982		1986	
1 Citicorp	U.S.	1 Dai-Ichi Kangyo Bank	Japan
2 Bankamerica Corp.	U.S.	2 Fuji Bank	Japan
3 Bank Nationale de Paris	France	3 Sumitomo Bank	Japan
4 Credit Agricole	France	4 Mitsubishi Bank	Japan
5 Credit Lyonnais	France	5 Sanwa Bank	Japan
6 Barclays Group	Britain	6 Citicorp	U.S.
7 National Westminster	Britain	7 Norinchukin Bank	Japan
8 Dai-Ichi Kangyo Bank	Japan	8 Industrial Bank of Japan	Japan
9 Société Générale	France	9 Credit Agricole	France
10 Fuji Bank	Japan	10 Bank Nationale de Paris	France

flow of funds. Meanwhile Japanese banks, securities firms, and insurance companies are fanning out around the globe to look after the downstream end of the business, gaining unprecedented influence over how global capital resources will be allocated, at what terms, and, most of all, to whose profit.

5

Burnt Teflon: How Reaganomics Sold America's Birthright for a Mess of Debt, and How Japan Became Banker to the World as a Result

There is nothing wrong with the economy.
　　　　　　　　—President Ronald Reagan,
　　　　　　　　reacting to the "Black Monday"
　　　　　　　　stock market crash[1]

A Bull Goes to Tokyo

Treasury Secretary Donald Regan arrived in Tokyo in March of 1984 determined to play "hardball" with the Japanese. Regan, who'd been chief of Merrill Lynch before joining Ronald Reagan's administration, was sick and tired of what he believed was Japan's unwillingness to strengthen the yen, liberalize interest rates, and open Tokyo's financial markets to American participation.

Regan had strong feelings on these subjects. In his Wall Street career, he'd been one of the original bulls arguing that government should get out of the financial community's way. Having fought and won the battle for financial deregulation at home, he now proposed to wage the same campaign on a global basis, zealous in his conviction that globalized financial markets would be in America's best interests.

Since coming to power in 1981, the Reagan administration had carried out a "strong dollar" policy. The secretary of the treasury himself was known for his belief that a strong dollar was synonymous with a strong America. But now American businessmen were saying that the dollar had simply become too strong. The Business Roundtable and other articulate representatives of corporate America lobbied Washington persistently, seeking an adjustment of the dollar so that U.S. business could better compete with foreign-made goods.

Toward the end of 1983 and beginning of 1984, the specter of the Japanese trade surplus began to worry even the White House team of ardent "free-traders" and "dollar bulls." The president refused to believe that American industry was no longer competitive, and he refused to give any credence to the protectionist talk of congressional Democrats. He wanted an explanation of the problem—and an action plan—more in line with his view of the world. Ultimately his Council of Economic Advisers told him what he wanted to hear: Japanese exporters were so successful because their yen was so cheap. The reason American exporters were losing market share was that the dollar was too strong. They showed the president how the trade deficit could be solved by forcing Japan to revalue its currency upward.

The president took the idea up with Prime Minister Nakasone toward the end of 1983. Immediately afterward Donald Regan pursued the subject in more detail with Finance Minister Noboru Takeshita. The two men chartered a "Yen/Dollar Working Group," made up of economists and government officials from both sides. From the American viewpoint, the group's purpose was to alleviate a brewing U.S.-Japan trade crisis by altering the yen/dollar exchange rate, which the American side argued was the nub of the problem. The working group met six times, but there was no progress. The U.S. trade deficit worsened, and the yen remained weak.

Now, Don Regan vowed to take charge personally. To those who traveled with him to Tokyo, he made it clear he wasn't going to pussyfoot around. He was going to tell the Japanese bluntly that they'd better get moving.

And he did. At a meeting sponsored by Keidanren, he harangued top Japanese businessmen with harsh words and high-pressure demands. "Your markets are not open to our financial institutions," he told them. "Your markets are not open to the capital for the rest of the world to enjoy, as is the United States market, and the message that I'm giving to your Ministry of Finance . . . is: action, action, action, that's what I want now. I'm through with patience. . . ."

Again and again, the treasury secretary underscored his chief demand—that Japan raise the value of the yen. "We think that the yen is probably weaker in relation to the dollar because of the fact that it's not an international currency. If there were more demand for the yen, the yen would be stronger in relation to the dollar. . . . In America we have a couple of car rental companies. We have number one, we have number two, and number two, the Avis Company, has a slogan: 'Number two tries harder.' And we're saying if Japan is number two, Japan should try harder."[2]

Regan's verbal barbs were backed up with every kind of pressure the United States could muster. "Commodore Perry was no shrinking violet, but even he would have swallowed hard at the Reagan administration's performance," recalled Jeffrey Garten, who headed up Shearson Lehman's Asian investment banking unit in Japan. "If Tokyo did not commit to further opening its capital markets, Washington threatened to unleash a protectionist Congress. It promised to veto Japan's promotion to higher voting status in the World Bank. The American government even hinted at retaliation against Japanese banks in the U.S."[3]

Like the president he served, Don Regan was so arrogant in his presumption of American invincibility that he could not see the fatal flaw in what he proposed. He lacked so much as a glint of recognition that in the near future it would no longer be clear which economy was Hertz and which was Avis.

Had the United States still exerted its prior hegemony over the industrial world's economy, or had Japan been economically weaker than it was, the opening of Tokyo's financial markets might have represented the dynamic new business opportunity for American interests Regan assumed it to be. But even London's Big Bang—the world's most dramatic financial market opening—proved to be of dubious benefit to Americans. There, U.S.-based firms were able to dive in as deep as they dared, buy top talent, and vault ahead of tradition-steeped British houses on their native ground. Today, however, only a handful of American financial companies are making significant profits from their U.K. operations. Many are retrenching, with some openly questioning their original assumptions about the cost/benefits of globalized markets.

That American firms only partially succeeded in London, where they didn't have to surmount Japanese-style barriers of language and culture, underscores the basic flaw in Regan's line of reasoning. In

London, well-endowed Americans went toe to toe with less well endowed Britons over a relatively small but truly open market that both American and British firms (as well as Japanese) could lay meaningful claims to servicing. In Tokyo, however, the fate of American firms (even after great progress in deregulation) is to compete against much more richly endowed Japanese in a tightly controlled and culture-bound market where no one believes Americans can gain more than a fractional share of domestic business.

The "opening" of capital-rich Tokyo, moreover, implied by definition that the flow of capital *from* Japan *to* the rest of the world would be greater than the reverse. This factor, American Treasury officials understood well. In fact, they thought it highly desirable. In trying to figure out how to finance the eye-popping Reaganomic budget deficits that were just beginning to reveal themselves, the idea of opening up Tokyo's capital markets so that Japanese trade surpluses could readily flow back to the United States seemed to be a plausible bandage for what otherwise might become a bleeding debt sore.

The long-range implications of that policy were lost on those trying to solve what they thought was only a short-term deficit problem. "I used to tell American bankers that the last thing they should be pressing for is an opening of the Tokyo financial market," observes MIT's Lester Thurow. "If it weren't for Japanese restrictions on capital flows, Tokyo would have already overtaken New York as the world's leading financial center."

But Don Regan didn't countenance second thoughts. History had cast him in a rerun of the Commodore Perry story, and nothing could dissuade him from bringing about the second opening of Japan.

Perhaps American negotiators were emboldened by briefings they received about *gaiatsu*—the Japanese tradition that venerates outside pressure as the best way to change the country. If so, they failed to understand its subtleties. The real history of *gaiatsu* is that the Japanese use foreigners as tools in their own factional arguments. Long before Commodore Perry arrived in 1853, indigenous political momentum had gathered in support of opening Japan. Perry's black ships, dramatic as they appeared on the horizon, really only served as the catalyst in easing the passage of the old order and advancing the Meiji cause.

Like the Meiji revolutionaries, powerful sections of the Japanese financial community saw an opportunity to put Don Regan's agenda to use for their own aims. Useful as the protected financial environment had been for Japan's past growth, it now manacled the ambitious dreams of the large financial institutions. Men like Tabuchi of Nomura, Komatsu of Sumitomo Bank, and Kurosawa of IBJ recognized that Japan could now become a global financial power. Their companies could stand at the forefront of world finance, if only they could break down some of the regulatory walls that kept Japanese money sealed off from world money. To do that, however, they had to overcome conservative domestic opposition that feared the transition from an industrial economy to a postindustrial one and sought to delay that change as long as possible. They had already made some gains—foreign exchange controls were lifted in 1980—but by and large the pace of deregulation was too slow for the Japanese financial community's ambitions.

In the American pressure to spur Tokyo's liberalization and to internationalize the yen, Japan's superbankers and financiers found the lever they needed to turn the tide against those seeking to preserve the status quo. This, more than American "hardball" tactics, explains why negotiators made such rapid progress over financial matters, compared with the drawn-out debate over trade, where the two sides never did seem to agree. "The Reagan administration has eagerly presented Japanese financial 'liberalization' measures as a fundamental breakthrough," noted Karel van Wolferen, a Dutch journalist who had spent twenty-five years covering Tokyo. But in point of fact, what the Japanese had agreed to was limited to a series of steps "designed to make Japanese financial institutions more internationally competitive rather than to give foreign financial institutions a larger share of the Japanese market."[4]

Within a few weeks of Regan's visit to Tokyo, a "Yen/Dollar Agreement" was reached in which "the U.S. side got almost all it asked for," according to Jeffrey Frankel, the exchange rate specialist who helped the American side prepare for the negotiations.[5] The Japanese would move to liberate barriers retarding the free flow of capital, they would allow the yen to play a greater international role and hence increase its value, they would open up the Tokyo financial market to greater participation by American financial institutions, and they would even take a few steps toward allowing interest rates to be determined by market forces.

Over the next few years, however, the results of the yen/dollar accord would prove to be diametrically opposed to accepted American wisdom about it in 1984. The yen would strengthen, yet the trade deficit would worsen. The strong yen and the weak dollar, moreover, would exacerbate all the other imbalances Don Regan sought to rectify. Yen-based Japanese financial institutions would obtain a far stronger role in world financial markets than dollar-based Americans operating in Tokyo, even after Americans finally gained greater freedom to do business in Japan. The weakness of the dollar and the towering strength of the yen would ultimately work to reinforce the long-standing disparity between interest rates in the two countries. In short, as Jeffrey Garten observed, "Tokyo, not Washington, may be the winner from the Yen/Dollar Agreement. . . . The ultimate irony may be that in finance, as in trade, Japan will beat America at its own game."[6]

The spring of 1984, however, was no time for negative thoughts about the American economy. The president had entrusted its future to that great crucible of unending virtue—the free market—and his trust was bearing fruit. The recession plaguing the early years of the administration had turned into a rip-roaring economic expansion, and the White House was basking in the light of what appeared to be a complete vindication of its policies. Production was up, the monster of inflation had been tamed, and unemployment was down. The youthful new rich were rolling out of computer labs and Wall Street offices as if the economy had suddenly discovered how to mass-produce millionaires. American business was being reenergized and restructured through the miracles of investment banking, venture capital, and corporate takeovers—led by a corps of uniquely American characters whose blatant greed was superseded for the moment by the public's fascination with their cowboy style and gold rush spirit. The "wealth effect" of the Roaring Eighties was rippling through the upper and upper-middle levels of American society, giving the impression of unlimited, unending prosperity.

Not since the 1920s had the sheer glory of money been such a captivating social force. Not since the 1940s had the public so believed in an American president. And not since the 1950s had the rest of the world so envied the depth and breadth of the U.S. economy, its capacity for technological innovation, and the vigor of America's commitment to the sanctity of capitalism itself.

Time and again Reagan's opponents backed down in the face of his political strength, admitting the futility of challenging it. Those who continued their criticism of White House policies had trouble being heard above the noise of the party, even when they sought to draw attention to major social issues like the swelling budget deficit, the cost of the huge arms buildup, the reckless excesses tolerated in the name of deregulation, and the systematic dismantling of the safety net for the poor and disadvantaged. America was feeling good about itself again. The 1984 Republican Convention's theme song said it all: "Happy Days Are Here Again."

True, there were a few problems with this otherwise magical president. Sometimes it was too obvious that his policies supported the rich and the special interests at the expense of the poor and the middle class. For a White House desperately concerned with "image," the black-tie parties and the new designer fashions swirling about Washington were at unfortunate odds with the growing dimensions of American homelessness and hunger.

True, most people were aware that the president was principally an actor, with little intellectual grasp of the issues at hand. But that was all right because people liked his general stance and trusted his intuition. If he had a penchant for citing facts that weren't facts, or letting slip glimpses of frightening subconscious thoughts, his reassuring mirth more than compensated.

True, he was a bundle of contradictions on matters from the personal to the political. He said that he was for a balanced budget, yet he proposed ever-bigger deficits. He said he was for the "three R's," yet he slashed government support for education. He said the family should be the cornerstone of American life, yet he was visibly estranged from his own.

True, Reagan's laid-back "management style" was a little too laid-back. There were too many incidents of snoozing through meetings with world leaders and too many long vacations. The willingness to "delegate" authority was a welcome relief from Jimmy Carter's "micromanagement," but this president had a nasty habit of delegating critical matters to a coterie of officials who believed that neither conflict-of-interest laws nor the U.S. Constitution applied to them personally.

Despite such problems, Ronald Reagan was thriving. He was unbeatable and unstoppable. Appropriately enough, he was dubbed the "Teflon President." No matter how bad his missteps, nothing seemed to stick.

It was right about this time (1983–84) that the Reagan White House began to take on the air of unchecked, undiluted power reminiscent of Nixon's "Imperial Presidency." The world was Ronald Reagan's oyster. The men who set his agenda—particularly Don Regan (who assumed such a powerful role as chief of staff in the second term that many would say he was the *real* president)—began seeking ways to extend the Reagan revolution's definition of "freedom" to every ideological battle they had always wanted to promote.

They dispatched the marines to Grenada and won widespread praise for an action that, in another time period, might well have been seen as little more than a jingoistic adventure against a tiny island nation. They dared to have the president declare publicly what many Americans had long believed—that the Soviet Union was an evil empire, and that American policy toward Moscow should proceed from the starting point of preparing for war rather than bowing to political pressure for arms treaties and summit meetings.

It was during that time too that the White House called upon its other old Wall Street hand besides Don Regan—William Casey, the CIA chief who had once served as chairman of the Securities and Exchange Commission—to begin building an "off the shelf" covert operations capability. The ensuing drama of Iranian terrorists and Nicaraguan contras, of what the president knew and what he forgot, of the National Security Agency and Oliver North, of congressional inquiries and the tangled tale they uncovered, does not concern us directly here. But its context is critical.

No one can doubt that Ronald Reagan and those around him despised Iranian terrorism. No one can doubt they passionately believed in the cause of the contras. Yet their complex machinations, based on erroneous assumptions of their own strength, a provincial American view of how the world worked, and a shameful ignorance about the real conditions in Iran, culminated in obtaining results that were *exactly the opposite* of what they intended. The antiterrorist Ronald Reagan actually ended up supplying notorious terrorists with additional weapons of terror! As for the contras (whose cause the president compared with that of the American Founding Fathers), they never even got much of the money that was supposed to come to them via the convoluted Iranian channel. Ultimately their credibility was eroded and their guerrilla war strangled by the web of deceit woven around them by the president's men in the basement of the White House.

The Yen/Dollar Agreement produced no scandal like the Iran/contra affair, although it may well turn out to have greater historical importance. But it was born of the same erroneous assumptions about American strength, the same provincial American view of how the world worked, and the same sort of shameful ignorance about the real conditions abroad—in this case, the Japanese economy.

Washington's efforts to rig the yen/dollar relationship even relied on the same clandestine approach to government that characterized the Iran/contra scandal. In 1985, when James Baker and Donald Regan swapped jobs and Baker took over the Treasury Department's task of driving down the dollar, he immediately moved to circumvent the established Economic Policy Council (whose members included all senior officials with an interest in economic matters). Instead he established a "special channel" within the administration for economic policy-making. "The hallmarks of the new group were secrecy, clandestine operation, and an absence of the internal dissent that sometimes leads to news leaks."[7] David Mulford, the obscure official recruited by Baker to head up the attack on the dollar, was chosen, among other reasons, for his ability to keep secrets—an ability demonstrated during the nine prior years he had served as an investment adviser to the Saudi government.

Given this context, it is no surprise that Washington's Japan policy yielded the same sort of ironic result as the one shaped by Oliver North. Don Regan got what he set out for in Tokyo. But like American negotiators who secured the release of a few hostages with their sale of arms in Tehran, it turned out later that what he wanted was *exactly the opposite* of what the United States needed.

Disaster in the Twin Towers

To explain the changed positions of the United States and Japan in the world over the eight years of the Reagan presidency, one must begin by giving the Japanese credit for their vision, their hard work, and their speed of adaptation to new conditions. But to fully understand the process, one must give substantial weight to the disastrous directions pursued in Washington—particularly those infamous twin towers (perhaps better thought of as towering infernos) that the Reagan administration has left as its monument to future Americans: the budget and trade deficits.

The Reaganomic budget deficit has been appropriately dubbed by investment banker Felix Rohatyn "a conscious policy of national economic suicide." Those who doubt the "conscious" part of Rohatyn's indictment should read David Stockman's insider's account, *The Triumph of Politics,* in which the former budget director describes Reagan's resistance to all meaningful budget cuts and his willful refusal to accept changes in his agenda. Near the end of his term, Reagan's profligacy was so great that without others in the Republican leadership to rein him in, the "1986 deficit would have exceeded 8 percent of GNP or $350 billion," a statistic, Stockman says, that would have turned the U.S. economy into a "banana republic" right there and then. Reagan's policies, rooted in "hundreds of decisions he and his inner circle have made since August 1981," were as deliberate and calculated as they were wrong, Stockman tells us. The American economy was "taken hostage by the awesome stubbornness of the nation's fortieth president," who in the short space of eight years managed to triple the debt accumulated by his thirty-nine predecessors.[8]

The dangerous implications such indebtedness holds for the future U.S. economy has now finally been opened up for public discussion. But aside from the generalized threat to American well-being, the legacy of more than a trillion dollars' worth of deficit spending in the Reagan years reverberates in the U.S.-Japan economic relationship in certain very specific ways.

The fact that so much of Reaganomic debt was financed by borrowings from Japan has planted a ticking time bomb. The threat of a Japanese pullout from the U.S. bond market gives Tokyo meaningful leverage in bilateral negotiations over trade, defense, and other issues —leverage it is already beginning to use. International unease over America's creditworthiness is also beginning to dim enthusiasm for dollar assets and raise questions in the minds of global bankers as to whether the dollar can or should continue to be used as the world's key currency.

Under the best of circumstances, U.S. economic growth will be constrained for the rest of the century owing to the high percentage of GNP that must flow out of the country to pay back debts to foreigners. But there is more to this story. Economists seeking to defend the Reagan record have correctly pointed out that the United States at various times in its history has run even bigger deficits in proportion to GNP. So too have other countries at other times, including Japan.

In the final analysis, *what is more important than the size of the deficit is the use to which it is put.* Deficit spending that creates future real growth can be justified on the grounds that as the economy expands, the burden of the payback will be eased. In the Reaganomic case, however, there was no specific economic development program. That was to be left to the private sector. The "supply-side" tax cuts, which helped create such a huge chasm between the government's revenues and expenses, did not trigger the new domestic investment that was promised. During the 1980s, in fact, American business maintained one of the industrial world's lowest investment rates in new plant and equipment. Washington also withdrew from its historic role as the leading investor in the nation's infrastructure, slashing outlays for "hardware" (roads, bridges, transportation, and the like) as well as "software" (education and training).

While wealthy Americans were busy putting their supply-side tax cuts into largely nonproductive paper investments, Japanese business (itself no slouch at speculation) managed to keep up its long-standing policy of reinvesting heavily in manufacturing. As a result Japanese processing machinery is, on the average, two years newer than American, the Japanese robot population is five times larger than the U.S. count, Japanese civilian R&D now leads the world, and the growth of Japanese industrial productivity continues to outpace the United States even though American productivity reversed its long decline during the Reagan years.

"It is a spectacle that ought to shock Americans," says Peter Peterson of the fact that Japanese net investment in 1986 was $30 billion larger than the U.S. figure—$300 billion vs. $270 billion. "A population half the size of our own, living on a group of islands the size of California, is adding more each year to its stock of factories, houses, bridges, and laboratories—in absolute terms—than we are to ours. And Japan still has savings left over, about $80 billion in 1986, to lend to thriftless foreigners."[9]

Had the U.S. government borrowed a trillion dollars to fund a retooling of basic industries and the development of new ones, or to educate and train American workers for new skills and new technologies, or to systematically target export products for the future, the mess of debt might have had pretense to an economic rationale. But this was not the case. Reaganomics undertook enormous debt in return for (1) a brief interlude of overindulgent consumption by the top half of society and (2) a vast expansion of weapons systems, which ultimately did less for world peace than the initiative Reagan finally took toward the end of his administration to seek an arms treaty with Moscow.

Given one last chance to minimize the damage of the debt bomb with the Tax Reform Act of 1986, Reagan created a curious spectacle in Washington with his insistence on a "revenue neutral" bill. Battle lines were drawn and redrawn, emotional rhetoric spewed from both parties, horse trading on a historic scale took place. The president stood firm and in the end won "victory." What was the victory? That he had "simplified" taxes—a dubious notion considering the 2,704 changes in tax law entailed by the bill.[10]

Reagan's real victory was that he managed to hold on to the tax tiger's tail through a two-year war with Congress, without ever having to admit how mistaken his spending policy was in the first place. Given the chance to engage in a lengthy national debate on the subject of taxes, Congress lacked the guts to insist that the president either raise revenues or cut swelling expenditures.

Thus the country emerged from the Reagan era weighted down by a $2.5 trillion national debt and $150+ billion annual deficits. We spent much but got little in return. In particular, there can be no doubt that America is far less competitive today than eight years ago in regard to Japan, our chief economic rival and now our chief banker as well.

Weak Dollars, Strong Yen

The Reagan administration's budget deficits created an open sore on the body of the American economy, allowing Japanese money to rush in. But perhaps even more suicidal from the standpoint of global economic competition was the White House decision to attempt to solve the trade problem by draining the blood out of the strong dollar and transfusing it to the yen.[11]

The belief that the trade deficit with Japan could be resolved through changes in currency values was an erroneous, contemptuous, and typically Reaganomic way to look at a very serious problem. It sought to reconcile two decades of Japanese manufacturing excellence and American manufacturing mismanagement with a cosmetic touch of bookkeeping, rather than put America through the necessary effort to restructure the way the country lives, works, does business, and is governed.

To imply that contemporary Japanese export products sell well chiefly because the yen is undervalued (as the Reagan administration argued for the last five years) is to miss the whole point of how Japan transformed its manufacturing sector since its "oil shock" experiences. Once upon a time, Japan did rely on cheap labor and a cheap yen to gain export market share. But today an increasingly large portion of Japanese industry gets its competitive edge from superior technology and processes, as well as macroeconomic planning by government and microeconomic planning by corporations. The root cause of Japan's trade surplus is not favorable exchange rates—although a cheap yen has obviously helped—but Japan's economic structure. The Japanese machine tools industry takes less than two months to ship an order, whereas the American average is nearly six months. Quality defects in American manufacturing run at 8–10 percent of production versus 1 percent in Japan. American business invests only $2,600 per worker annually, while Japan's commitment to new equipment, training, and improvements in the production process is two and a half times as great.

The problem with Reaganomic logic on exchange rates is illustrated dramatically in the charts below:

PROBLEMS CHEAP DOLLARS CAN'T SOLVE
U.S. vs. Japanese production of 256K RAM computer chips[12]
(Typical yields of good chips per wafer)

	U.S.	Japan
Start of wafer fabrication	100%	100%
After first quality check	66	88
After final wafer test	20	57
Salable chips after assembly	17	54

Costs and Output, General Motors vs. Toyota[13]

	GM	Toyota
Passenger vehicles produced per employee	11.7	57.7
Labor cost per vehicle	$4,148	$630
Earnings per vehicle	$ 343	$466

Now it is true that automobiles and computer chips are two areas in which Japanese production technology is at its most advanced. A standard for automation and quality has been achieved in these sectors that still eludes other Japanese industries. But others *are* moving in this direction. Autos and computer chips, moreover, are exactly the kinds of products the Japanese export to compete with American-made products in the U.S. market.

The implications of the chip figures are mind-boggling even though they represent an extreme case: if only 17 percent of the chips produced in American wafer fabs are usable, compared with 54 percent in Japan, the attempt to make U.S. chipmakers competitive through currency rate juggling alone (rather than massive new investment in retooling the American industry) would require a dollar valued around sixty yen. Somewhat less extreme is the case of the auto industry, where a dollar pegged at ninety yen might make GM truly cost competitive with Toyota.

Leaving aside the global financial panic and domestic inflationary hurricane that would be triggered by the dollar's fall to those levels, such currency juggling would create a vicious cycle in its own terms. At sixty yen to the dollar, a Japanese chipmaking giant like NEC could easily afford to buy up the entire U.S. chipmaking industry. Toyota would be capable of buying General Motors.

Ignoring these kinds of realities, and believing the United States still had the power to will its economic aims into being, the Reagan administration launched headlong into the insidious swamp of dollar bashing. The assumption was that a cheaper dollar would give Japan "a taste of its own medicine" by making American goods supercompetitive and pricing Japanese goods out of the market. The burden of U.S. industrial decline could be pushed onto Japan's back for a while.

For almost a year after the Yen/Dollar Agreement, the yen remained weak. But in February of 1985, with the dollar trading at 260 yen, even many in the Japanese business community had come to agree that the dollar was too strong. Thus the Bank of Japan curtailed its resistance to American downward pressure on the dollar, and the great financial role reversal finally began. By the summer of that year the yen had strengthened 30 percent.

Even that was small change for James Baker, the new U.S. treasury secretary. At New York's Plaza Hotel, Baker brought together the finance ministers of the world's leading economies. He cajoled and threatened them, ultimately convincing them to join the United States in a sustained, coordinated attack on the dollar. Six months later the dollar was down to 180 yen. A free fall had commenced. Like a man tumbling off the top of a mountain peak, the greenback was occasionally snagged by a branch as the Japanese or others in the global currency game attempted to break its fall. But the plateaus were short-lived and the descent absolute. Continued inaction by Washington on the budget and trade deficits spurred world currency traders into dumping dollars every time new figures were reported. By the end of 1987 the dollar had collapsed to what many had thought was a "never-never land" near 123 yen.

REQUIEM FOR THE DOLLAR

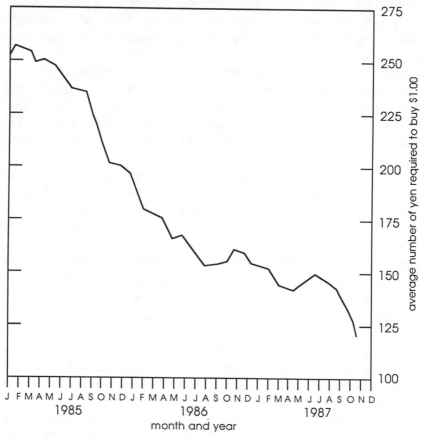

From 1985 to 1987, the Reagan administration drove down the value of the dollar from 263 yen to 123.

Japanese reactions to this dollar/yen reversal were intriguingly schizophrenic. In the beginning, *endaka* was portrayed in the Japanese media as a disaster that could crush the economy. Government spokesmen acted as if the rising yen were a cruel and unusual punishment meted out by the United States for Japan's minor crime of having carried trade surpluses to an extreme. Their dour forecasts indicated that the country was preparing for years of low-growth, high-unemployment, profit-squeezed penance. Yet within these pious pronouncements one could detect a hint that many Japanese businessmen didn't really believe a strong yen spelled disaster. What they said out loud often sounded like cant; not a few were crying all the way to the bank.[14]

Unlike their American counterparts, Japanese financial officials had long historical memories. Toyoo Gyohten, MoF's man charged with international affairs, had gone through all this once before in 1971. The "Nixon shock" had just taken place, decoupling the U.S. dollar's link to gold and triggering a major devaluation of the dollar against other world currencies. The yen was then pegged at 360 to the dollar. Under intense pressure from the United States, Japanese negotiators reluctantly accepted nearly a 17 percent strengthening of the yen to 308.

"Popular opinion in Japan was so convinced that appreciation of the yen of more than 10 percent would immediately bring about recession, stagnation, or depression," recalls Gyohten. But those with real financial acumen thought otherwise. "In hindsight, there were many people who actually did not believe this—because the stock market went up on the news that the yen would settle at 308." Indeed, the yen has continued to strengthen ever since, and Japan has continued to thrive.

Gyohten also understood something about the bluster of American treasury secretaries. At the 1971 Smithsonian meeting, he notes, "The star of the show was John Connally. . . . He believed in conducting the negotiation in a high-handed posture. . . . Judging from the discussions, there was an impression that Connally won. But later, if you look back, you are certainly sure that Connally didn't get very much."[15] Fourteen years after the Smithsonian meeting, the same syndrome was in effect at the Plaza with Jim Baker standing in for John Connally.

The gnomes of Nihonbashi did genuinely worry about the future profitability of export-dependent Japanese companies. They had real fears about the slipping values of dollar-based Japanese investment portfolios abroad. They sincerely questioned whether the yen was ready to play the international role its new strength would confer upon it, whether Tokyo was really ready to serve as the international finance center it was fast becoming, and whether Japan itself was ready to play the leading international role the United States was abandoning with its policy of cannibalizing its own dollars. But despite these reservations, they also saw fantastic possibilities looming on the horizon.

Such mixed feelings were reflected not only in differing opinions at the desks of currency traders, but in the mazelike buildings where the MoF decided policy and the BoJ strategized about its implementation. On some days it looked as if BoJ were the lone force on the planet holding up the dollar's value. On others the Japanese central bank's lack of intervention encouraged open season on the falling buck. On those days when BoJ frantically bought dollars and dumped yen, it was tempting to believe that the Reaganomic dollar policy was working. Logic seemed to suggest that if Japan's top monetary experts were intervening to put the brakes on the dollar's fall, they must be doing so because Japan was losing competitiveness and the United States was gaining it back.

It was *American logic* that suggested such a conclusion, though, not Japanese logic. Americans tended to see the issue in stark absolutes—either a strong dollar or a strong yen. Japanese tended to look at the subtleties in between, more concerned with the velocity of change than the change itself. If the United States insisted on forcing the yen up and the dollar down, few Japanese economic experts believed the trend could be resisted. It could, however, be *managed*. "We are not afraid of a certain level of currency rates in the abstract," BoJ economist Yoshio Suzuki observed after the dollar had already slipped below 140 yen. "What we fear is lack of time to adjust."

So BoJ bought time for Japanese exporters to adjust their business plans by cutting costs, moving production overseas, resourcing components that could no longer be produced competitively at home, getting out of unprofitable sectors, and adding new technology. By 1988, when the full impact of *endaka* was being felt, Japanese industry was a fundamentally different force in the world from the one the White House had sought to restrain four years earlier at the time of Don

Regan's fateful trip to Tokyo. Japan's way of doing business had undergone such a transformation, in fact, that BoJ governor Satoshi Sumita and his aides now dared to admit in public that "the merits of the strong yen are numerous."[16]

The Reagan White House, however, never noticed that the world had changed.

J-Curve or Heisenberg's Principle?

If James Baker and Ronald Reagan believed a lower dollar and higher yen was what America needed, they had certainly gotten what they wanted by the end of 1987. Now came the shocking news: despite a 100 percent increase in the value of the yen (and a similarly dramatic increase in the value of the German mark), no fundamental improvement had taken place in the U.S. trade deficit, nor had the Japanese and German surpluses begun to shrink anywhere near the expected degrees.

Pro-White House economists had caveated their forecasts from the beginning by warning of the "J-curve" effect. The trade deficit, they said, would actually worsen before it got better, because the same volume of imports bought with suddenly cheaper dollars would temporarily raise the gross total of the import sector. Over time, they insisted, as American consumers switched to cheaper domestically produced goods and U.S. exporters began capitalizing on their new price advantage abroad, the trade deficit couldn't help but fall in line with the change in currency rates. The most optimistic of the "J-curve" theorists suggested the trade deficit would begin to show a marked improvement in six months; the more conservative said the proper time frame was a year. A few said it might take eighteen months for real progress.

They were all incredibly wrong, to say the least. Twenty-five months after the Plaza Agreement, the October 1987 monthly trade figures showed an all-time record U.S. deficit of $17.6 billion. Within that record the United States ran a deficit with Japan of almost $6 billion for the month, compared with an average deficit of $3 billion a month in 1984. Not only was the Reaganomic policy wrong, it had once again achieved exactly the opposite of its intention. *The dollar had been halved, yet the trade deficit with Japan had doubled*.

The White House declared victory anyway, patting itself on the back in those months when small improvements in trade figures did show up and terming every new increase in the deficit an "aberration" explained by variations on the "J-curve" theme. Indeed, Ronald Reagan himself continued to talk the dollar down, although he often did so at photo opportunities in half sentences that weren't always crystal clear from a macroeconomic viewpoint. Jim Baker, however, made it quite clear that he planned to continue driving the dollar down to pressure Germany and Japan into further conformity with American economic policies. He made his position so clear, in fact, that some Black Monday—morning quarterbacks charged him with lighting the fuse of the October 1987 crash on Wall Street—the result, they said, of further devaluation threats he'd made the prior weekend.

Yet the administration persisted in its "see no evil, hear no evil" stance. Even the official White House statement on the stock market debacle claimed that "the trade deficit, when adjusted for changes in currencies, is steadily improving."[17]

The implications of that little phrase "when adjusted for changes in currencies" were astounding. It was as if the White House were saying, "If we could go back and value today's volume of imports and exports at currency levels that existed two years ago before we started attacking the dollar and raising the yen and other currencies, then you would be seeing a steady improvement in the trade deficit." The notion of "adjusting for changes in currencies" implied that the White House didn't believe we were really living in the new world economic order its own dollar-bashing policies had created—a world where Americans imported a smaller volume of goods, exported a greater volume, and still faced the same drain of cash out of the economy. In the Reaganomic dream world, the benefits of the lower dollar could be enjoyed without suffering the consequences of stronger foreign currencies.

In the real world, there was no such luck. From the beginning, the effort to solve the trade deficit through manipulation of currency exchange rates was like a physics professor studying the aerodynamics of the curve ball and then trying to pitch a big-league ball game. It made textbook sense, but not common sense. It worked in econometric computer models, but not on the fiercely competitive battlefront of world trade.

The relevant phenomenon was not so much the "J-curve" as Heisenberg's uncertainty principle—the dictum that the very act of studying a problem, let alone attempting to correct it, can fundamentally alter the nature of the problem itself. In this case, radically different reactions by the business community on either side of the Pacific to the changing dollar/yen relationship introduced radical new variables into the balance of trade.

After the Plaza meeting, Japan went into its bunkers. Big corporations assumed the worst. They prepared for painful, structural changes to cope with a long period ahead of cheap dollars and strong yen. Even before the new currency rates began to show up in statistics, Japanese leaders were warning of a national crisis and encouraging rationalization measures even more severe than those undertaken during the "oil shocks."

Knowing they were headed for much tougher price competition with domestic American industry, Japanese exporters grimaced yet managed to hold the line. The yen would rise 10 percent; Japanese export prices wouldn't budge. Another 10 percent, and reluctantly the Japanese would post a 3 percent increase. And so on. Instead of simply passing along a higher dollar price to American consumers, as the econometric models assumed, they dug in their heels, cut costs, cut profits, and even accepted losses to hold on to market share. Nissan, for example, reduced annual costs by $1.5 billion without reducing output.

Because of the strong yen, Japanese manufacturers were also able to cushion operating losses with profits from *zaitek*-style investments. On the operating side, Nissan actually slid into the red in the first half of 1986 before cost-cutting efficiencies began paying off. But when the year was over, the company still showed a profit—nearly three-quarters derived from returns on its investment portfolio. This certainly helped the company keep U.S. price increases to a minimum. A Nissan automobile that sold in the United States for $9,000 in 1984, and should have sold for $18,000 in 1987 according to changes in yen/dollar exchange rates, actually sold for only $11,000. If it had really sold for $18,000, it might well have been priced out of the market. At $11,000 it may not have been quite as popular as before, but it was still highly competitive. In fact, Nissan's total U.S. car sales for 1987 fell only 3 percent from the prior year—considerably less than the drops experienced by Chrysler or GM, both of which, in theory, should have been gaining colossal competitive advantages from the currency swings. Honda, which raised its prices 1 to 3 percent nine different times over the two years of the dollar's free fall, actually *increased* its share of the U.S. auto market during the same period from 6 percent to more than 7 percent.

Ample evidence suggests that rather than attempting to use their newfound currency advantage to wrest back market share from the Japanese, domestic U.S. automakers consciously chose to raise prices instead, thus boosting profitability at the consumer's expense. Studies by auto market research firm J. D. Power & Co. confirm that while Japanese manufacturers were raising U.S. prices an average of 9–13 percent from 1985 to 1988, GM, Ford, and Chrysler were raising prices by even more vigorous factors of 12–15 percent. As a result, the Reagan administration's "dollar protectionism" protected nothing but short-term corporate profits, while the Japanese auto giants continued to defy gravity and gain market share.

Nor was this pattern limited to the auto industry. Years of groundwork laid in the U.S. market by a wide range of Japanese exporters was paying off in spades. Their strategy for building market share had created several near monopolies that they continued to exploit despite increased prices. Desktop copiers, VCRs, DRAM chips, and computer printers were areas where American manufacturing had become all but extinct. Burned once, Americans who abandoned these businesses in the face of prior Japanese competition were twice shy. Unlike the econometric models, few were willing to reenter the fray, no matter how substantial the currency advantage.

The Japanese were also aided by the reputation they had built for quality and value. Automobiles, cameras, TV sets, and a host of other Japanese products that once attracted U.S. consumer attention because they were cheap were now considered the quality leaders worthy of a *premium* over comparable American products. Marketing experts had begun to speak of a growing segment of American consumers as "import-intenders"—meaning people who intend to buy imported products in order to get the quality they desire. Washington may not have understood this, but it was a known fact in shopping malls and auto garages across America. "General Motors and Toyota are turning out identical cars on their joint venture assembly line in California, but the GM car has to be priced hundreds of dollars less in the showrooms because it's got an American name," noted a Maryland auto mechanic.[18]

American-imposed *endaka* also provided Japanese exporting industries with the pretext to initiate overdue but never before tolerable restructurings. Specifically, the new conditions allowed companies to break the much vaunted Japanese "lifetime employment" guarantee. They laid off workers, closed down factories, and shifted production offshore where their newly strong yen found extraordinary bargains in land, facilities, and labor. In Korea, Taiwan, Hong Kong, and Singapore, where labor costs were already low, Japanese employers gained a further advantage every time the dollar fell, since the currencies of these Asian NICs remained closely pegged to the U.S. dollar. While Washington assumed that Japan could be squeezed into submission by a yen doubled in value, Japanese business avoided the squeeze—and in some cases even gained ground—by evacuating to nearby Korea, where industrious and skilled workers could be hired for one-eighth the hourly pay of Japanese workers.

This trend carried with it the danger that Japanese industry would be "hollowed out," as domestic American manufacturing had been by the flight of multinational corporations to low-wage countries in the 1970s and 1980s. Japanese industry was—and is—alarmed by that prospect. The threat of "Korea doing to Japan what Japan has done to the United States" is used by industry and government to encourage a continued atmosphere of vigilance and austerity among workers. But while "hollowing out" may prove to be a serious problem in the future, so far it has been a less pernicious trend than either American or Japanese experts anticipated when the yen began its rise.[19]

The jobs eliminated to date have been concentrated in inefficient factories and workshops still making the pre-"oil shock" products dependent on cheap labor. Excising such employment contributes to the country's competitiveness, especially since retraining programs are available for many of those displaced. Despite official moaning and groaning about what was originally expected to be Japan's first serious unemployment crisis in three decades, joblessness peaked at a little over 3 percent in 1987 and has been receding since.

Whereas "surviving *endaka*" became the subject of animated Japanese industry forums resulting in specific government initiatives to aid business, no comparable "benefiting from the weaker dollar" programs were organized in the United States. Many American businessmen weren't even aware the Reagan administration was trying to "help" them by driving the dollar down. Even fewer had any idea where the dollar would stop or what it would mean for their business.

Instead of pressing their new currency advantage, U.S. companies often let it slip away by raising their own prices as soon as the Japanese were finally forced to hike theirs.

Ironically, small and medium-sized American companies, conscientiously trying to use the opportunity of the lower dollar to crack the Japan market, found themselves forced to bear exorbitant yen-based costs to do so. Although cheap dollars *did* make some of their products more attractive, they discovered that price was by no means the first concern of Japanese consumers. More important to the success of a product was adapting it specifically for Japanese needs. Supporting, servicing, and marketing American products the "Japanese way" meant incurring yen-based costs in higher yen. No matter how enticing the size of the marketplace, few American companies warmed to the thought of export sales in a country where housing for an expatriate executive could generate a six-figure annual expense item.

For Americans operating in many parts of the world, the biggest problem in competing with the Japanese is not price, but the favorable financing terms Japanese companies can offer as a result of their low cost of capital and government guarantees. The Reagan administration had no help to offer on this score. With the Export-Import Bank already requiring a $3 billion bailout, nobody in Washington dared propose new government programs to support export financing.

With no idea how long the administration would hold to the weak dollar course, some American businesses were simply not interested in taking the risk of ramping up for global exports. Noted Eaton Corporation vice-chairman Stephen Hardis: "Our experience has been that the advantage you get from a weak currency only lasts a few years. You don't rush out and add capacity for what is a pretty ephemeral advantage.[20]

Part of the Reagan program called for pressure on Japan to stimulate its domestic economy. In an expansionary Japan, low-priced American goods would theoretically rack up significant export sales. This was another fallacy that presumed American logic over the realities of Japan. Tokyo *did* stimulate the economy. By the third quarter of 1987, Japan's GNP was growing at a phenomenal 8 percent rate—shocking for a country that was supposed to be reliant on exports and reeling under the blows of losing its exporting advantage. American exports *did* improve somewhat. But there was little large-scale benefit to American exporters. For high-end imports, the Japanese looked to Europe.[21] For low-end imports, they looked to Southeast Asia and China. The Asian NICs saw their exports to Japan grow 400 percent faster than American exports once Japan's expansion got going.

Having shunned Western-style consumerism for so long, there were many holes in Japanese domestic product lines that American companies should have been well positioned to fill. But once again theory was one thing and reality another. As Tokyo took Washington's advice and spurred growth, Japanese companies losing export markets moved rapidly to convert redundant factories and work forces to production of consumer items.

Symbolic of why Japanese consumers were not likely to constitute the export market anticipated in Washington was the story of 1987's best-selling new electronic product in Japan—a tiny, computerized bread baker that could mix ingredients, knead dough, and bake a small loaf of fresh white bread automatically. Bread itself is a relatively recent American life-style import into rice-centric Japan. One would have thought that if there were a market for white bread or for bread-baking machinery, Americans might have captured it. But no. Matsushita, Sanyo, and other Japanese companies came up with the idea and promptly sold nearly a million units in the first year—at prices averaging $300. The Japanese bread bakers are now even showing up on American store shelves. Meanwhile Japanese electronics companies declared the white bread baked by their machines to be the definitive standard—more suitable to Japanese tastes than imported American bread.

Then too there were the residual blatant cases of out-and-out Japanese "unfairness." Until 1988, American construction companies were consistently barred from participation in building the new Kansai Airport, a model for the large-scale public works projects Japan plans to unfold in the 1990s. Tokyo was making it clear that while it might accept American demands to stimulate the economy (a sensible idea that could be implemented in a way that appeared to be a concession to American pressure), Americans were not necessarily going to share in the benefits.

That many of the expected results from a falling dollar haven't yet accrued to American business is not all that surprising when one considers how the policy was implemented. Reagan's attack on the dollar represented a sweeping high-stakes initiative put into play without planning, without support, without consensus, without subpolicies to leverage it, without fail-safe measures to limit its damage, without a vision about how to control it and where to end it—in short, with no strategic plan whatever. Arguably, devaluing the dollar could have been a powerful tool in promoting U.S. trade competitiveness, *if* it were linked to government support for export industries, credits for trade financing, tax incentives for restructuring domestic industry, and a control mechanism to prevent business from squandering the currency advantage on price hikes. But those ideas stood in contradiction to the Reagan administration's basic article of faith: let the free market decide.

Because the free market is one major force in world trade—although not the omnipotent one imagined by the ideologues of the Reagan administration—the weak dollar is inevitably helping many American businesses. Americans selling fungible goods like peanuts or citrus fruit, which require little or no adaptation to foreign markets, have already received a lift. Some traditionally export-conscious companies that had been hamstrung by the high dollar have also begun to regain market share—so much so that some economists are predicting that U.S. growth in the next few years will come largely from the export sector. Hewlett-Packard and Caterpillar, for example, have been the subject of frequent stories in the business press about the revitalization of their export businesses. But these companies represent the best of American industry, not the norm. They are the ones Peters and Waterman had to *search* for when they wrote *In Search of Excellence*.

The cost of obtaining these benefits, however, may prove catastrophic. The *monthly* trade deficit that is hailed in 1988 as showing "great progress" is still significantly larger than the *quarterly* trade deficit at the beginning of the Reagan years. Despite price increases, American consumers spend more on imported goods today than before the dollar's fall. With foreign imports still pouring into the United States—but at substantially higher prices—and with weakening dollars tempering foreign enthusiasm for investing in American bonds, the possibility of a return to double-digit inflation is growing. "Like drugs, devaluation gives you a breather, a small kick," says British financier Sir James Goldsmith, who lived through Britain's plunging pound in the 1970s. "Then it becomes an inflationary merry-go-round to hell."[22]

Ugly though inflation will be, it pales in comparison with much more disturbing long-term forces set in motion by the attack on the dollar, as we shall see below.

Bringing the War Home

The dollars and yen the Reagan administration juggled were targeted to affect sectors of both economies involved with trade. Yet foreign trade represents less than a quarter of total economic activity in both countries. Washington's doubling game couldn't, of course, discriminate between the value of yen used for different economic purposes. Strengthening the yen involved in Japan's foreign trade meant strengthening the value of every single yen in all of Japan. As a result, ordinary housewives in Tokyo have become buyers and sellers of not inconsequential blocks of American stocks. Moderately prosperous Japanese companies have become financial giants by world standards. Wealthy Japanese individuals have been transformed into powerful international tycoons. Japanese industrial corporations and financial institutions, which were just beginning to explore the wider investment world, have been given the enormous boost of doubling their already staggering assets.

The capital advantage is *the* competitive advantage of the future. With its dollar policy, the Reagan administration voluntarily relinquished it. The globalized economy will be dominated by those who can best penetrate each individual market, control production and distribution of products within it, and capitalize on the particular financial opportunities presented. Enriching Japanese companies and forcing them abroad to take advantage of such opportunities, while simultaneously impoverishing American companies and erecting a barrier to their international growth, is about the least intelligent competitive strategy imaginable. The cost of weakening the dollar sufficiently to make American crops and smokestack industrial products "competitive" again globally has been to strengthen the yen and other foreign currencies to such a point that the very nations we are supposed to be "competing" with are now able to buy into America's most advanced high-technology companies, own America's choicest real estate, and build the world's most advanced factories for their own purposes inside the United States—all at prices they consider to be bargains.

The same economists who once predicted the "J-curve" would run its course in six to twelve months now say the reduction in the trade deficit will be dramatic in 1989–90. Perhaps this time they will be right—but for the wrong reasons.

At the moment, the main factor capable of significantly reducing the American trade deficit with Japan is *not* increased American exports or foreign imports being priced out of the American market, although both trends are observable. Instead it is the strategy of yen-based Japanese exporting companies using their doubled financial resources to underwrite a massive, accelerating shift of production to the United States.

While Caterpillar may have gained a short-term competitive lift from the dollar's decline (Caterpillar's Lee Morgan was one of those business figures who lobbied the White House most persuasively to bring down the high dollar in 1983), it never needed such a shocking drop to compete against the Japanese. As things have turned out, Komatsu, Caterpillar's arch rival from Japan, may be the bigger beneficiary of the Reagan policy. In the short run, Komatsu has lost North American market share back to Caterpillar. But using its hoard of strong yen, Komatsu invested in constructing a sparkling new plant in Chattanooga, Tennessee, and has begun to shift production there. In addition, Komatsu created a joint venture with Dallas-based Dresser Industries (analysts expect the Japanese to buy out Dresser in due course) to produce and market construction equipment at four existing U.S. plants—including one in Caterpillar's hometown of Peoria, Illinois. If Caterpillar believed the strong yen had "blunted the Komatsu threat," speculates *Business Week,* these events make it "clear that the duel will continue well into the 1990s."[23]

Caterpillar may be healthy enough to survive that type of challenge, but much of the rest of American industry is not. Even for Caterpillar, going head to head with Komatsu right in the United States does not necessarily mean the competition is moving to a level playing field. Komatsu has access to lower cost capital, is under less short-term pressure from shareholders, faces fewer union problems, and is even getting public funding to train workers for its new American facility.

Komatsu earth movers built in Chattanooga, Hondas rolling off assembly lines in Ohio, NEC desktop computers assembled in Massachusetts—none of these products show up as Japanese exports in the trade statistics because they are "Made in USA."[24] The electronic components made at a Matsushita *maquiladora* in Tijuana (under a special program originally established to give the Mexican economy a lift by encouraging U.S. companies to establish factories in border towns) disappear completely from the U.S.-Japan trade picture. They cross the border not as "Made in Japan," but as *"Hecho en Mexico"* —part of the U.S.-Mexico trade balance. No wonder Japan is now Mexico's fastest-growing foreign investor.

Money is now no object for Japanese companies desiring global expansion. What they could once achieve only in Japan, they can now replicate within American borders or nearby, thrusting their companies into the epicenter of the market and removing the great competitive handicaps they have endured all these years. No longer will they have to gauge American needs from ten thousand miles away and ship their exports across an ocean.

We thus come at last to the most nightmarish aspect of Reagan's dollar policy. It is not simply that weakening the dollar contributed so little to restoring balance in the U.S. trade account. The bigger problem is that it has taken what was still largely an external problem and internalized it. In effect, Reagan brought the trade war home. Japan has gained unimpeded and unprecedented direct access to the American market, while giving up little in return.

"The United States welcomes foreign direct investment," the ever-ebullient Ronald Reagan once remarked. "We believe that there are only winners, no losers.[25] In this view, the president was supported by many economists who explained that the transfer of large sectors of Japanese manufacturing to the United States will benefit the American economy by generating jobs, broadening tax revenues, and heightening competition. Observed Edward Lincoln, a Brookings Institution scholar, of the Japanese industrial challenge in the United States: "If we can't meet it, well, we deserve to work for the Japanese." Lincoln asserts that the benefits to the United States will be such that "the issue shouldn't even be debated."[26]

Yet those who choose to look on the bright side of this question ignore some decidedly darker issues: What kind of jobs? Where do the profits go? What are the broader implications of an American economy with a Japanese engine at its heart? Looking at those questions, it becomes apparent that some definite winners and losers are shaping up in the process of Nipponizing American business.

Already the pace of expansion by Japanese automakers has led to predictions that by 1995 half the U.S. auto market will be dominated by Japanese companies either exporting from Japan or building in the United States. Even today, U.S. automakers are so outclassed by Japanese production standards that GM, Ford, and Chrysler have each entered into arrangements that amount to putting their names on cars built *in the United States* by Japanese manufacturers.

The "ripple effect" that economists have long described in connection with the auto industry is now a Japanese ripple running through the American heartland. Rather than buying from indigenous U.S. auto parts suppliers, Japanese manufacturers are making it easy for their suppliers from home to set up shop alongside them. American parts firms now report that it has become as hard to sell air conditioners, steering wheels, and motor mounts to Japanese carmakers in the United States as it would be to sell to them in Japan. The newly arrived Japanese parts companies, however, are selling successfully to U.S. automakers.

Ohio Congresswoman Marcy Kaptur accuses the Japanese of running "a completely closed system" and establishing "what amounts to colonies in the U.S. with their suppliers."[27] More than a few experts believe the home-grown segment of the $60 billion annual U.S. auto parts industry is jeopardized and possibly doomed by Japanese competition.

As for the jobs the Japanese are creating, Harvard political economist Robert Reich sees a conscious—and perfectly understandable—pattern of keeping the most strategic parts of the production process at home and exporting only those aspects of manufacturing that "involve relatively few workers, or else entail skills that have little value in trade."[28] If this is true, then the United States is likely to gain no more benefit from Japanese production than other low-wage countries historically obtain from foreign-owned factories. It sops up some unemployment, to be sure, but hardly advances the U.S. economy along the challenging lines needed for world leadership in the future. Those who believe that the American labor movement is a social force of some value are also concerned that the Japanese, setting up new production facilities in largely nonunion areas, have been highly successful at excluding unions. Executives of the Big Three, on the other hand, wonder why they have to deal with the UAW when their Japanese competitors right down I-75 do not. Whether you look at the issue from the vantage point of labor or management, the fact is the Japanese are able to do things in the United States Americans are not able to do so readily.

Some two thousand Japanese companies have already come to the United States. More than thirty of these companies would currently rank in the *Fortune* 500 if they were counted as independent entities. But the roots of the trend reach far deeper than the visible surface of big Japanese companies with well-known names. Obscure regional banks from Japan are opening offices to help their customers diversify into the American market. The Hokuriku Bank, for example, which has become the ninetieth largest bank in the world by accumulating the yen deposits of customers in distant rural reaches of Japan, published a glossy English-language annual report recently, depicting its efforts on behalf of those customers now building U.S. subsidiaries, such as Ise America Inc.—a poultry company with twelve million hens scattered through nine plants in eastern states.

Japanese money may well drive the next wave of large-scale U.S. mergers and acquisitions. Yamaichi, the Japanese securities firm with the longest experience in the mergers field, expanded its American subsidiary's M&A staff from two to fifteen between 1986 and 1987. Says Masaaki Yoshida, the general manager of M&A for Yamaichi in Tokyo, "People say that Japanese don't do M&A business. That's wrong. Japanese don't do hostile takeovers the way Americans do. But Japanese companies do many friendly takeovers." Whereas Yamaichi's M&A business was once made up almost exclusively of Japanese domestic transactions, its deal stream today comprises 50 percent of Japanese investments abroad.

Drawing the line between hostile and friendly, of course, is not so easy. Hideki Mitani, a Goldman Sachs investment banker who advises Japanese clients on United States expansion opportunities, offers a sobering vision of the future: "If Japanese continue to come to the U.S. with state-of-the-art manufacturing plants, the profitability of U.S. companies will decline, and they could face takeover bids resulting in the replacement of American management," he warns. "U.S. companies must decide whether to continue operations on their own and risk a takeover or consider combining their operations with Japanese companies."

Those who wish to put the best face on what is happening insist that the surging Japanese presence is not tantamount to an economic

invasion, but part and parcel of the broader process of economic globalization rendering national borders obsolete as accounting units.
There is a certain amount of truth in this argument. Just as Hondas
assembled in the United States don't show up as Japanese exports,
neither do IBM computers built in Japan show up as American exports. As business globalizes, thousands of quirks in the old way of
maintaining trade statistics confuse the issue. How to best account for
the flow of services as well as goods? How to calculate "invisible"
income from investments, patents, and copyrights? What to do about
Japanese production from those Mexican *maquiladoras* or IBM's exports to other Asian countries out of its factories in Japan? When
buyers and sellers of financial instruments meet on electronic global
networks, where is the profit actually being made?

These kinds of questions reveal some of the inadequacies of trade
statistics. In his thought-provoking book, *Beyond National Borders,*
Kenichi Ohmae even goes so far as to suggest that "there is no imbalance between the United States and Japan," when the extenuating
circumstances of American companies producing goods in Japan and
Japanese companies producing goods in the United States are factored
into the calculations.[29]

Yet a certain profoundly simple macroeconomic reality transcends
all the ways of keeping the statistics. Dollars are piling up in Japan;
yen are *not* piling up in the United States. In the new world of globalized markets, Americans may well invest in Japan while Japanese
invest in America, but an obvious and overwhelming imbalance char-
acterizes these investment patterns. The Japanese-owned portion of
American business is growing four times faster than the U.S. economy; the U.S.-owned portion of Japanese business is actually shrinking. Japan in 1987 made $34 billion worth of direct investments
around the world; the rest of the world made less than $1 billion
worth of direct investments in Japan. In the 1960s nearly half of
Sony's stock was owned by Americans; today Sony buys a large
American company like CBS Records outright. Sumitomo Bank becomes a significant minority partner in Goldman Sachs, testing the
limits of Glass-Steagall relaxation American firms had not yet tested;
no American banks are able to become equity partners in prestigious
Japanese investment houses.

These new imbalances are potentially more dangerous than the
trade imbalance. Ownership of a chunk of the American economy

gives Japanese business qualitatively more leverage than trade ever could. Japanese lobbyists are already an influential force on Capitol Hill, where some say they specialize in "threat power." Senator Tom Harkin of Iowa observes that "over time, as ownership of our assets is transferred overseas, so is the authority to make important business and economic decisions affecting the prosperity and independence of our nation."[30]

Black Monday and Terrible Tuesday

History may judge the Reagan administration's wholesale deregulation of the U.S. financial system as a national disaster almost on a par with the budget deficit and the dollar policy.

The process itself began long before the Reagan era. The successive administrations of Nixon, Ford, and Carter all took away pieces of the regulatory mosaic, leading up to and following the fateful May Day on Wall Street in 1975 when the brokerage industry deregulated commission fees. The exigencies of high inflation, floating exchange rates, recycled petrodollars, and new computerized information systems, not to mention changing perceptions about how and where value itself would be produced in the future, all tore holes in a regulatory structure whose weight-bearing walls had been erected in response to events half a century earlier.

Most of the ideas behind financial deregulation have merit. But as was the pattern in so many areas during the Reagan years, the government was unwilling to couple the principle of deregulation with mechanisms capable of properly minimizing the dangers and maximizing the benefits. The result was that American capitalism in the 1980s came to be characterized by what *Business Week* called "the casino economy."

Shocking abuses of the new system captured headlines, notably the insider trading scandals. But more important than the illegal acts of the few were the newly legalized and encouraged directions taken by the financial community as a whole. Financial products were thrown on the market with the risks poorly understood and the economic value questionable. Investment bankers, arbitrageurs, and leveraged buyout specialists gained a disproportionate share of power, spreading the cancer of "management for short-term financial return" at the expense of building sound long-term businesses. Wall Street reversed its historic role as corporate America's adviser and broker, becoming instead the master of corporate America's destiny. In the name of improving market "efficiencies," options on nonexistent products came into vogue along with program trading, portfolio insurance, and a batch of other "innovations" whose raison d'être was not to minimize risk, as was often claimed, but to expand risk and, once it was expanded, to seek maximum advantage from it.

From junk bonds to home equity loans, from new securities backed by mortgages to those backed by credit card receivables, the center of gravity in the American financial system swung from equity to debt, with the debt portion pyramiding toward chaos.

As regulatory distinctions between banks and brokers were relaxed and historic boundary lines separating the activities of many types of financial institutions were dropped, those wishing to stay in the game were compelled to abandon long-standing conservative philosophies in favor of more speculative ones. New entrants as well as old veterans now competed for higher stakes. To do that they needed vastly greater quantities of capital. And the best place to look for capital— as Goldman Sachs, Shearson Lehman, Paine Webber, and a host of other companies discovered—was Tokyo.

"Deregulation is a good idea, but there's just one problem," observes Perrin Long, the Wall Street analyst who analyzes Wall Street itself. "No one realized that by the time deregulation got rolling, the U.S. was going to be the world's biggest debtor economy. If you turn the system upside down, double, triple, and quadruple the capital requirements, and create new opportunities for the very biggest players—and you do all this while you are in the process of becoming a debtor nation—all you've really done is set the table for your friends in the creditor nation to have a good time at the feast."

From the way the debate over financial deregulation was carried out, one would never have guessed that Washington was even aware of Japan as a competitive financial power. Watching the action of the American side of the yen/dollar committee on the playing field (level or otherwise) of global economic strategy, one was reminded of Casey Stengel's question to the original New York Mets: "Can't anybody here play this game?" The demands pushed so hard by Americans and resisted so hard by Japanese until they finally acquiesced always seemed to aid the Japanese side once adopted.

Opening American markets wider than any financial markets had ever been in world history, subjecting them to increased volatility and risk of every kind, and removing even the semblance of coordinated oversight was an ill-advised course under optimum circumstances. But the confluence of those policies with the rise of Japan as a financial superpower has written the recipe for the loss of American financial leadership.

American negotiators may well have extracted commitments from Nakasone, Takeshita, and Miyazawa to join the United States in the spree of deregulation, but the Japanese side always made it clear that it would do so slowly, carefully, and in the context of their own financial culture. American negotiator Beryl Sprinkel once tried to convince MoF's Toyoo Gyohten that the best way to chop off a dog's tail was in one chop rather than inch by inch. Gyohten responded that in making a wooden wheel, it is necessary to bend the wood into the right shape slowly and steadily.

That difference in philosophy is a crucial one. According to Wall Street's best-known economist, Henry Kaufman, the United States now has "specialized regulators looking at segments of the market rather than an overall regulator that looks at all financial institutions and the markets in totality."[31] At Gyohten's MoF, on the other hand, Japan has yet to dispense with overall regulators looking at the big picture. That control Japanese authorities have maintained over their nation's vital financial functions—even as they deregulate—is a strategic advantage in an unstable world.

The global aftermath of Wall Street's Black Monday crash on October 19, 1987 (or "Terrible Tuesday," as it was known on the Asian side of the dateline), offers a window on this difference.

In the United States—a debtor nation with colossal budget and trade deficits, a weak currency, and a disparate collection of new, volatile, and little-regulated financial strategies at work in its markets—Black Monday was experienced as a devastating "meltdown" of the system, which triggered a monstrous evaporation of wealth overnight. As the New York Stock Exchange cannibalized 30 percent of its peak value in the plummet, it was later learned that the exchange itself came within minutes of collapse under the pressures of program trading and portfolio insurance.

In Tokyo, MoF officials met quietly with the big financial firms in the wake of Wall Street's crash. Ideas were exchanged about how best to ensure stability in the market. Big price declines took place, but without pandemonium. Among the TSE's many regulations, those that keep a stock price from falling too far within specified trading periods prevented a free fall, as did the lack of options, futures, index trading, and short selling. In the end, the Tokyo market—which many American experts had previously thought far more precariously overvalued than the American market—fell only half as far as New York.

Confidence, the key to financial power, was badly shaken in the United States, but not in Japan, where Finance Minister Miyazawa publicly proclaimed that Tokyo had nothing to fear from Wall Street's crash other than the inconvenience of a few "aftershocks." One of Nomura's top money managers summed up the mood, noting, "Whatever happens in the rest of the world, the Japanese market will resist it."[32]

The top portfolio manager for a Tokyo capital management firm put it best when he said, "Japan is the world's leading creditor nation. We have the money; we should just relax and buy stocks. That will have a very positive influence on world markets."[33] Wall Street itself looked to Tokyo for leadership, and when the Nikkei index rebounded, it helped pull the Dow, London's *Financial Times* index, and the rest of the world back up with it. For the first time in history, Nihonbashi was leading; Wall Street was reacting.

When the smoke from Black Monday cleared, Nomura placed a full-page ad in *The Wall Street Journal* featuring three big graphs showing how much more resilient and buoyant the Tokyo market had proven compared with New York and London:

Tokyo	-17.8% from its 1987 peak during crash week
New York	-32.1%
London	-36.1%

"When the crash came, all markets were not created equal," Nomura's ad gloated. "The fundamental strength of Japan's economy has instilled confidence in both individual and institutional investors, which in turn has provided stability in otherwise volatile financial markets. Investor confidence and economic strength make Tokyo the safest market in volatile times."[34] Indeed, six months after the crash, Tokyo's Nikkei index soared to a new all-time record, while New York's Dow Jones still languished several hundred points below pre-crash levels.

The crash also demonstrated that it was Japanese investors, not Americans, who were most committed to global markets. Most big sellers in Tokyo during the crash were Americans, frantically pulling money out of that market to cover losses back in New York. The Japanese in New York, however, stood pat in their positions, selling precious little and picking up bargains afterward. When 1987's roller coaster finally ended, Japanese investors held a record high share of NYSE equities; American investors held fewer TSE equities than at any time since the 1970s.

American brokerage houses, reeling from losses for their own accounts, began laying off staff the morning after the crash. By year's end more than fifteen thousand employees had lost their jobs at U.S. financial firms. *The New York Times* observed that some Wall Street firms "lapsed into civil war" following the crash, fighting over who was to blame and even triggering splits in the highest ranks of houses that had so recently been on top of the world.[35] A recession within the economy of New York City was predicted as a result of the financial community's contraction.

Japanese brokerage firms laid off very few people. Tokyo didn't skip a beat in its plans for renovating the city toward the goal of making it the world's financial capital. Generally speaking, Japanese firms moved ahead cautiously after the crash—but deliberately, just the same.

Tokyo may be in for some hard times ahead, even another crash. No financial market is immune to such a possibility. But the difference is that the Japanese have consciously tried to keep Tokyo safe. The Reagan administration took no such precautions with the deregulation of American markets.

The most disquieting note of all was struck in a speech by Nicholas Brady half a year after the crash. Cochairman of Dillon, Read & Co., and a confidant of Vice President George Bush, Brady headed the presidential task force empowered to investigate the debacle's causes. Long after he submitted his report (virtually ignored by the White House, which had commissioned it), Brady addressed a Washington meeting of institutional investors. He used the occasion to make explicit something left out of the written report—his own personal opinion about what really triggered the crash. It was a startling revelation:

> People ask me: What was it that blew it off on the ninteenth of October —was it the twin deficits, was it the Rostenkowski legislation, what was it? The *real trigger was that the Japanese came in for their own reasons*

and sold an enormous amount of U.S. government bonds and drove the thirty-year government [bond] up through 10 percent. And when it got through 10 percent, that got a lot of people thinking, "Gee, that's four times the return you can get on equity. Here we go, inflation again." *That, to me, is what really started the ninteenth—a worry by the Japanese about U.S. currency.*[36]

Once again, the message was clear to those willing to hear it: Even in the absence of any malevolent agenda on the part of foreign investors, the porousness of the U.S. economic system, combined with the concentrated power of Japanese capital acting in its own perceived self-interest, could lead to previously unimaginable financial disaster *accidently.*

Part III

SNAPSHOTS FROM THE TRENCHES OF THE COMING FINANCIAL WAR

6

Twenty Times Bigger Than Merrill Lynch: A Look Inside Nomura Securities

> Sometimes when American friends talk to me about the heights of their innovation and the excellence of their research, and then go on about how backward the Japanese are, I ask if they've studied their history lately on who won the war between Athens and Sparta. It's really a rhetorical question, although I've discovered that a lot of them actually don't know the right answer.
>
> —A British broker in Tokyo

Placement Power

At precisely 7:45 A.M. the meeting came to order. Ten relatively young men, all coatless in the Tokyo summer heat, gathered around a few simple folding tables. Seven in white shirts, three in light blue. Their faces scrubbed, their hair cropped close. Each one had pen and notebook at the ready. They'd commuted as long as two hours to get here, sandwiched like sardines into trains and subway cars, but they showed no sign of fatigue. Just the opposite. The energy level was like that in a locker room just before a championship football game.

These were the *kachos* (section chiefs) of the Shinjuku branch of the Nomura Securities Co., Ltd.—the number-one branch office of the number-one securities company in the world. Their *bucho* (general manager) was Masahiro Aozono, a squat, barrel-chested man whose success in attracting three thousand small business portfolios to this branch and increasing their aggregate value by 350 billion yen over the preceding year had earned him the appellation "Young Lion of Nomura." Pointing to his own outsized gut, however, he noted that "Young Pig" might be more appropriate.

Aozono was soon to become one of the youngest members of Nomura's board. On this particular day, however, he was still sweating his way up the corporate ladder of success. So too was every man in the office, along with twelve thousand others who were also convening their morning meetings at the very same moment in Nomura's 131 branches dotting the Japanese archipelago.

Statistics can only accomplish so much in trying to depict the Japanese financial world. To really understand its inner workings, one needs to see it up close. And there is no better place to look than inside Nomura, the biggest and boldest of all Japanese financial houses. Nomura is many things to many people. It is a huge retail brokerage house similar to Merrill Lynch in the United States. It is a global bond trading house like Salomon Brothers; a corporate underwriter and investment banking partner to industry like Goldman Sachs. Its mutual fund management subsidiary is rapidly becoming the world's largest fund manager. Nomura Research Institute is Japan's premier economic think tank, reputed to be the proving grounds for many new LDP economic initiatives. Other subsidiaries are engaged in real estate, venture capital, and the China trade. Even bioengineering and computer software development are housed under the Nomura umbrella, emphasizing the link company strategists perceive between capital surpluses and investment in new technology.

Financial firms the world over talk about serving as global financial supermarkets. Nomura is one of the very few with the resources to discuss the idea *seriously*. It is the world's single most profitable financial services company, earning a flabbergasting $2 billion after taxes in its most recent year. That was an extraordinary year to be sure, but even under less torrid growth conditions, its pretax profits nearly match the pretax profits of the entire U.S. brokerage industry. Assets in custody—about a quarter-trillion dollars—are greater than the asset base of any private sector bank. Judged by the market value of its stock, Nomura is at least twenty times bigger than Merrill Lynch.

Through its network of offices in twenty-one countries, Nomura is a vital player in every international market. In far corners of the world, Nomuramen carry on all manner of headline-making transactions, functioning as primary dealers in U.S. Treasuries, market makers in British equities, and underwriters of Eurobonds.

But the heart and soul of its business still lies in selling stocks and bonds to a Japanese nation with a seemingly inexhaustible appetite for stocks and bonds. Its "placement power" is so great that there is literally no new issue too big for Nomura to manage—even the largest stock issue in world history, NTT's $20 billion initial share offering in 1987. "Nomura," says an envious foreign broker, "can place anything with its Japanese clients. *Anything.*"

The key to "placement power" resides in the branch network. Every day fifty thousand customers visit branch offices. Every day salesmen are spurred on by management to meet a quota of one hundred phone calls. And here, in the Shinjuku branch, Nomura's engine was roaring into gear to begin a typical day.

Like a drill sergeant barking out orders to his troops, Masahiro Aozono reviewed what had happened in New York and London during the few hours of sleep permitted in the life of a *kacho*. Behind him, a Cushman & Wakefield real estate map of Manhattan was studded with magnets representing Japanese investments. Electronic screens flashed with the latest dollar/yen quotations, LIBOR and overnight Fed fund rates, gold fixes, U.S. Treasury yields, and the full complement of other world investment barometers. Nearby, an electronic scoreboard showed the previous day's closing prices of the most actively traded companies on the Tokyo Stock Exchange. The board flickered indolently, awaiting the frenzy that would begin at 9:00 A.M. when the TSE's two-hour morning session opened.

The Young Lion of Nomura exhorted his troops to remember the commitment to research and information demanded by the company's founder. Tokushichi Nomura II, the son of an Osaka money changer, had toured the world in 1908. After an epiphanous visit to the research department of the Wall Street firm Post & Flagg, he returned to Japan, vowing to make research the cornerstone of the Nomura financial empire he sought to build. Later he published Japan's first investment newsletters and research reports. Nomura's job, he said, was to "scientifically analyze the merits not only of the speculative stocks that were most talked about in the investment community, but of all stocks available to the market—to determine their true value and assess them as possible investment vehicles."[1] With that premise, he built Nomura into one of Japan's giant pre–World War II *zaibatsus*. Although it would be taken apart and transformed after the war, the commitment to research would remain a central theme in Nomura's modern reincarnation.

"It's hard to manage so much money as this branch now has in custody," Aozono told the *kachos*. "You must raise your knowledge and find new opportunities for your customers. Research, research, research. Study every report carefully." Then he saluted them for having met yesterday's quota of two hundred million yen each for a new Nomura-sponsored mutual fund. He informed them of an upcoming lecture at the branch for customers interested in one of the hot financial products of the moment, convertible bonds. Then he dismissed them. The whole session was over in minutes.

Like most Japanese companies, Nomura's internal hierarchy is not only chartable on paper, but physically evident. Everyone in the Shinjuku branch works in the same big, drab, unpretentious room, presided over by Aozono. Each *kacho* heads up a table of subordinate troops. Breaking out of the meeting room in formation, the section chiefs convened quick submeetings of subordinates to personally transmit the day's marching orders. When those meetings ended, the entire staff came to its feet at the middle of the room for a few more last-minute thoughts and inspirational words from one of the *kachos*.

"In the last week the market has been trending down," he told them. "Explain this to your customers. Show them why this is only temporary. And tell them we are recommending chemical and pharmaceutical stocks!"

With that, a huzzah went up from the room. Each man hurried to his desk to get on the telephone. Young women in their twenties, all attired in the summer uniform of striped blouses and blue skirts, rushed to pass out chemical company reports arriving via fax from Nomura headquarters across town in Nihonbashi.

When Nomura talks, people listen. Company spokesmen deny any disproportionate influence over the market. But Nomura's properly proportioned influence alone represents the most monopolistic force in any major world exchange. With four million customers in Japan and direct control of roughly 20 percent of all Japanese stock and bond trading, Nomura's recommendation of a stock is usually enough to drive up the price, even against the grain of a down market or negative fundamentals. Nomura's share of TSE trading is greater than the *combined* share of NYSE trades handled by seven leading American firms. And that doesn't include the trading volume of an estimated fifteen smaller brokerage houses in which Nomura is a minority shareholder. "When Nomura makes a strong recommendation, it's as if Merrill, Salomon, and Goldman all came out with the same idea at the same minute."[2]

Nomura underwrites 40 percent of initial public stock offerings in Japan and more than 50 percent of convertible bonds. It is the biggest single financier of the Japanese government's long-term debt, holding a share of the government bond underwriting syndicate two and a half times larger than its rivals from the banking sector.

Encouraged by Nomura's bullish pronouncements about the opportunities ahead for Japanese finance in the age of deregulation, the company's own stock has been a darling of Japanese investors, rising nearly 2,000 percent during the decade between 1977–87. That run-up made millionaires out of hundreds of Nomura's profit-sharing employees who had labored long years at lowly wages but clung fast to their stock.

Untold Nomura customers also became millionaires in the recent stock market boom simply by playing Nomura's "stock of the week" picks. All the Japanese brokerage houses practice this supermarket-style hawking of "weekly specials," usually based on "sectorial themes" about where the future economy is headed—real estate stocks are hot for a while, then biotechnology, leisure-time industries, and so on. When Nomura picks a stock, it has the power to ramp up its price to where Nomura's research says it ought to be.

"In a rising market, Nomura's recommendations are virtually self-fulfilling," says one executive. "There is so much liquidity in Japan, and so many young, inexperienced people managing it. They just do what their brokerage firm tells them. If the stock goes up, they come back for more. It's a virtuous circle."

Those customers who do a reasonable volume of business with Nomura often get a bit of advance insight into what the company might promote next. In Japan such talk is not considered "insider trading," as it might be in the United States. Instead it is all part of an unending cycle of "relationship building" that keeps customers loyal to their salesmen, salesmen working hard for their customers, and foreign brokers with little hope of coming between them. If an important customer loses money on a Nomura-touted investment, his salesman will be able to "go to his branch manager and suggest that he be tipped off about the next juicy new issue" as compensation.[3]

Like other kinds of Japanese businesses, Nomura takes "customer service" extremely seriously. It is the first lesson young recruits are taught. Following the morning meeting at the Shinjuku branch, the newest recruits took turns exiting via the main door. Before doing so, each one turned back toward the department and bellowed out at the top of his lungs a Japanese line whose proximate translation was, "I am off to serve the customers and inform them of the latest trends!" Then they would bow low to their colleagues and literally sprint out the door, looking like kamikaze pilots running to their aircraft.

"Out there, they will learn the hard way what it's like to be the most important thing a man can be at Nomura: a salesman," remarked Aozono of his corps of newcomers. He knew theirs would be a frustrating day pounding pavements, ringing doorbells, and visiting shopkeepers again and again in search of their first customers. New salesmen are considered lazy if they don't use up a pair of shoes in a month. Doors will be shut in their faces—even in polite Japan—but still they have it easy compared with their legendary Nomura forebears. Minoru Segawa, president of Nomura in the 1950s, recalled visiting a leading industrialist at home in the days when Nomura was first trying to build its reputation. Segawa was ordered to enter through the kitchen door, since he was deemed no better than a peddler.[4]

That history is deliberately kept fresh at Nomura, where toughness is more highly prized than polish and where the charge of "aggressiveness" is considered a compliment rather than an insult. Unlike most Japanese companies, Nomura is unafraid of the appearance of immodesty in promoting itself. It publishes annual factbooks showing the many ways in which it dominates the Japanese financial markets —and, increasingly, some world financial markets as well. Its own publications declare Nomura to be the biggest, the most innovative, and the most excellent.

Nomura is arrogant, but not pretentious. In Tokyo it is the American firms whose offices look the way one would expect Nomura's offices to look: stunning Japanese screens, ceramics, woodblock prints, and elegant antique furniture all carefully interwoven with the general decor of hushed high-tech electronic minimalism. Nomura's offices, on the other hand, are Spartan, overcrowded, linoleum-tiled, and virtually undecorated (except for the executive level in the Nihonbashi headquarters, which does have a carpet and a few original European paintings).

At Nomura retail brokers see themselves for what they are: hard-working salesmen selling financial products not to "clients" but to customers. Highfalutin titles like "account executive" or "personal financial consultant" are rarely used. Unlike American financial companies, where vice presidents are counted in triple digits, Nomura's vice presidents can be counted on one hand. The corporate culture sees little need to glorify its business beyond its evident reality. The Nomuraman has been trained to believe that the twin causes of customer and corporate profit should be glory enough for any man.

A Warrior Culture

About three hundred new recruits join Nomura every April first. Most expect to spend the rest of their professional lives at Nomura. In principle this will not be too difficult, since the only grounds for actually getting fired are fiddling with customer funds or fiddling with married women. But the pressure will be intense and the hierarchy unforgiving. The first few years are like boot camp, during which time many drop by the wayside of their own accord. Later, those whose work doesn't make the grade (or those who lose one of the company's periodic power struggles) are politely exiled to meaningless jobs, unimportant offices, or dead-end subsidiaries. For the majority of Nomuramen, though, there is a sure and steady path through the hierarchy to responsible positions. Sustained hard work, company loyalty, and self-effacement will get you there.

True superstars will be promoted to the top at a younger age than at most Japanese companies, provided they manage to demonstrate their mettle without stepping on the toes of their superiors. With many directors now in their forties and a president in his mid-fifties, Nomura is setting a model of youthful leadership at odds with the geriatric one that has traditionally dominated Japanese business. Even the president will not age much in office. After a brief chance to run the company for a few years, he will be retired to the more honorific role of chairman and replaced with a younger man.

Nomura is a cradle-to-grave establishment. New recruits frequently live in company-provided dormitories. In return for the arduous commitment Nomuramen are expected to make—so arduous they don't have time for dating girls outside the office—the company's personnel department deliberately chooses the comeliest females for its staff of OL's (office ladies). "Nomura girls" are graduates of Japan's best universities, but they will get little chance to put their education to work. When a foreign visitor arrives at headquarters, he is likely to encounter a dozen Nomura girls on his way to the executive floor, each one bowing and pointing the way to the next. They will spend several years greeting visitors, operating elevators, fixing tea and coffee, and doing light secretarial work until they pair off with a Nomuraman. Then they will marry and go home to look after the family and the household. As many as half of today's managers are married to Nomura girls they met at the beginning of their careers.

To speed up the pairing-off process, Nomura sponsors its own marriage brokerage service. Department chiefs invariably help out as well, seeing it as an integral part of their job to help subordinates find mates. Years later, if the marriage falls on hard times, the couple will seek help in settling disputes from the mentor who introduced them.

Few women actually make professional careers at Nomura. Yet oddly enough, one of the backbones of the company's much vaunted "placement power" is its 3,500 "midis"—middle-aged housewives—who work "part-time," meaning they "only" work nine to five. Nomura began using them in 1953 as part of a campaign to promote public interest in the stock market. Throughout Japan they distributed piggy bank-like devices known as *ryo* chests designed to hold spare coins. Nomura kept the key. When the *ryo* reached five thousand yen, the saleswoman came to collect it, exchanging the money for a share in an investment trust. Eventually a million new participants were attracted to the Japanese stock market this way, helping to ignite the TSE boom of the 1960s.

The approach has since been modernized, but Nomura's team of "midis" still comprise what the company calls its "front line of customer service." Today saleswomen organize Tupperware-style parties to introduce small groups of housewives to the company's bond offerings, mutual funds, and other new products. Largely as a result of this effort, Nomura's retail customers can be found in one out of every six Japanese homes.

The fact that Nomura's heritage lies in Osaka gives it an edge in the rough-and-tumble world of the stock market. "Tokyo people care about titles and refinement, Osaka people care about making money," says one insider. Japanese society's bias against the brokerage profession has never stood in Nomura's way. Even today an important Tokyo family would much rather see their son join status-rich Mitsubishi Bank than Nomura; the imperial family still reportedly maintains a policy against its princesses marrying men who are either journalists or stockbrokers. Thriving on this prejudice, Nomura recruited hard-working "country boys" in the past. Bringing them to Tokyo as "blank slates," molding them in the company's image, and laying a lifetime career path before them, Nomura instilled a sense of superloyalty even stronger than the rest of loyalty-conscious Japanese business. This history, in part, is responsible for the attitude both inside and outside Nomura that the company functions like a fanatic religion, zealously rewarding its own and lashing out ferociously at those who cross it.

Today most new recruits are college graduates. But unlike other leading Japanese companies that make a fetish of hiring only the graduates of Japan's Ivy League (Tokyo University, Waseda, and Keio), Nomura assigns more weight to a prospective candidate's desire than where he obtained his degree. Physical strength is high on the list of qualities sought by the company. "The life of a Nomuraman is a hard one. We need men who can withstand the stresses and strains," says a company spokesman.

Even though the company sends a crop of its rising stars annually to the Harvard Business School, Wharton, Cambridge, London School of Economics, and other prestigious Western universities, many are reluctant to go. They know that even now, in the midst of Nomura's efforts to bill itself as a sophisticated global firm, a Harvard degree gains them little inside the organization. It is more likely to arouse the suspicion that they are too soft or too foreign-influenced. Room at the top, with certain notable exceptions, is reserved for those who've worked their way up through the bread-and-butter of the retail branch network.

Recruits typically spend a few years doing a bit of everything: salesman, trader, analyst; retail and wholesale; stocks and bonds; front office and back office. Generalists are revered; specialization is denigrated. The goal is to create a company resembling the Japanese candy known as *kintaro-ame*—a log-shaped sweet in which the interior filling has been swirled into the design of a face. "Wherever you cut the candy, you get the same face," says one who went through the Nomura training process.

Even the superstars must be cut of the same company fabric. Take Koji Higashi, the top salesman of the Shinjuku branch, who is in his early thirties and has spent ten years at Nomura. He manages multi-million-dollar portfolios for a long list of corporate customers. One of those is Promise, itself a thriving group of wheelers and dealers in the household finance business. When it comes to investing its own $14 million equity portfolio, Promise relies on Nomura—and Higashi. The president of Promise is so enamored of Higashi's good advice that he has dubbed him the "Henry Kaufman of Shinjuku."

An American broker on Wall Street managing similarly sized portfolios would likely make $200,000–$500,000 from salary, commissions, and bonuses. At Nomura there is only one salary scale—a modest one, based on seniority. There are no commissions. There are bonuses—but the amounts are derived almost entirely from the firm's total results, not individual achievements. The "Henry Kaufman of Shinjuku" makes a grand total of about $35,000 a year. For Higashi, the fast track doesn't mean Ferraris and cocaine. A big thrill for him is having the money to buy tickets to the Whitney Houston concert. He gets frequent calls from headhunters trying to lure him to one of the American firms in Tokyo. He's been offered as much as ten times his current salary to move. His answer: "Of course I would like to earn more money, but money is not the only thing in life. Loyalty to Nomura is more important."

Nomura is the well-oiled fighting machine of a warrior culture. Its men are veritable samurai of stocks and bonds.

Foreign Cassandras, Foreign Pollyannas

Like any army, Nomura has its weak points. It even has its share of deserters. Not all Nomuramen can be quite as certain about their future with the company as Higashi. In the past, quitting Nomura meant looking for a job far afield, since only in rare circumstances would another Big Four company hire one disloyal enough to have resigned a Nomura position in the first place. The particular circumstances would be considered irrelevant; the act of disloyalty absolute.

The arrival of a multiplicity of foreign securities firms in Tokyo—all in desperate need of experienced Japanese staff—has promoted an increasing flow of human resources out of Japanese companies. Those uncomfortable with the suffocating environment at Nomura ("any man who wants to avoid brain death and any woman who wants to see what else she can do besides serve tea," according to one acerbic observer) can now move to foreign houses, where they will be better paid and given more responsibility.

Brave enough to risk ostracism by leaving Nomura, such people are rarely foolish enough to burn their bridges completely by talking publicly about their experiences. But another group of ex-Nomuramen has also begun to grow: foreigners, hired by Nomura in its dizzy pace of internationalization, who ultimately find themselves unable to adjust to the corporate culture. Foreign defectors *do* tend to be more voluble. As their numbers have increased, so too have the horror stories about life inside.

The recent internal power struggle described in chapter 1 between Masaaki Kurokawa and Yoshio Terasawa, which focused on how much emphasis to give to doing things the traditional "Nomura way" in foreign financial markets, expedited the departure of a number of prominent Americans within the firm who disagreed with Kurokawa's Tokyo-centric policies. Despite Nomura's verbal commitment to build "local" operations in its London and U.S. offices—and despite the fact that less than 10 percent of Nomura's staff abroad is Japanese — American, British, and other foreign nationals hired by the firm are losing what little local decision-making power they once had.

The trappings of internationalization are all in place, but the core of the firm is more Japanese than ever. The frightening part, say those close to the scene, is that the new orientation is working. "Terasawa was very well liked, but Nomura Securities International [the U.S. subsidiary] wasn't that successful. Now it is," says one Nomura watcher, adding, "Terasawa was well suited for the days when Nomura was trying to be a good neighbor and a good partner with American firms. Kurokawa is better-suited for the new order of things, where Nomura has the power to go it alone and beat the Americans at their own game."

Over the years the bill of particulars American Nomuramen have cited about their employer has run from the sublime to the ridiculous:

A group of Americans in the New York office once staged a well-publicized "strike" to dramatize their dissatisfaction with Nomura's unwillingness to pay Wall Street–style salaries and bonuses.

A frequent complaint is that foreigners are invited to participate in high-level meetings, only to find the discussion dwelling on mundane topics. When the foreigners leave, it seems, the real meetings begin.

Brokers say they were pressured into making repeat overtures to unresponsive American institutional client prospects, even multiple telephone calls on the same day. In Japan, they were told, one demonstrates sincerity by keeping up an excessive level of contact even in the face of persistent rejection. Japanese managers believed the same approach would work in the United States. When Americans didn't adhere to it, they were accused of being "lazy."

One foreign analyst working for Nomura wrote an English-language report critical of a Japanese company. When the report was translated into Japanese, however, it read like an enthusiastic "buy" recommendation. Apparently someone at headquarters believed it was important not to offend the subject company.

An American working in Tokyo was told to write a brief thank-you note to an English-speaking customer. His text was not only criticized by his Japanese superior once, it was subjected to six revisions on matters of grammar and nuance. In the end the American was ordered to send out a letter that included obvious misspellings and grammatical errors conforming to his Japanese superior's limited grasp of English.

Personalized as the above experiences may be, foreign critics say they add up to a trend: Nomura will never be able to achieve its stated goal of transferring its domestic strength to the international investment banking arena if it continues to do things the Nomura way. The company, they say, lacks the spirit of innovation, flexibility, and the partnering sensibilities crucial to investment banking success.

Foreign Cassandras see other problems looming as Nomura is compelled to rely less on size and more on agility in the deregulated Tokyo financial world. What will Nomura do when the main source of its current profits—domestic commission income—is reduced by the knife of deregulation slicing through the world's fattest margins? What will happen to Nomura's leadership in underwriting if and when article 65 is relaxed and the mighty Japanese city banks are allowed to go after this lucrative business? As for Nomura's often biased research and blatant share ramping, critics argue such practices will cause Japanese money managers to seek business relationships with more independent foreign houses. Even the worldliness of Nomura's current president, Yoshihisa Tabuchi, is a subject of foreign derision. One former Nomuraman says Tabuchi "talks a good game about international finance for fifteen minutes, after which it becomes obvious that he's a domestic retail man all the way and doesn't know much else."

The theme of Nomura as a Japanese giant unable to make more than a cosmetic breakthrough into the global marketplace is evidenced again and again in the comments about the firm that show up in the American business press: Nomura has brawn but lacks the brains to wrest plum business away from Wall Street. . . . Nomura is a one-product house—distribution power in Japan and not much else.[5] . . . Nomura is weak in corporate finance. They can place bonds in Japan, but they can't structure deals.[6] . . . Nomura lacks the flexibility and imagination needed from world players. It has the latest computer technology, but not the trading mentality to go with it.[7] . . . Nomura's insularity and inbred culture have produced managers who have spent most of their time in Japan, speaking only to other Japanese in trading rooms, boardrooms, noodle shops, and bars.[8] . . . Being biggest in the world is not necessarily an advantage in New York, where success depends on speed, creativity, and complex deal making. . . .[9]

The American consensus, in short, is that with all due respect to the enormity of Nomura's power inside Japan, its corporate culture and operating style prevent it from competing seriously with foreigners for non-Japanese business. Its current visible role in global finance is only a function of Japan's capital surpluses; when those are reduced, Nomura's global stature will shrink too. Wall Street concedes that American pension funds may call on Nomura to help manage the small portion of their assets they wish to invest in Japan; but the notion that they would, in any significant number, call on the U.S. arm of Nomura to manage their U.S. equity portfolio is considered implausible.

The American criticisms of Nomura all have basis in fact. Yet the rush to judgment that Nomura is unlikely to pose a direct threat to American and European financial service companies on their native ground is recklessly naive. It is Pollyanna-ish thinking from men who are supposed to be the ultimate pragmatists.

"Nomura is a company with loads of problems," observes an American who recently ended a lengthy stint in the New York office. "But they're made out of a material their American competitors can't match: *muscle, pure muscle*. I've seen all the mistakes they make. I'd give them a 'D' on style and no better than a 'B' on content. But they are so strong and so determined, I don't see anything that will stop them."

London Game, New York Set, Tokyo Match

In the year 2000, Nomura's headquarters will not be in Tokyo but on a satellite orbiting the Earth, uplinking and downlinking information and electronic transactions instantaneously across the globalized axis of the London, New York, and Tokyo markets. Such was the oft-proclaimed vision of Nomura's most recent past president and current chairman, Setsuya Tabuchi (known as "Big Tabuchi" to distinguish him from the current president, Yoshihisa Tabuchi, to whom he is not related). "Big Tabuchi" established much of the groundwork of the international expansion "Little Tabuchi" is now carrying out.

Despite his nickname, there is nothing "little" about "Little Tabuchi." Burly and tough, he is a salesman's salesman who worked his way through the ranks to the company's presidency. Today he exudes confidence and power, without a trace of the mildly humbled aspirations that have invaded the vocabulary of his American counterparts since Black Monday. One former Nomura executive says of Tabuchi, "If he had lived in another time period, I'm sure he would have been a shogun." Other insiders refer to him as the "Mao Zedong of Nomura"—in part because of a slight physical resemblance to the former Chinese leader, but more because like Mao, Tabuchi wields power ruthlessly and strategically. If Mao borrowed freely from Sun Tzu's ancient writings on the art of war to make his revolution in China, Tabuchi is borrowing some of the same pages to steer Nomura toward leadership of the global financial revolution.

Speaking in Japanese with an imperious, electrical whisper, Tabuchi explains Nomura's strategy, sometimes running far ahead of his translator but peppering his speech with enough Anglicized concepts so that the English-only listener can catch his drift: "expansion," "world investors," "investment banking supermarket," and "Londonnewyorktokyo" as if it were a single word. Seated beneath an original painting by Marc Chagall (in which a red sun is visible), Tabuchi holds himself bolt upright, every sinew taut, ready to pounce. Chainsmoking furiously, sometimes shrouding his own visage in a mysterious swirl of smoke rings, he declares:

"We want all customers. We aspire to serve all nationalities, all borrowers, all issuers, and all investors. We wish to be like Japanese manufacturing companies which sell the same products to people in every part of the world. I think my friends like John Gutfreund at Salomon and Bill Schreyer at Merrill Lynch have the same sort of ambition as we do. Right now, it is hard to tell who is ahead. In the future, it will be clearer.

"The growth of our company is a function of the Japanese capital market being opened and liberalized. History shows money *must* circulate out of a capital-surplus nation into the world economy. The London merchant bankers played this role when capital accumulated in London. For most of the twentieth century, the United States played this role. Now the time has come when the Japanese must fulfill their responsibilities. It is in this area that Nomura finds its reason for being."

Actually the vision is not new. Even in Nomura's earliest days, when founder Tokushichi Nomura II was trying to elevate the Japanese securities business above the level of the gamblers, pawnbrokers, and pickle dealers who then populated its ranks, he dreamed of building Nomura into a company that would "stand side by side with the investment banking firms of Wall Street."[10] As early as 1927, only two years after the official incorporation of Nomura Securities, an office was opened in New York's financial district.

A turning point in the life of postwar Japanese financial markets occurred in 1961 when Sony became the first Japanese corporation to issue its shares in ADR (American Depository Receipt) form, readily tradable on the NYSE. Nomura had been intimately involved in preparing this breakthrough deal, which allowed Americans a practical way to buy shares in the Japanese economic miracle for the first time. Free-market forces would now be applied to what was otherwise a tightly controlled and lackluster Tokyo Stock Exchange, and prices would begin to rise dramatically on the TSE as a result. Smith Barney, Sony's U.S. underwriter, was skeptical about including Nomura in the deal. But Sony and Nomura insisted, and eventually the gentlemen of Smith Barney were convinced to allow Nomura to comanage the ADR offering in the United States.

According to Nomura's official corporate history, "As soon as actual sales began, the phones at Nomura's New York office were ringing nonstop. There was only one brief message for callers: 'Sorry, Sony sold out.' Through the end of September, buy orders for the Sony issue outnumbered sell orders by a ratio of over thirty to one.... 'Nomura of Japan' was on its way to becoming 'Nomura of the World.' There would be no looking back."[11]

Throughout the 1960s Nomura expanded aggressively abroad, chiefly with the intention of capitalizing on the new foreign interest in the Tokyo market. Meanwhile Nomuramen assigned to the United States studied everything about the functioning of the American market. In particular they studied Merrill Lynch. Merrill was the company they most admired, and the one best known in Japan, since it was the first U.S. securities firm to open a branch in Tokyo. It is said that Nomura studied Merrill down to the last detail, even measuring the desks in its offices.

In 1965 Yamaichi Securities, the leader of the Japanese market, nearly collapsed in the speculative wave that engulfed the TSE, and Nomura leaped to the number-one spot as a result. Being number one in Japan is very important; those who perceive themselves as number one in their own field want to do business only with those who are number one in theirs. The idea of a big firm seeking innovative solutions or more attentive service from a boutique firm—as so often happens in the United States—rarely happens in Japan. Thus, when Japan's great outward march of exporters began in the 1960s, the biggest among them insisted upon Nomura's financial services, compelling Nomura further and deeper into global finance.

Servicing Japanese industrial companies in their transnational journeys would have generated enough business to make any securities firm into a world-class player. But the need to recycle Japan's capital surpluses in the 1980s radically altered the nature of Nomura's corporate mission. This was especially true after 1984 when Japanese insurance companies and other large institutional investors gained greater freedom to invest part of their assets overseas, and the capital came flowing out of Japan in torrents.

To accommodate the deluge, Nomura's U.S. operation grew from less than fifty employees in 1983 to nearly seven hundred by the end of 1987. The London office experienced similar growth. Nomura transformed itself from a little-known comanager of underwritings involving transpacific business into a towering force in the U.S. government bond market, Eurobonds, and other fixed-income areas.

In 1985 a middle-level Nomuraman unaccustomed to speaking with the foreign press confidently proclaimed Nomura had a thirty-year plan for dominating world financial markets. When asked about it in 1987, Tabuchi laughed at the absurdity of attempting to write down an actual plan to cover the next thirty years of developments. In a rare display of Nomura modesty, Tabuchi argued that while Nomura wants to compete in the domestic U.S., British, and other markets, it does not expect to ever have the power to "dominate" them.

Whether Nomura's time horizons are five, ten, or thirty years, and regardless of just how big a market share the firm really seeks in each local market, there can be no doubt that Nomura is pursuing a cohesive, rational strategy aimed at nothing less than emerging as the biggest and most efficient vendor of financial services in the unified twenty-four-hour global market of the future.

In London, where the markets are wide open and the British firms themselves lack deep capital resources, Nomura expects to be able to exert a hegemonic influence sooner rather than later. It is already doing just that in the Eurobond business, which is headquartered in London and is the most important financial market outside the United States and Japan. Nomura came out of nowhere five years ago to emerge as the number-one underwriter of Eurobonds in 1987, unseating all the great names of American and European investment banking. Nomura is assiduously stockpiling talent, watching and waiting as American and European firms pull back from their overinflated expectations of profits to be made after the Big Bang. In London Nomura has done what regulations prevent it from doing in either Japan or the United States—it has opened its own commercial bank.

In New York Nomura first plunged deeply into the high-volume fixed-income markets such as U.S. government bonds, requiring the least complex level of local involvement and making the best use of the firm's "placement power" back in Japan. But big *American* investors now feel *compelled* to do some of their bond buying through Nomura, because Nomura presumably has the best answers to the biggest question hanging over the market: "What are the Japanese going to do?"

From that starting point, Nomura has begun to find its way into equities, fund management, real estate, M&A, and other investment banking functions. Nomura's U.S. subsidiary plans to enter virtually every nook and cranny of the American securities and investment banking environment, with the possible exception of retail brokerage. Although Nomura believes in growing from within rather than buying other firms as a matter of philosophy, it has already demonstrated a willingness to dip into its war chest in order to enter businesses where it lacks expertise. Its acquisition of a stake in Eastdil, the premier real estate investment banking firm in New York, positioned Nomura overnight as one of the most important forces in New York City's commercial real estate development. A similar purchase of Babcock & Brown has thrust it to the front of the lease-financing business.

Whether local American staff members have real influence or not, the company has certainly given itself a local look. What could be more all-American than Don McKinnon, a strapping former linebacker for the New England Patriots and longtime Wall Street veteran, heading up Nomura's New York equity trading department? What could be more blue chip than clients like AT&T? S. Lawrence Prendergast, AT&T's treasurer, indicates that the Nomura way in the United States is beginning to work. Nomura, he says, has been "calling on us for about fifteen years and didn't generate any business for the first ten. Their persistence and the wealth of Japan . . . have paid off for them."[12]

Nomura executives talk about achieving a fifty-fifty balance between domestic and foreign revenues by 1991. That would be a dramatic shift from 1984 when 90 percent of Nomura's income came from Japan-to-Japan transactions. The muscular Nomuramen don't plan to lose any Japanese business in making that shift. Instead they expect only to *add* business abroad.

To those who think them crazed megalomaniacs for believing they could generate $4 billion worth of additional annual pretax income from activities in highly competitive foreign markets, Nomura allows as how it counts in the "foreign" column commissions and fees earned on behalf of Japanese clients investing abroad. If Nomura's projections are accurate, the company could become the biggest brokerage house in the United States solely on the basis of selling American stocks to Japanese investors. But Nomura doesn't intend to stop there. No matter how long it takes, Nomura fully intends to become a player in the U.S.-to-U.S. side of the business. It has already lost a lot of money in the United States trying to do this over the years, but that doesn't matter. Nomuramen believe passionately in what they call *dochakuka*—the policy of burrowing deeply into a market, working it, and patiently waiting for it to yield results. By the time *dochakuka* has succeeded in the United States, the Tokyo market will be fully liberalized and prepared to play its role as the key financial center in the world.

Innovative Enough

For those who fault Nomura in that ephemeral department known as "innovation," the Eurobond market shows the Nomuramen capable enough on this front. The company's own favorite contribution to the giddy world of new international financial products is the "Heaven and Hell" foreign exchange–indexed bond it originated for IBM Credit Corp. Developed by a young mathematician in Nomura's new product group, the "Heaven and Hell" issue involved three interest rate swaps and five foreign currency swaps, with the net result that IBM issued its paper via Nomura forty basis points cheaper than it might otherwise have been able to.

With considerable fanfare, Nomura's publicity materials trumpet the "Deal of the Year" award won by the IBM offering as vindication that the company really is as brainy as it is brawny. The "Heaven and Hell" swap, it says, caused a "lot of eyebrow raising and heart searching because U.S. investment banks and European merchant banks had been suggesting that their Japanese rivals might be big and strong in capital and distribution, but that they were weak in financial engineering."[13] In a backhanded riposte to Wall Street, however, Nomura declares that it has no interest in "innovation for innovation's own sake"[14] and only creates new products where they serve useful purposes.

Nomura has pioneered a diverse lot of such useful innovations: high-coupon Euroyen bonds, Dutch florin warrant bonds, Euroyen convertible bonds, Euroyen dual-currency bonds, and all manner of "Sushi," "Shogun," "Samurai," and "Yankee" bonds. Nomura is currently working on swaps technology so secretive that its swaps department in Tokyo has been declared off limits to visitors.

The first private company in Japan to use any kind of computer system (a Univac 120 in 1955), Nomura is now plowing its profits heavily into futuristic databases and trading programs. Its computer subsidiary, one of Japan's largest software-writing enterprises, is reportedly working on an artificial intelligence–driven global equity trading program. Its CAPITAL information system is installed on-site with more than two thousand institutional investors. By the early 1990s Nomura expects to have a million retail customers using its desktop computer trading network.

While the London-New York-Tokyo axis consumes most of Nomura's corporate attention, its activities are by no means limited to those markets. Extremely active in Hong Kong, Singapore, Toronto, and most European financial markets, Nomura hopes the availability of Japanese investment capital will stimulate stock exchanges all over the world to expand and diversify. Nobumitsu Kagami, managing director of Nomura's investment management company, NIMCO, expects to handle the flow of $25 billion into global equities over the next few years. Although he looks first and foremost at the United States, Europe, Canada, Australia, and New Zealand, he also sees significant Japanese equity investments flowing into the stock markets of the Asian NICs in the early 1990s and into the emerging markets of Brazil, Mexico, and other high-growth countries in the late 1990s. "This is where the opportunities of the future are, and in these areas you can afford a little higher risk in return for a little higher return."

Executive Vice President Yoshiji Fukushima has a bolder, more startling vision of Nomura's sweeping global role. A consummate "retail man" who rose to the number-two position with virtually no experience abroad, Fukushima confidently predicts that in ten years' time Japan's net external assets will be one trillion dollars. Of all the financial companies in the world, he says, only Nomura has the capacity to do the job of recycling that capital and "apportioning it to the advanced countries, the less developed countries, and the communist world, to best revitalize the economy of the world as a whole."[15]

7

Tulipmania or Hidden Assets? Understanding the Japanese Financial Revolution

All that money, chasing a limited supply of Japanese land and Japanese stocks, is blowing the markets sky-high. In *Extraordinary Popular Delusions and the Madness of Crowds,* Charles Mackay wrote chillingly about mass hysterias of the past, when rising prices became their own justification and reason was thrown to the wolves. What has happened recently in Tokyo bears more than a few resemblances to past manias like the Dutch tulip bulb craze or the South Sea bubble.

The Japanese, proud of presiding over the world's biggest stock market, are reduced to justifying stock prices by citing "hidden values" in land or in investment portfolios. When you're at the point where you use one aspect of a boom to justify another, you begin to sound like *Popular Delusions.*

——Forbes[1]

Of PERs and NAVs

Paul Aron looks like George Smiley, the legendary hero of John le Carré's espionage thrillers: dapper in an absentminded sort of way, pudgy, and avuncular, with a kindly air that belies the cutthroat business in which he works. Inside the skyscraper aerie in lower Manhattan's Battery Park City where Daiwa Securities America is headquartered, Aron putters past trading desks as if he were an Oxford don groping his way through a world that long ago decided to eliminate thought in favor of action. Like George Smiley, Paul Aron prefers his own standards to those of the rest of the world. And like Smiley too, he believes that rational analysis is man's best revenge in a chaotic cosmos.

Aron was among the first American portfolio managers to bet heavily on Japan. At Dreyfus in 1969, he launched a $100 million mutual fund as a vehicle for Americans to invest in the coming Tokyo Stock Exchange miracle he forecast. Most professionals disagreed sharply with his optimism about Japan. At 1,800 the Nikkei index was already deemed "astronomical." But time proved Aron right: the Nikkei soared in the 1970s, and his investors enjoyed results that ranked alongside the most spectacular ever returned by a mutual fund.

Even after that success, Wall Street pros continued to view Aron as overly enamored with Japan. When he announced that he was signing on with Daiwa, a Tokyo-based securities house virtually unknown in the United States, they thought he'd gone off the deep end.

Under Daiwa's aegis Aron stumped the United States, organizing conferences and seminars to educate Americans about the great potential in Japanese equities. Most of his audiences were skeptical. Some even laughed. But those who listened to Aron's recommendations continued to be richly rewarded.

Years later, when the great Tokyo bull market of 1985–87 got under way (and Daiwa had become one of the biggest securities firms in the world), Paul Aron was familiar with the syndrome that seemed to be dogging him: the more events proved him right, the crazier everyone else thought he was. "At 1,800, they said the Nikkei index couldn't go any higher," he noted with some frustration. "At 7,000, they said the same thing. At 13,000, we heard it again, and I suppose we'll keep hearing it. We hear it from people who believe Tokyo's PERs [price/earnings ratios] are dangerously inflated. But what they don't always understand is that PERs are calculated differently and interpreted differently in the U.S. and in Japan."

To prove his point, Aron did a detailed analysis of PERs in both countries. In a seminal series of reports, he demonstrated that astronomical-sounding Japanese PERs had more to do with differences in accounting methods than with madness in the Tokyo market. Using his own PER leveling model, Aron concluded that the leading stocks traded on the Tokyo and New York stock exchanges were almost identically valued. Portfolio managers who continued to stay away from Japanese equities, he predicted, would frustrate themselves and their investors by missing great opportunities. "In my experience," he wrote, "the nay-sayers have been correct really only . . . after the initial oil shock in 1973–74. I am not so arrogant as to deny that they may be correct again, but I submit that to be right a couple of times over the last eighteen years does not contribute to good performance."[2]

Aron and his colleagues at Daiwa continued to turn out favorable recommendations on Japanese stocks. A few American portfolio managers followed their advice and earned stunning returns, especially when the strengthening yen began to multiply the heady underlying gains in Tokyo share prices for dollar-based investors. Other managers reached similarly bullish conclusions about Japan independently. A wave of U.S.-based global equity funds sprang up and leaped successfully into the Tokyo market to record some of the best performance records of 1986—Merrill Lynch and Fidelity to name but two. Yet most American money managers could not bring themselves to accept Aron's thinking. Tokyo remained synonymous with rigged markets, volatile speculation, and aberrant circumstances likely to jackknife at any moment.

Under the best of circumstances, the TSE is difficult for foreigners to comprehend. For those who don't speak or read Japanese and aren't well connected, the task of keeping tabs on the inner life of Japanese companies is nearly impossible. While the frenzy of buying and selling on the TSE floor may *look* familiar enough to Americans watching it from the gallery, what's *really* going on is another story altogether.

Monopolization of trading by the Big Four creates one of the world's most intense expressions of the "herd" mentality. Kabutocho, the neighborhood surrounding the TSE's Nihonbashi headquarters, is so rife with purported inside information that Westerners who have worked in other financial centers claim Tokyo as the most rumor-driven market in the world. The rumors, however, along with real facts and knowledge, pass through an intricately designed hierarchy. "If you don't mind playing follow-the-leader behind Nomura and Nikko here, you can do all right," says the research director of a British house in Tokyo. "Those who like being contrarians should take their marbles elsewhere if they don't want to lose them all."

The oddities of Japanese financial culture put foreigners at a distinct disadvantage in trying to develop market strategy: hand-picked "stocks of the week" selected and touted by the Big Four based on investment "themes" that are sometimes scarcely plausible . . . "election stocks" that zoom up when politicians need money and then collapse after the campaign . . . "ambulance stocks" to rescue important clients who've lost money on brokerage house recommendations . . . *sokaiya* (thugs) paid to carry out harassment and physical assaults at shareholders meetings . . . *jiageya* (sharks), who are not averse to using murder as a tactic to force small landowners to sell prime parcels of real estate . . . huge *tokkin* funds, where major corporations farm out asset management to gunslingers to circumvent an otherwise unfavorable capital gains tax basis . . . an analyst community that would rather say nothing about a Japanese company than say something negative, and much, much more.

Over and above these cultural differences, Tokyo's so-called fundamentals scared the daylights out of most American institutional investors from 1985 onward. As the Tokyo bulls ran, the TSE appeared increasingly decoupled from reality. Wall Street's own boom drove the S&P 500 to what was considered a highly speculative average PER of 20 shortly before the October 1987 crash. If that dizzy multiple turned the Street's bulls into Ferdinands as well as outright bears, what were they to make of Nikkei index stocks trading at an average PER of 60? Of Japanese blue chips that paid virtually no dividends and enjoyed PERs of 100, 200, or more? Of more than one hundred stocks with PERs over 1,000?

Regardless of what Paul Aron had to say about accounting methods, how could the total market value of the 1,500 stocks on the TSE be worth more than the 2,250 stocks listed on the NYSE? What sense could be made of a Japanese stock market that valued NTT more highly than IBM, AT&T, Exxon, General Electric, and General Motors *combined*?

At one American brokerage house in Tokyo, an analyst submitted a report to the newly arrived American president suggesting a "buy" recommendation for All-Nippon Airways (ANA). The president reviewed the report, saw a PER for the company of 305, and assumed it was a typographical error with one decimal place too many. When he found out it wasn't, he summoned his analysts and reminded them, "ANA might be the greatest company in the world, but how can we recommend a Japanese airline stock with a multiple of 305 to American investors, when the whole U.S. airline industry is trading at a multiple of 15?"

Some Americans made a fortune in those heady Tokyo days. But most of those responsible for investing sizable pools of money in Japan looked at triple-digit PERs and shuddered. "Sell," they said. And they kept selling, believing each new thousand-point rung on the Nikkei's ladder was unsustainable. From 1985 straight through 1987, Americans were net sellers of Japanese equities. As a result they missed most of the action in what turned out to be the greatest bull market in modern financial history—a bull market that distributed gains to its participants three or four times greater than those produced by the run-up on Wall Street during the same time period.

To those standing outside Japanese financial culture and trying to peer in, Tokyo didn't look like a bull market. It looked instead like a very serious case of "Tulipmania." Prices seemed to have about as much to do with real value as in the seventeenth-century Dutch tulip bulb craze when trading in a single rare bulb shot up as high as 5,500 guilders (about $45,000 today) before crashing down to 300 guilders. Thoughtful global investors listened carefully to all the rationalizations from the experts—Paul Aron included—and promptly rejected them as utterly irrational.

The most popular of these rationalizations was the notion that the market's rise resulted from analysts uncovering "hidden assets" of Japanese corporations. Why was the share price of Nippon Steel skyrocketing when the company itself was reeling under the blows of *endaka* and facing fierce competition from steel exporters in lower-wage countries? Because of "hidden assets"—namely, its massive real estate holdings. Carried on the books at prices paid decades earlier, the market value of the land beneath the company's steel-making complexes had now risen by ten, fifty, or one hundred times. At 349 yen, each Nippon Steel share actually represented 992 yen of net asset value in the company.[3] If Nippon Steel never hauled another ingot out of its blast furnaces and turned itself into a realty company instead, stockholders would make out like bandits.

"While American investors study the ratios, Japanese investors study maps," observed *The Wall Street Journal*. "A company may report dreadful earnings, but if it sits on a choice plot of land, its stock could soar. Shares of Tokyo Gas Co., Nippon Steel Corp., and Ishikawajima-Harima Heavy Industries Co. are hot now because the companies are situated near Tokyo Bay, where the government is in the throes of a major redevelopment project."[4] Most intensely affected were realty and land development companies themselves, which held portfolios of properties sometimes carried on their books at prices paid in the nineteenth century.

Virtually every Japanese industrial company is a landowner. Most service companies own prime chunks of downtown Tokyo real estate. Thus the "hidden assets" explanation was widely applicable. If you can't understand Japanese PERs, then look at the NAVs and PBRs instead, explained the best of the foreign analysts, referring to net asset values and price/book value ratios. "In terms of real asset value as opposed to simply conventional valuation, some of the cheapest stocks in the entire world are in Japan," reported George Noble, portfolio manager for the Fidelity Overseas Fund—one of the few foreign funds to buy Japanese equities aggressively in 1986, loading up on property-laden railroads, real estate companies, and insurance carriers.[5]

Hogwash, replied most American investment sages. In the first place, the real estate market suffered from even greater Tulipmania than the stock market. What businesses could possibly generate enough cash flow to warrant paying $10,000–$20,000 for a single square foot of space in Tokyo? How could the sum total of Japan's land area, roughly the size of California, be more valuable than the entire North American continent? Yet that's what the logical (or illogical) extrapolation of Japanese real estate values suggested. Americans who believed property prices would soon come crashing down also believed that stocks would follow head over heels. "The world economy rests under a giant inverted pyramid of inflated values, with its tip centered in downtown Tokyo," reported an investment newsletter expressing the collective fears of many foreigners.[6] This view held that when Tokyo's real estate market began to crumble, Japanese banks (representing about 40 percent of TSE market capitalization) would collapse like a house of cards, since most of them were heavily exposed to real estate loans. Because of the prominent role of Japanese banks in the world economy, their fall would in turn trigger global hysteria, with blood running through the streets of every financial capital.

If dizzy Tokyo property prices didn't offer enough evidence of the plausibility in that scenario, the other major expression of "hidden assets" added to the case. This part of the argument focused on the portfolios of "relationship shares" held by most TSE companies. To cement business relationships, corporations doing business with each other typically buy blocks of each other's stock. This is especially true of banks, which are often the leading shareholders in the companies to which they lend. Yet even though "relationship shares" account for 50 percent of all outstanding stock, such shares have historically been locked away, never to be traded—turning what should be a thick, liquid market into a thin, illiquid one. The shortage of readily negotiable stock exaggerates price movements, especially in an up market. Relationship shares, moreover, are carried on corporate books at their original par value, just as real estate is carried at its purchase price. Marking these "hidden assets" to current market values would obviously have a radical impact on a company's book value.

But this too had an unconvincing ring. John Templeton, the dean of American global investors (who along with Paul Aron had been one of the big winners in the Japanese markets of the 1960s and 1970s), now shied away from the TSE. "Adjusting asset values would be a valid method if you were going to liquidate the company," he said. But "when was the last time you heard of a large Japanese company being liquidated?"[7]

On the surface, Templeton was right. Japanese companies are not being liquidated and broken up en masse, as in the United States. But as Paul Aron urged investors to note, the restructuring of the Japanese economy *is* beginning to cause companies to think about their futures in new ways. Some relationship shares are being sold to offset the negative impact of *endaka* on exporting companies. Corporate properties have started to change hands rapidly. In the same way that "merger mania" altered perceptions about where the value lay in American companies, Japan's restructuring is legitimately giving long-dormant assets new vitality. "Americans," declared Aron, "are making a big mistake by not observing the transformation taking place in Japanese life, much as Japan's unusual GNP growth of the late fifties and sixties was almost completely ignored while it was taking place."[8]

The Price/Culture Ratio

A few of the bright young analysts on the Tokyo staffs of foreign securities firms had begun to understand that it wasn't all Tulipmania. At Goldman Sachs, Salomon, Baring, and other foreign houses, they did their homework and came up with good insights on stocks likely to benefit from economic restructuring.

When they issued their buy recommendations, however, they found relatively few American takers. Tokyo seemed too dangerously over-bought, too close to collapse. Throughout the summer of 1987 many on Wall Street believed the only thing that could stop the Dow from reaching 3000 would be a panic in Tokyo. If the "Nikkei takes a real tumble, it could drag Wall Street with it," reported *Business Week*.[9]

"Japanese markets have gone berserk," said the editors of *Strategic Investment*. "Japan will trigger the next worldwide financial collapse."[10]

The notion of Tokyo's imminent demise became so popular that Wall Street traders who'd never before followed the TSE took to beginning the day by checking to see if anything untoward had happened overnight in Tokyo. Every wobble of the Nikkei was rumored to be the beginning of the big global quake. Until Black Monday, that is, when it became excruciatingly clear that one did not need to look across the Pacific to find an overvalued stock market.

Even when invited by the October 1987 panic in New York and London to join the world sell-off, Tokyo more or less demurred. "The Nikkei's performance was a lesson learned hard by the vast majority of the U.S. investment community," said *Asset International* in its year-end postmortem of 1987—a year in which the supposedly over-blown Nikkei led all world exchanges in continued gains (+44 percent in dollar terms, compared with the Dow's +2 percent). "For Tokyo, 1987 was pretty much business as usual, and that can be said of no other major financial center."[11] Even then, Americans remained wary. Merrill Lynch's international investment strategist Thomas Robinson summarized the U.S. consensus when he peered into 1988 and said, "The Japanese equity market is not attractive" because "potential returns are not sufficient to offset the considerable risks."[12]

Yet the other shoe never seemed to drop. Halfway through 1988, the Nikkei index was setting new all-time records, even as Wall Street languished well below pre-crash levels. By the verdict of the market-place—supposedly the ultimate arbiter of such things—Japanese investors remain more convinced of the inherent value in their companies whose PERs average 60 than Americans were with their companies whose average PER hit 20 just before Black Monday.

Why? One answer certainly lies in Paul Aron's PER calculations showing that some of the extremes of the Tokyo market are less extreme than they appear. Another lies in the basic validity—despite some overstatement—of the "hidden assets" thesis. Much is also attributable to the inner workings of the Tokyo market (such as the limited supply of tradable shares, the absence of short selling, and the limits on daily price volatility), which predispose the TSE to upward motion or none at all, rather than sharp downward spikes. TSE prices didn't fall as far as NYSE prices in the Black Monday crash quite simply because they couldn't. Tokyo's price limit system ensures that a stock closing at 999 yen yesterday is confined to a 10 percent trading range today. It can rise to 1099 or fall to 899, but on reaching either limit trading is halted. What's more, *saitori* (the equivalent of NYSE specialists) are only allowed to drop prices of a 999-yen stock by ten yen at a time. They must allow enough time to pass to establish an absence of buyers at that level before they can drop the price another ten yen. Under this system, it can take all day for a stock to fall its limit.

All these microtrends are pieces of the puzzle. But there is a larger, macrolevel answer as well, a sort of price/culture ratio in which the Japanese and American conceptions of value are at opposite ends of the matrix.

A profound bias is at work in Japanese financial markets—a bias that places a higher value on companies precisely because they are *Japanese*.[13] One facet of this idea is sheer xenophobia: "Given a choice, the Japanese generally prefer to invest at home, even now that it is easy to invest abroad," observes Shijuro Ogata, deputy governor of the Japan Development Bank. "Rightly or wrongly, they see safety at home and risk abroad."

Another facet derives from the high level of virtue ascribed to Japanese business.[14] "If a Japanese company announces plans for diversification, its share price shoots up because the investing public believes management knows what it is doing, whereas in the U.S. or the U.K. the investment community will have its own opinion about whether or not a company's diversification plan will improve stock value," notes David Dible, the outspoken Tokyo research director for Hoare Govett.

Layered on top of such biases is the belief that the Japanese economy is not yet mature but still in for enormous growth. American investors are quite familiar with how the prospect of high growth skews a company's stock price. In the early 1980s those willing to believe in the future that lay beyond astronomical PERs of new U.S. technology companies like Genentech or Apple experienced excellent appreciation in their portfolios.

To foreign eyes the TSE looks as if it is filled with aging companies that ought to be valued as similar mature American stocks are. To Japanese investors, however, the TSE represents fifteen hundred potential Genentechs and Apples. Bolstering this new Tokyo investment zeitgeist are some of the following assumptions:

- Japan will continue growing faster than the United States (and the rest of the industrial world, for that matter) in GNP size, per capita income, and productivity. Burgeoning consumerism and public works will stimulate the economy for the rest of the century, allowing a multitude of opportunities for traditional companies to convert their prodigious resources to new uses.[15]
- In the areas of high technology most relevant to the information age economy (microelectronics, robotics, new materials, biotechnology, aviation and space science, superconductivity), Japanese companies are already world leaders or will be soon.
- In financial services, the world's most strategic economic sector in the next century, Japanese companies are already dominant, even though they are just beginning to develop the global infrastructure to match their domestic strength.
- The Pacific Rim will remain the world's most dynamic region, creating vast new markets for Japanese companies as well as major new investment opportunities. Japan will be the de facto metropolitan heartland of the Pacific century.

For those who agree with such assumptions, TSE prices make perfect sense. IBM's scientists won the Nobel Prize for their superconductivity discoveries, but few American investors took large positions in IBM based on anticipated profits from superconductor-related applications. In Tokyo, meanwhile, stocks of companies likely to benefit from the incipient superconductor industry (like Furukawa Electric, Fuji Electric, Mitsubishi Metal, and a dozen others) jumped 20–75 percent in the days following a series of revolutionary announcements about superconductors.[16]

NTT may be an exorbitant stock that will never perform at the level anticipated by its current share price. But a certain viable argument runs beneath all the political and cultural distortions involved in arriving at its $20,000-per-share value. Even though the Japanese telecommunications market is being deregulated, NTT's overwhelmingly dominant position is assured. NTT's laboratories will produce the world's state-of-the-art telecommunications technology of the future. NTT will not only provide the essential network for Japanese life in the information age, it will export that network to the largely undeveloped telecommunications markets of Asia and to the United States, where a market once dominated by AT&T is now a battleground of warring American competitors bleeding each other to death.

Hoare Govett's Dible believes that British managers in Tokyo are achieving a better performance record than Americans because they understand what's happening around them. "Having lost an empire once, the British recognize the process when they see it happening again. Americans run around Tokyo saying, 'This stock can't possibly be worth this much.' What they really mean is, 'This stock can't possibly be worth more than a similar American stock.' But it is. It isn't funny money they're playing with here in Tokyo. The funny money is in New York."

Deregulation, Tokyo Style

The Okura Sho (Ministry of Finance) is a mazelike building located in the very heart of Tokyo's central government district, Kasumigaseki. Its dimly lit corridors, each a city block long, wind their way past hundreds of identical offices staffed by teams of white-shirted bureaucrats, all of whom seem to have the same arrangement atop their ancient wooden desks: sky-high piles of paper, a tea cup, a Thermos, and an old black telephone. Lots of abacuses and cheap electronic calculators; few computer terminals. Lots of beat-up typewriter relics; few word processors. It is hard to believe that under this roof beats the heart of the world's leading creditor nation.

MoF men are some of the world's most incorruptible and indefatigable civil servants. They are bureaucrat's bureaucrats; accountant's accountants. Their ministry predates most of the rest of the Japanese government, and it is considered the most prestigious career track in government. Once upon a time MoF's regulatory grip was so tight that it could have accounted for just about every yen in the country.

At the end of a deregulatory decade, MoF men are at last curbing their own vaunted impulse to vigilance—but not too much. Markets and institutions are still subject to more careful scrutiny in Tokyo than in any other world financial center.

Over the last few years, *gaijin* have beaten a well-trodden path through the byzantine halls of the Okura Sho to the office of Toyoo Gyohten, the vice-minister charged with international affairs. They have pleaded, demanded, lobbied, argued, insisted, requested, petitioned, implored, haggled, threatened, and otherwise made their case for the particular kind of access to the Japanese financial market they desired. The observant among these visiting *gaijin* have noticed an antique European map hanging below the digital display of the day's yen/dollar quotation at the far end of Gyohten's office. Like most maps of its period, this one depicts the Japanese islands as if they stretched horizontally from east to west across the same latitude, rather than descending from north to south in the longitudinal arrangement shown on modern maps. Gyohten is an avid map collector, but in a land that specializes in nonverbal symbols, this map serves as more than decoration. It is a gentle reminder to foreigners that the West has a long history of approaching Japan from an erroneous viewpoint.

A cool head in the frantic world of global finance, Gyohten is one of those who have made Herculean efforts to speed Japan's financial liberalization. For many years he himself was critical of the MoF bureaucracy for moving too slowly. But now that Japan has made radical changes in a relatively short space of time, Gyohten is visibly disappointed with some of the foreigners. He believes many new international companies arriving on the Tokyo scene are failing to make maximum use of the new opportunities created, while continuing to complain about cumbersome regulations.

"When American business tries to penetrate another market, its first thought is to change the other market to suit its needs," he muses. "Such an approach will not be successful in Japan. Here, it is the other way around. American business must change to suit the needs of the market."

An admirer of much that is good in the American financial system, Gyohten confesses that the extent of deregulation in U.S. markets makes him nervous. There is a delicate balance, he says, between freedom and creditworthiness; between chaos and stability. It troubles him that foreigners encountering the Japanese equation of freedom and creditworthiness reject it out of hand, insisting on the superiority of their own standards. The verdicts on American and British deregulation are not yet in, Gyohten warns. Both countries may well have gone too far. Whether they have or haven't, Toyoo Gyohten and his colleagues are certainly not prepared to let Japan go *that far.*

Japan, however, has come considerably farther down the road of financial deregulation than most outside observers would have believed possible five years ago. Interest rates have been liberalized for large depositors. An auction system for some government bonds (rather than preallocated syndicates alone) has been initiated. A stock futures market has been created in Osaka.

Commercial paper, yen-denominated banker's acceptances, yen swaps, corporate bonds with separable equity warrants attached, sector-oriented mutual funds, Samurai bonds (yen-denominated foreign bonds issued in Japan), Shogun bonds (foreign currency–denominated bonds issued by foreign borrowers in Japan), Sushi bonds (foreign currency bonds issued in Japan by Japanese institutions for Japanese portfolios), and dozens upon dozens of other financial products have been introduced. The net effect is that even though Japan remains more regulated than other financial centers, most of the products and markets that exist elsewhere now exist in Japan in some stage of development.

The rigid separation between types of financial institutions is fast disappearing. Securities companies are allowed to engage in practices that clearly look like banking (customers can get cash from their medium-term government bond accounts with an automatic-teller card, for example), while banks, pressing for the free run of the securities underwriting business, are increasingly winning entry into newly evolving financial markets that once would have been the purview of securities companies alone (such as commercial paper). City banks, trust banks, long-term banks, and regional banks are all now stepping on each other's toes so frequently that it is often hard to tell them apart.

Since the mid-eighties, foreign financial firms have won the right to be members of the Tokyo Stock Exchange, to participate in government bond underwriting, and to enter into trust banking and other fields once consciously designated as "Japanese only." Some fifty foreign securities operate in Tokyo along with ninety foreign banks.

Soon one hundred foreign companies will be listed on the TSE.

The Japanese financial world, in short, is not the tightly controlled, rigidly segmented, insular environment it was until very recently. Mr. Gyohten's ministry still has its work cut out in deciding how and when to permit the complete deregulation of small-deposit interest rates, brokerage commissions, security companies entrance into the foreign exchange business, and other politically charged areas that remain subject to archaic regulations. MoF must eventually come to grips with article 65's line of demarcation between banks and securities firms and articulate a clear policy on just how far it will let the distinctions blur. Ultimately the entire Japanese government must also arrive at a clearer consensus on the pace of the yen's internationalization, the growth of Tokyo as a world financial center, and other strategic matters.

For now, however, foreigners can no longer make the claim that Tokyo is isolated from the rest of the world or that it has failed to join the international wave of deregulation. With that smoke screen removed, it becomes evident that deregulation was always first and foremost a Japanese response to perceived Japanese needs, not the product of a reluctant Tokyo bowing to outside pressure, as some Americans have flattered themselves into believing. It is now also obvious that the mere fact of deregulation in Tokyo is not enough to improve the competitive potential of foreign companies there.

"It wouldn't make sense for Japan to change its financial system simply to please foreigners, would it?" asks Gyohten with understated irony. And Japan didn't. A brief look at some of the forces driving Japan's deregulatory process is here in order.

The first impetus was the changing needs of the Japanese government itself. In the 1970s, when breakneck economic growth began to slow and the oil shocks triggered retooling of the entire economic machine, the Japanese government assumed the role of key domestic investor earlier played by private industry. As a result, the prior flow-of-funds setup became outmoded. The bond market had to be greatly invigorated in order to meet the government's financing needs. A secondary market was required, as well as more competitive interest rates. These shifts demanded more creative, active, and dynamic markets, which in turn required a measure of deregulation. (The securities firms that best grasped these changes—Nomura and Daiwa, for example—won significant market share from others, like Nikko, which faltered for a time by underestimating how big the government bond market would become.)

Next came the imperative to recycle the trade surplus. Japan had no intention of allowing trade surplus dollars to come to rest inside Japan, where they could have triggered massive inflation and disturbed economic equilibrium. Controls that previously worked to wall off the Japanese financial market from the rest of the world in order to keep capital *in,* now had to be lifted in order to let it flow *out.*

Third, domestic banks and securities companies exerted critical pressure on MoF to allow new, more efficient uses of the vast reservoir of liquidity in the financial system. Japanese banks in the early 1980s had staggering deposit bases but dwindling loan customers, because industrial corporations themselves had become so cash rich and so capable of accessing the global bond market. Securities firms, riding the twin rails of the booming domestic bond market and trade surplus–driven global expansion, suddenly had the capital, customer base, and staff in place to expand into new products and new markets. These could be up, running, and thriving as soon as MoF approved them.

Fourth, no one in Japan wanted the domestic financial services industry to lose ground to foreign competitors whose deregulatory processes were allowing them to enter new businesses, gain new skills, maximize the use of new technology, and gear up for international financial leadership. A new world economic order of floating exchange rates, fast-moving petrodollars, high-tech financial products, and omnipotent investment banks was born around 1980, and American institutions were at center stage of this new transborder action. Recognizing the strategic character of financial services in the twenty-first century, Japan wanted to be sure its companies would be capable competitors in the new great game.

Here, much grander ambitions came into play than the pragmatic problems of financing government debt, recycling the trade surplus, or responding to pressure from domestic institutions. The most farsighted among Japanese leaders understood that the "oil shocks" were not really oil shocks at all, but industrial shocks warning Japan that the long, successful period of reliance on smokestack industries—and the Industrial Age social organization it had excelled in building around them—was drawing to a close.

One particularly visionary MITI strategist, Naohiro Amaya, delivered a report as early as 1970 calling for Japan to switch its emphasis from an industrial to a postindustrial economy. Criticized at first, his ideas became accepted wisdom after the oil shocks. More recently, Amaya observed that the Japanese financial system rests on an accumulation of capital analogous to "nineteenth-century British hardware," but that its future success depends on how fast it moves to develop "twenty-first-century intellectual software" of systems and techniques possible only in a liberalized environment. Japan's business has become international, he says, but its thinking is still domestic. This situation must change not so much to please the rest of the world as to assure Japan's survival in it.

In a series of lectures to top Japanese business and government leaders in 1980, futurist Alvin Toffler crystallized the key message: "Japan's stunning economic success in the sixties and seventies meant that Japan had learned how to play the game of industrialization. But . . . a new era [is] approaching and . . . just because Japan knows how to make cheap, high-quality cars, steel, or TV sets doesn't mean it will necessarily do well in the restructured economy of the future."[17]

Unlike "Atari Democrats" and other politicians who dabbled briefly with the idea of restructuring the U.S. economy, the Japanese listened to Toffler. They adopted preparation for the information age as their national goal. Education, science, and other sectors presumed vital to the twenty-first century began to be overhauled, subjected to fewer central controls, and encouraged to "be creative." Recognizing that Japan had caught up to the West, MITI proposed that new targets for the 1980s and 1990s be picked to make Japan a "technology intensive nation" gaining its "bargaining power" in the world from intellect and technology more than industrial exports. To do that entailed "reexamining social systems beginning with those old institutions, practices, and authorization-licensing systems which block freedom and mobility."[18] In that context, much of the drive toward financial deregulation can be read as a recognition that more flexibility, diversity, and international connectivity was needed in the system to ensure that Japan would get the most future mileage from its financial resources.

Eisuke Sakakibara, director of MoF's Treasury Department, confirms that MoF never thought of deregulation as something that would benefit foreigners, but always as something necessary for Japan. The willingness of foreigners to make a ruckus about deregulation allowed

MoF a chance to gracefully deploy *gaiatsu* to overcome inertia elsewhere in the Japanese system.

Sakakibara cites the auction of Japanese government bonds as an example. From 1984 onward, with increasing intensity, American securities firms in Tokyo insisted that the all-Japanese club of bond syndicators unfairly prohibited foreign access to this lucrative and growing business. Backed up by Washington negotiators, they lobbied hard for Japan to adopt a U.S.-style auction system to distribute bonds. Eugene Atkinson, president of Goldman Sachs in Tokyo, once called the bond auction his number-one priority issue in discussions with the Japanese authorities. Congressman Charles Schumer visited Tokyo and argued that a bond auction was one of the reciprocal market-opening measures he considered mandatory before dropping legislation he proposed in Washington to curb Japanese financial activities in the United States.

Finally, in 1987 MoF agreed to allow about 20 percent of Japanese bonds to be auctioned. Small as it was, this appeared to be a victory for foreign pressure in opening the Tokyo market. Yet according to Sakakibara, "This is what Japan wanted to do anyway. Incorporating the auction system makes the market more efficient." Foreign pressure was just a tool MoF exploited. "Without American assertiveness, it would have taken us longer to reach consensus about when to begin introducing the auction system."

The Japanese process of "controlled decontrol" may well be winding down in terms of breaking new conceptual ground, although specific rules and procedures are sure to undergo continued relaxation. Sakakibara believes that from here on in, the American and Japanese financial systems may gain greater resemblance not so much because Japan will continue with wide-ranging liberalization, but because the United States will move back toward reregulation. "Following the pendulum of history, we can expect that the process of deregulation will soon swing back from the extremes it has reached," he said shortly before Black Monday. "In all probability a catastrophe will occur in the next few years that will bring about new regulation in the West."

Achilles' Heels and Crash Scenarios

Is Japan's financial machine so successful that it has become crash-proof? Almost, but not quite.

As Tokyo officialdom is fond of pointing out, because of Japan's small size and lack of raw materials, the country as a whole remains more vulnerable to vagaries beyond its control than other rich nations. In particular, the Japanese worry about the possibility of another oil shock. To a lesser extent they fear the scourge of the long anticipated earthquake that some predict will devastate Tokyo.

On the oil issue, Japanese forecasters say the question is not if but when the next crisis will come. Currently Japan is about 30 percent less reliant on foreign oil than it was fifteen years ago. Even so, another precipitous rise in oil prices in the near term would no doubt wreck havoc with the Japanese economy. The experience could be even worse than those in the past, because Japan's ability to survive and thrive in the era of the strong yen is bound up with low oil prices. Longer term, however, Japan is becoming less vulnerable. Alone among developed economies, it continues to pursue synthetic fuels, solar power, and nuclear energy with an enthusiasm unabated from energy crisis days.

Like the threat Californians live with, the great Tokyo earthquake could come tomorrow, a century from now, or three years from now and not cause as much damage as worst-case scenarios predict. The Japanese have developed some of the world's best earthquake-detection technology. Nonstop research is continuing in the Tsukuba Science City. New buildings are theoretically capable of withstanding earthquakes of significant magnitude. Even so, the fact of the matter is that Tokyo's Marunouchi-Otemachi-Nihonbashi corridor lies near the epicenter of a major earthquake fault.

Aside from perpetual question marks posed by the threats of oil shocks or earthquakes, other systemic flaws loom on the Japanese horizon. MoF's strategists have done a good job of limiting excesses, weeding out extremes, and emphasizing gradualism in the deregulatory process. That process, though, is bigger than they are. Liberalization and internationalization have brought the Japanese economy to a stage where market forces beyond Tokyo's control are finally beginning to influence business developments. Japanese deregulators have systematically reduced the risk inherent in such large-scale change, but they have not eliminated it. In this new situation anything *could* happen. It is therefore worth contemplating some of those possibilities.

Protectionism in the West is clearly the greatest threat to Japan's economic health. The recessionary impact of any real movement to close Western trade doors would be large, although less so as Japan's domestic economy moves onto the high-growth track. Japanese business continues to work feverishly to reduce the protectionist threat by moving production overseas and investing in foreign economies. But future protectionism may not be of the expected variety. Already, for example, some U.S. auto executives are calling for cars built by Japanese-owned companies at U.S. plants to be included in Japanese import quotas. A few other industries are starting to grumble about unfair competition from U.S.-based Japanese manufacturers. If the U.S. economy enters a severe recession, the lobby of threatened American industries could grow vociferous quickly, bringing about political action that would ultimately unravel Japan's whole U.S. manufacturing strategy. There is no doubt that such a scenario would inflict heavy damage on the Japanese economy and financial markets.

The notion of the Great Tokyo real estate crash triggering in turn the Great Tokyo stock market crash—as predicted by foreign analysts who pooh-pooh the "hidden assets" thesis about Tokyo values—is a danger, although not quite as palpable as some pundits suggest. Because the current supply of prime metropolitan real estate is so minuscule, a total price collapse resulting from cyclic oversupply is unlikely.

LDP leaders, however, are consciously trying to reengineer land policy. They recognize that the nation's growth is constrained by the absurd cost of property. The government's own program to create jobs through public works is severely hampered by having to allocate most of its pump-priming budget just to acquire the necessary land. To some, the answer lies in man-made islands for Tokyo Bay, where the government can reclaim ocean land by fiat, although the cost of developing it is immense. To others, no real solution will be achieved until today's massive subsidies to Japan's inefficient agricultural sector are ended and farmers are driven off the land, freeing up large tracts that are now woefully underutilized. One oft heard scheme is to clear farmers out of a one-hundred-kilometer belt around Tokyo and

Osaka, using the land to develop housing, factories, and new industries.

With its propensity for consensus and gradualism, the Japanese government is obviously not going to implement such an extreme policy overnight. Steps toward it, however, could ignite unpredictable responses since so much of Japan's new wealth—including most of its very richest individuals—today rests on real estate. Even ordinary middle-class households have borrowed heavily against the inflated value in their homes to speculate in stocks, creating a pattern of pressures and choke points running through the basic fabric of the entire banking industry as well as the stock market. More than a quarter of total Japanese bank loan exposure may now be tied up in one way or another with property.

Certainly the Japanese government knows all this and will endeavor to bring real estate prices in for a soft landing that doesn't precipitate a panic. So far, that approach has been relatively successful. New capital gains taxes have slowed the speculative flipping of residential property in Tokyo. This, in turn, has brought prices down 20 percent from their 1987 highs without the stock market batting an eyelid. In a daring game of Russian roulette, MoF and BoJ have succeeded in getting the banks to curb real estate lending, even though the loan reductions are working to squeeze speculators who carry hefty obligations to the banks.

Experts in the banking industry say Tokyo land prices would have to fall at least 40 percent from their peak before even the weakest of financial institutions felt a whisker of discomfort.[19] That would seem to give government planners considerably more room to work with than some foreign Jeremiahs think.

Whether or not it is possible to continue bringing realty prices down gently remains to be seen. In an age of wealth and liberalization, the Japanese citizenry is not as pliant as it once was, as Mr. Nakasone discovered at the end of his administration when efforts to impose a 5 percent sales tax had to be shelved in the face of unexpected public outrage. If government land policy were suddenly to run into broad-based political opposition—from farmers, homeowners, bankers, or the new merchant-bourgeoisie that has made its fortune in real estate—it is quite possible that the speculative atmosphere would be rekindled, producing in turn the possibility of a panic.

Interestingly, there appear to be some within MoF who think a "minicrash" wouldn't be such a bad thing for the stock market to blow off some of its speculative dust and keep financial institutions from getting too uppity. But MoF also knows which levers to pull to stimulate recovery. At the beginning of 1988, with the TSE still haunted by the specter of Black Monday, and with Japan's voracious appetite for equity facing the challenge of digesting a new multibillion-dollar issue of NTT shares, MoF suddenly reversed prior skepticism about the growth of *tokkin* funds, announcing it would relax rules restricting life insurance companies from investing through them. The TSE was so enthused by this prospect that the Nikkei average immediately jumped 1,215 points in its second-best one-day performance on record.

Deregulation, gentle as it has been, is thrusting some financial institutions into waters too deep, while putting new pressures on others whose markets were once assured. Regional banks in a few hard-hit agricultural areas, for example, are unable to keep up with the new competitive demands as their rural depositor base disappears. Even some of the giant city banks sitting atop mountains of assets are in trouble. Their old-core lending business is eroding as industrial companies increasingly bypass them in favor of securitized bonds and commercial paper.

The last few years of wild financial growth have also produced alarming speculative habits concealed by the general upward drift of the market. *Zaitek* practitioners with little risk or lending knowledge are temporarily showing profits on relending activities that often look suspiciously like Japanese versions of junk bonds. In tighter economic times, those junk debtors will be pushed into default, zapping unticipated *zaitek* revenue. Similarly, many Japanese companies are counting on guaranteed returns promised by *tokkin* fund managers—although guarantees are nominally improper. In an up stock market, there has been little difficulty delivering the anticipated returns. But if the market starts heading down, the *tokkin* industry itself could be jeopardized, weakening one of the market's most enthusiastic props and feeding the downward spiral.

What all this means is that the danger of financial institutions failing is increased. Even the overconfident giants may not be completely immune. Scott Pardee, vice-chairman of Yamaichi's U.S. subsidiary, points out that his parent company, still wounded from its speculative fall from grace in the 1960s, has practiced a conservative policy toward business growth in the recent boom. "Other Japanese companies haven't learned that lesson. They are encouraging speculative behavior that cannot be sustained. At some point, it all begins to backfire. A securities company that doubles its profits this year and assumes it can do the same thing next year is riding for a fall."

The Japanese social system is notorious for its inability to cope with failure. The financial system in particular has been regulated on the premise of maintaining it as a failure-free zone. The collapse of a well-known institution—not necessarily even one of the giants, just an important regional bank or second-tier securities company—would shake Japanese confidence much more deeply than the failure of a similar institution in the United States.

The above are some (by no means all) of the short- and midterm threats to the Japanese financial miracle. They are quite real, and some portions of these scenarios will come to pass. But the worst cases probably won't. Japan appears to be getting what it needs from the new age of deregulation without inciting the system itself to riot. As Jared Taylor, a bilingual and bicultural former Tokyo loan officer for Manufacturers Hanover Trust, suggests, "If any society can square the circle, it is Japan. After all, it has been brilliantly successful in teaching its citizens to mind the rules. What is to prevent it from teaching them just as successfully to break a few? A 'homogeneous people on an island nation' might just be taught to bubble with creativity without boiling over."[20]

Thus, despite the bubbly appearance of Tulipmania, Japanese financial markets are not headed for chaos. At the fundamental level, they aren't decoupled from reality. Instead they are deeply connected to the new reality of Japan's increasing role as the world's economic and financial leader. That reality is likely to withstand oil shocks and earthquakes, protectionism and falling property markets.

8

Rising Sun on Wall Street/Home Boys in Tokyo

This crazy globalization thing is coming back to haunt us.
—Peter Solomon, vice-chairman,
Shearson Lehman[1]

The Short View at Harvard

In the summer of 1986, the Harvard Business School sponsored a colloquium on the subject of the changing financial services field. Among those in attendance were many high-ranking Wall Street figures. A sizable group of them turned out for the session on globalization led by Carl Kester, a thirty-four-year-old professor who'd recently begun to study Japanese finance.

Kester began by presenting the usual stunning array of facts showing how the world was moving toward integrated capital markets and twenty-four-hour trading days. This was the very dream the financial community had coveted for so long. But he cautioned his audience: "The barriers to entry are falling all around you. You're going to be raising capital at competitive prices and selling it at competitive prices. How are you going to do more than pay the rent? What's your competitive advantage?"

The young professor was hoping to get this high-demographic group of Wall Street intellect to target inefficiencies in the system they planned to correct, new niches to be explored, and new ways they could add value. Instead he faced an audience of puzzled stares. "We're making more money today than ever, and we're America's

209

most competitive industry," was the tenor of their reply to his challenge. Then Kester asked them what they were going to do about the Japanese. A barrier-free world was one that benefited Japan the most, he argued. Bigger, better-capitalized Japanese financial institutions would soon be challenging American banks and brokerage houses just as Toyota and Honda had challenged American automakers. "You can run from the Japanese, but you can't hide," Kester cautioned.

The audience simply refused to accept Kester's premise. To them, financial services was a field synonymous with American leadership. In the cocktail session afterward, a man who'd made his career at Morgan Stanley sought Kester out and told him squarely, "In this business, there is no Japanese threat." Others made similar remarks, arguing that unlike automobiles, finance was a field where Americans still had a big lead on the Japanese in new products, new technology, and management techniques.

"I just couldn't believe the shortsightedness," Kester mused later. "Some of these people don't realize how protected their own business has been until now. Others are talking about globalization without any real understanding that Japanese institutions pose a much greater competitiveness problem to them than they do to the Japanese."

Rising Sun on Wall Street

Is it really possible that Japanese companies will succeed in winning market share and besting American rivals in the U.S. financial marketplace as they have with their industrial exports?

It is tempting to draw a close analogy between contemporary experiences in financial services and what went before in steel, autos, and electronics. From the viewpoint of structure and process, marked similarities exist. As with those earlier exporters, the Japanese companies now participating in the U.S. financial sector are those that grew inordinately large and brawny in the protected environment of their home market. They have entered the United States relatively unimpeded, choosing as their first targets a few key sectors of the financial business where they could best deploy their strategic Japanese strengths in capital and placement. They have concentrated an overwhelming force on those areas and been willing to cut profits to levels unacceptable by American standards in order to build market share.

They have begun to commoditize parts of the business once regarded as highly specialized, such as government bond trading.

In all these respects and more, the Japanese entry into financial services *looks* a lot like the pattern established with industrial products. In finance, the pattern seems to be unfolding even faster than it did in other industries, reflecting the greater velocity at which money flows as opposed to goods. The weighty presence of Japanese institutions in the United States was built up almost entirely in the explosive years since 1984. Extrapolating from the trends exhibited since 1984, one would conclude that sometime in the 1990s, 10 percent of Wall Street employees will be working for Japanese firms, Japanese investors will be responsible for a fifth of trading volume on the NYSE, Japanese banks will service a quarter of U.S. retail bank customers, and Japanese interests will own a piece of every leading American investment bank.

Simple extrapolation of current trends, however, is almost always an erroneous methodology, especially when starting from ground points near zero. Certainly much of the Japanese activity in recent years has been inspired by a confluence of extreme circumstances— such as Japan's relaxation of controls on capital outflows, its unprecedented trade surplus, its inordinate supply of domestic liquidity, and the awesome capital-borrowing requirements of the U.S. government. Although none of these trends will disappear, the extremity of their force is already tapering off.

Regardless of the weight of Japanese money, there is also merit in the argument proffered by confident Americans who say that the particularities of financial services are *not* all that much like the other businesses where Japanese competitors have come to play a major role. Investment banking, they say, is not terribly analogous to making steel. The skills involved with managing portfolios bear little similarity to what it takes to build automobiles well. Unlike auto and steel companies, American financial services executives argue that their business hasn't lost its hardworking, hard-driving, highly competitive edge.[2]

"It comes down to this: Japan's much paraded management style— which emphasizes consensus building and strong central control— works well for assembly-line manufacturing. But it is a clumsy instrument in the split-second decision making required in financial markets," said *Forbes,* summarizing this view. "If Wall Street continues to be flexible and innovative, finance is one area in which Japanese ambitions can be contained."[3]

Wall Street *is* continuing to be flexible and innovative. No one can deny that. Yet Japanese financial firms *are* gaining U.S. business. Not so much from the man in the street (aside from Japanese banks in California, the retail end of financial services is not yet what the Japanese are after), but from the large American corporations, pension funds, and money management groups that are themselves increasingly globalized.

As we saw in chapter 6, Nomura has a well-developed strategy for attracting substantial American clients. At the moment, it has little interest in competing with Merrill Lynch for the brokerage accounts of widows and orphans. It *is,* however, keenly interested in competing for the right to do business with the two thousand largest American corporations and institutional investors whose activities drive the financial services industry. In fact, it is already doing business with four hundred of them. As the world's number-one Eurobond underwriter, Nomura's client list is studded with such names as IBM, AT&T, and other blue chips. As the frequent leader of the pack at U.S. Treasury auctions, it commands the attention of American bond buyers and adds considerable value to such growing relationships.

Currently Nomura is trying to expand its presence in U.S. equities. When it announced a plan to steer about $10 billion worth of Japanese money into U.S. stocks, more than a few American portfolio managers picked up the phone to start doing some business with Nomura in order to draw a bead on where that money would be headed and when. Don McKinnon, Nomura's U.S. equities chief, predicts that in three more years the firm will have a "research, trading, and sales capability competitive with the best American firms." Investment banker Steven Looney, who heads Nomura's fledgling M&A (mergers and acquisitions) department, foresees Nomura routinely functioning as lead underwriter for the equity offerings of *Fortune* 100 companies in the near future.

With its powerful reach into the low-cost supply of Japanese capital, Nomura is expanding its involvement in U.S. public finance just as majors like Salomon have announced their retreat. Unprofitable as this field may be in the existing climate of cost cutting and changed tax laws, Nomura is smart enough to know that American states, cities, and counties will always need to raise money. In the long run the tax law will change again. Public finance will once again become a profitable business. Meanwhile Nomura's exercises in this direction will connect it to a grass-roots network of domestic American political allies, helping to render it impervious to future tendencies toward financial protectionism.

Nomura, in short, is evolving along the path its leaders first announced when they undertook a quantum expansion of the firm's U.S. presence: "We don't want to be a Japanese restaurant in New York serving only sushi and sukiyaki. We want to serve French cuisine, American fast food, everything in the future."[4]

Daiwa is pursuing a similar strategy with similar success. It has become one of the world's top Eurobond underwriters and is sometimes just as big a U.S. Treasury buyer and dealer as Nomura. Inside Japan Daiwa is known for its corporate and institutional relationships rather than retail strength. In a sense Daiwa is simply doing abroad what it has always done well at home. In 1986 the Daiwa America team raised more than a few investment banking eyebrows by gaining sole underwriter status for an important U.S. bond offering by a U.S. client—a $125 million GTE issue. Leveraging its excellent reputation among U.S. institutions in the U.S. Treasury market, Daiwa has also begun to build an American clientele in trading mortgage-backed securities and a wide assortment of fixed-income products. A sophisticated new equity research model developed by American analysts for tracking three thousand North American stocks has been acquired and perfected by Daiwa and is now being sold to a list of institutional clients whose aggregate money under management is one trillion dollars.

At Nikko's U.S. subsidiary, chairman Toshio Mori is in a hurry. "We are latecomers to the U.S. market, so we have to be very aggressive." Nikko has buttressed that rubric by repeatedly hiring executives right out of the U.S. Federal Reserve system, gaining a primary dealership, staffing up with a slew of respected American researchers, building a U.S.-to-U.S. equities sales force, and committing $100 million to the Blackstone Group's merchant banking fund. "American companies who want to do business in Japan come to us for help," Mori says. "But as we help them with their needs in Japan, they discover we can serve their U.S. needs as well."

Even the "smaller" Japanese securities firms are elbowing their way into New York. Yamatane Securities (number eight in Japan with net profit around $40 million) startled many on Wall Street who'd never heard its name when company president Tomiji Yamazaki heralded the opening of the firm's New York office by plunking down $500,000 to help underwrite the new Japanese gallery at New York's Metropolitan Museum of Art. Sanyo, Wako, and New Japan are giants by American standards even though few American financial professionals are aware of them. They generally share the Big Four's sweeping enthusiasm for global expansion, even if the resources they bring to such efforts are not quite as great.

"We fully intend to be one of the mega–financial institutions of the future," predicts Sanyo's Yoichi Tsuchiya, who at forty-five is the youngest CEO of a Japanese securities company. With a billion dollars in 1987 revenues and over $100 million in after-tax profit, Sanyo is well on its way. The company is devoting 13 percent of expenditures to computer systems and plans to outcomputer even Nomura (which is one of its biggest stockholders). It has built the most technologically impressive trading room in Japan, a football field–sized affair near the TSE. Sanyo claims its technology allows it to cut by two-thirds the American brokerage industry's ratio of back office staff to salesmen in the field. By 1990 Sanyo plans to have five hundred employees in its New York office; it has already acquired an equity stake in Spear Financial Services, a California-based discount broker.[5]

Each Japanese financial company has its own particular business plan in the United States, and as a group they are quite competitive with each other. But the fact that they are all driven by such similar forces emanating from their domestic market means they end up approaching the U.S. market in a relatively homogeneous way. If one Japanese house decides to become a major player in U.S. equities, others can't afford to tell their Japanese clients they lack that capability. This conforming pressure, combined with intuitive loyalty to Japanese national interest (enforced when needed by the inescapable guiding hand of MoF), results in turning the already weighty Japanese presence in American markets into a particularly concerted, cohesive force.

Consider, for example, the case of Houston Industries on August 7, 1987—a day when trading in its normally placid shares was so huge (24.5 million shares) that it accounted for 10 percent of the entire NYSE volume. Wall Street was confused. Who was the corporate raider putting Houston "in play"? As it turned out, there was no raider. Japanese investors were simply buying and selling Houston's shares back and forth between each other like so many hot potatoes. They were trying to circumvent the Japanese tax consequences of holding the stock on the day it paid its dividend. Using the stratagem of settling sales in five days and purchases in six, Japanese brokers in the United States shifted taxable dividends into nontaxable capital gains and vice versa for investors who benefited from such moves.

What is now known as "Japanese dividend arbitrage" has become an overwhelming factor in NYSE trading patterns, reaching its current high point on January 25, 1988, when Southern Company, the Atlanta-based electric utility, set a one-day NYSE volume record: 65.9 million shares, or about a quarter of all stock traded that day. Another thirty-five million shares of Arizona Public Service and Cincinnati Gas & Electric also changed hands—meaning that more than one hundred million utility-company shares were in motion. Most of them were being swapped back and forth between Japanese investors.[6]

The implications are staggering. If a small number of Japanese investors can move millions of shares in three American companies on a single day simply to gain a modest tax advantage, what would that concentration of power mean if applied to takeover stocks or to a politically motivated move out of the U.S. market altogether?

The concentrated nature of Japanese activity has already provoked allegations of anticompetitive practices. Authorities at Chicago's futures exchanges, for example, uncovered a pattern on the part of Japanese traders of getting together to balance buy and sell orders from customers in Japan in order to reduce the margin requirements they had to put up. A CBOT official noted that there appeared to be "a consortium of Japanese brokerage firms that get together at the end of the day [in Japan] and work things out."[7] Trading in this way gives them much greater leverage than American competitors.

A related phenomenon could be seen on a far grander scale in currency trading shortly before the close of the Japanese fiscal year on March 31, 1988. New accounting policies promulgated in Tokyo required insurance companies to report unrealized currency losses incurred during the year of 15 percent or more. The companies, preferring not to make such disclosures, scrambled madly through the month of March to prop up the dollar at levels that would prevent reporting requirements from being triggered. When their goals were met, they apparently abandoned the dollar, causing a steep 3 percent drop in its value in a matter of days.

The general strategy was clear from afar. But only the Japanese

seemed to know the specifics. Reports from Tokyo varied as to
whether the trigger figure would be the dollar/yen exchange rate *on*
March 31, or the *average* rate throughout the month of March. American analysts and investors thus found themselves at a severe handicap
in determining strategy. It was a game in which all the players on the
Japanese team knew the rules, while the American side had to guess
at them. Quite an irony considering that the object of the game was to
set the value of the American dollar!

The propensity of the Japanese to act in objective concert can be
seen all over the financial map. Following roughly similar domestic
policies, Japanese commercial banks have ended up with roughly similar international credit ratings, and many of them are tops—AAA.
When a U.S. municipality seeks a letter of credit guaranteeing its
obligations, debt-issuing guidelines often mandate that the letter of
credit *must* come from a AAA-rated bank. In other cases the presence
of a AAA guarantor minimizes costs. With AAA-rated American
banks now nearly nonexistent, Japanese banks have discovered an
obvious niche—and they've all plunged in together. The result is that
Japanese banks have a lock grip on the majority of transactions in this
market.

In Boston, Sanwa Bank won a bid to issue a letter of credit backing
the city's short-term notes by undercutting competing American
prices by half. One of the losing American bankers observed, "I suspect the city of Boston would be loath to buy a fleet of Hondas for its
police force. But they don't have any qualms about Japanese letters of
credit—because police cars are visible, but you don't see letters of
credit."[8]

Rather than fanning out across the United States, Japanese commercial banks have clustered their operations in California, where five
are now among the ten biggest, and 20 percent of all bank assets are
now Japanese-owned. Californians, it is true, are more open to new
trends than the rest of the nation. But the success of Japanese retail
banking on the West Coast gives the lie to the popularly held Wall
Street notion that Americans will be uncomfortable turning their financial affairs over to foreign-owned institutions. Bank of California,
acquired by Mitsubishi Bank, has successfully targeted the private
banking business for wealthy individuals and is on track to meet its
goal of doubling its asset base by 1990. Sumitomo Bank and Sanwa
Bank, among others, are becoming names as well known in California as Toyota and Nissan.

Branches of Japan-based banks operating abroad do not have to conform to American or European standards for capital requirements —which are typically far stricter than Japan's. Although this became a hotly contested issue briefly during 1987, the U.S. and British banking communities have now accepted a compromise whereby Japanese banks are boosting their capital reserves but are also allowed to count more of those famous "hidden assets" in order to match international standards. The effective result is that Japanese banks can still lend out more of their deposit base than their international rivals.

Increasingly, Japanese institutions are in the middle of big U.S.-to-U.S. business lending deals. When Northwest Airlines wanted to buy Republic Airlines, it borrowed $500 million from Mitsubishi Bank. The business pages of American newspapers are now filled with "tombstone" ads, announcing huge corporate loan packages sponsored by Japanese banks. A typical sample from *The Wall Street Journal* tells the story in a nutshell:[9]

UAL, Inc., $600,000,000 credit facility for the acquisition of Hilton International Hotels. Funds provided by:

The Bank of Yokohama, Ltd.	New York Branch
The Fuji Bank Limited	Chicago Branch
The Mitsubishi Bank, Ltd.	Chicago Branch
The Mitsui Bank, Ltd.	Chicago Branch
The Sumitomo Bank, Ltd.	Chicago Branch
The Yasuda Trust & Banking Co., Ltd.	New York Branch

Like their parent companies back home, Japanese financial institutions in the United States are not averse to cutting margins close to the bone—and even below—to establish business relationships. "The photocopying bill for Nomura's deal is higher than the profits," a U.S. syndication manager observed contemptuously of a Japanese bond offering for Rockwell International.[10] In the American view this is a weakness. In the Japanese view it augurs well for future strength. Patience, say the Japanese, is rewarded in the end with profits. Fuji Bank stuck out its horrific $425 million purchase of the Chicago-based finance company Walter Heller International, infusing it with an additional $725 million over four years, before Heller at last turned the corner and was restored to fiscal health.

In addition to building market share with low-profit deals, Japanese houses are also very keen on gaining experience, particularly in the high-fee-generating areas of American investment banking like M&A, real estate, and corporate restructurings. In these areas Japanese financial services companies have begun to discover an advantage unknown to their industrial forerunners: a "home market" of Japanese right inside the United States.

Until 1985 Japanese corporate customers relied almost exclusively on the knowledge of American investment banks to help put together big deals in the United States. When Sumitomo Bank went after a stake in Goldman Sachs, it relied on Lazard Freres as an intermediary. Sony was aided by the Blackstone Group in acquiring CBS Records. Dainippon Ink & Chemicals used Dillon, Read to negotiate its acquisition of Sun Chemical. Morgan Stanley has done more than $2 billion worth of Japanese M&A work in the last few years; Goldman Sachs handles $1.5 billion of Japanese investments in U.S. real estate deals annually. Most of these American investment banks plan to continue strengthening their capabilities to service Japanese investors. Yet at the same time they realize that the American monopoly on this lucrative slice of the pie has already ended.

Indications of how Japanese firms are starting to reach into traditionally American areas of M&A work could be seen as early as 1986–87, when the Long-Term Credit Bank helped arrange eight midsized deals, including Sumitomo Rubber's quarter-billion-dollar acquisition of 80 percent of Dunlop Tire. Sanwa Bank put together the $319 million purchase by Kokusai Motorcars of the Hyatt Regency Hotel in Maui and trumpets itself as number one in transpacific takeovers. Nomura married off T-Cell Sciences, a small Massachusetts biotechnology firm, to Japan's giant Yamanouchi Pharmaceutical.

The M&A business, once stigmatized in Japan as a dreaded American syndrome involving destruction of the sanctified corporation, has now lost its stigma. A new breed of Japanese investment bankers has been born, with its younger transpacific jet-setters likening themselves proudly to *ninja* (the famed secret agents of the Japanese feudal court) or *kuroko* (the silent, black-clad figures who help Kabuki actors make quick costume changes on stage).

The new *ninja* and *kuroko* are not yet working on billion-dollar deals in the United States, which remain the exclusive domain of the lords of American investment banking. But over the long haul they are well positioned to gain a sizable share of that business. The new Japanese investment bankers usually have ongoing institutional relationships with their clients spanning long years of mutual knowledge and trust. Industrial Bank of Japan, for example, does business with 90 percent of the top two hundred Japanese companies and the vast majority of them are keenly interested in foreign acquisitions. The key ingredients IBJ and others lack are in-depth knowledge of the business opportunities in the United States and skills in tailoring big, complicated deals workable in the American context. But they are gaining in those areas.

"Japanese corporations want to be sure they are represented by the very best people," says Tetsuo Okaya, VP in Yamaichi's fast-expanding M&A department. "But if they have a choice, they will feel more comfortable being represented by other Japanese companies which understand their needs and see the business the same way they do." In a few more years, he predicts, Yamaichi will be perceived as both Japanese *and* as competitive with the best American investment banks in identifying U.S. opportunities and structuring deals. American firms, meanwhile, are gaining little expertise in M&A work *inside* Japan since foreign takeovers of Japanese companies are still rare.

"The process of internationalizing Japan's wealth is ironically making the Japanese more Japan-centric," observes Merrill Lynch senior VP Tetsundo Iwakuni. "At the beginning, Japanese companies in the U.S. had no choice but to learn English, intergrate themselves with the American mainstream, and find American corporate partners. Now that they have become so rich and powerful, they have created a 'mini-Japan' inside the United States." He cites the case of Yamaha, which historically maintained a commercial paper underwriting arrangement in which Merrill Lynch was first and Nomura second. Under pressure from Nomura, Yamaha recently reversed that order.

These kinds of changes signal the beginning of a larger strategic shift. "The Japanese have thirty-year plans, while American firms think strategic planning means, 'What will we be doing twelve to eighteen months from now?'" says Perrin Long. As one of the few who makes his living by independent analysis of Wall Street's business, Long has cast a cold sober eye over some of the American investment community's egocentric claims. "I'm surprised at these folks," he says in his gentlemanly drawl. "They speak about innovation and such, but they ought to know this is a business where *money talks*. There are no patents on Wall Street. If one company comes up with an innovation today, everybody else will be doing it tomorrow. He who has the capital usually wins in the end. The Japanese are much stronger in that department than anyone else."

As for the vaunted "risk-taking" abilities of American firms, Long sees such pyrotechnics as important to capitalizing on short-term opportunities, but not decisive. "Most American financial institutions have been built on conservative values, exactly the kind held so dear by the Japanese."

Michael Schrage, a journalist attuned to the flow of power and wealth on Wall Street as senior editor at *Manhattan inc.*, shined a hot white light on the essence of the change taking place: "The value of innovation as a competitive edge in global financial markets now needs sharp reassessment. . . . Like automotive engineering and computer-chip design, financial engineering—the expertise needed to craft new options, swaps, futures, etc.—is devolving into a global commodity. As America's financial services industry 'downsizes,' it will become easier and cheaper for foreign firms, particularly Japanese banks and securities houses, to acquire the intellectual seed capital for innovation." Schrage quotes Peter Rona, CEO of IBJ/Schroder (a U.S. subsidiary of the Industrial Bank of Japan), as saying innovation alone "will not get you real financial clout. Whatever this highfalutin financial engineering talent is, it could be bought with a month's trade surplus."[11]

Wall Street's own domestic growth strategy may lead it unwittingly into Japanese pincers at both low and high ends. With costs escalating and profits eroding, more American firms want to move out of the high-overhead parts of the business and into the more glamorous and more profitable position-taking forms of investment and merchant banking. Defecting from the commodity-oriented sectors, they are inviting a growing Japanese presence in those areas, as in the case of government bond trading. "The Japanese are prepared to lose money in the U.S. for five more years. By that time, they may wind up *dominating* fixed-income, corporate, and municipal trading and corporate underwriting of debt and equity," Perrin Long warns.

At the same time, American firms that have chosen to focus more narrowly on higher-margin merchant banking activities will require greater supplies of their own capital to support the scale of position-oriented operations they desire. To give but one example, First Boston earned a whopping $100 million from its role advising Campeau Corporation on its takeover of Allied Stores. But to earn that fee, it had to risk $865 million of its own capital as a bridge loan to Campeau to seal the deal. First Boston CEO Peter Buchanan admitted afterward that although this particular case was a big success, another such adventure might fail, tying up the firm's capital for a lengthy period.[12]

The implications are obvious: to be in that kind of business, American firms that fancy themselves merchant bankers will have to turn to deep-pocketed partners from the outside. The Japanese institutions, eager for access and know-how, will be perfectly willing to oblige, as has already been proven by the infusions of capital provided Goldman Sachs by Sumitomo Bank, Paine Webber by Yasuda Mutual, and Shearson by Nippon Life.

Nor is it just the traditional giants of Wall Street that now look east. After M&A gurus Joseph Perella and Bruce Wasserstein made headlines by splitting off from First Boston and forming their own investment banking boutique, they immediately dispatched Perella to Tokyo, where he reportedly sought to raise $200–$300 million for his takeover and buyout fund.

The magnetic force of Japanese capital is so great that for American financial companies in trouble, Tokyo has become the obvious, and at times the only, place to go to solve the problem. When General Electric found itself unhappy with its acquisition of venerable Kidder, Peabody, the first thing GE's executives did was call in Nomura to find out if the Japanese would like to take all or part of Kidder off their hands. When Bank of America chairman A. W. Clausen sought to shore up the once proud bank's collapsing position, he went hat in hand to Tokyo and pounded pavements until he put together a $350 million bailout package. According to one executive, the terms of the deal were "pretty much dictated" by the Japanese—and they were very expensive.[13] Yet there was literally nowhere else Clausen could go to raise the kind of money he needed.

With insufficient capital to engage in long-term business development strategies, Bank of America, like other banks, can't keep some of its best business builders from defecting to the Japanese. Peter Nevitt, a leasing specialist, and two of his associates recently left Bank of America to form a leasing venture with the Japanese trading company Mitsui. Nevitt observed that American banks had become too timid for his taste in taking on new business. "Quite frankly, the banks have been in asset contraction rather than expansion, and they are risk averse, selling off loans and leases where they can. I wanted to be where the action is."[14] And the action, of course, is with the Japanese.

Perrin Long is sanguine about where these difficulties will lead: "The Japanese have the money, and most Americans have a price."

A Buddha in Disgrace?

Four decades ago Koh Komatsu was among a handful of survivors on a Japanese naval vessel hit by U.S. torpedoes off the Philippines at the height of the fighting in the Pacific war. Somewhere not too far away, another young sailor, John Weinberg, was on a ship pressing the American war effort.

In 1986 Komatsu was president of Sumitomo Bank, the crown jewel at the center of a vast group of interlocked businesses that have operated under the Sumitomo name for more than four hundred years. The bank has an asset base greater than Citicorp's. Although it is only the number-three bank in Japan in terms of deposits, it is generally considered one of the country's most profitable, prestigious, and forward-looking financial institutions. Komatsu—one of those Osaka types famed for getting right to the point—declared the short, sweet goal of making Sumitomo "the best bank in the world." To help accomplish that goal, he wanted to buy into a top-tier American investment bank whose staff could teach his army of young recruits from the best families and the best universities in Japan how to engage in this American style of wheeling and dealing.

John Weinberg was the chief executive of Goldman Sachs, and he was the man Komatsu had come to New York clandestinely to see. The irony of these two veterans of the Pacific theater sitting down to put together the investment banking world's most earthshaking marriage was not lost on either man. Their staffs urged them not to talk about the war, since both men had strong feelings about it. Inevitably, however, the two came to swap war stories, establishing a nervous kind of common ground.

It was McKinsey & Co. that had suggested Sumitomo buy a stake in Goldman. Felix Rohatyn of Lazard Freres had been retained to help put the deal together. Weinberg, after first expressing surprise, soon became seriously interested. For exactly the reasons discussed earlier,

Goldman needed capital to face the new era in investment banking. Despite 117 prestigious, successful years as a private partnership, it couldn't continue that way much longer. Privately Goldman's seventy-nine partners understood that even a billion dollars wasn't enough in today's world to compete at the top of their business. Accepting a passive Japanese equity investment sounded like a better course than going public. It offered the added kicker of enhancing Goldman's stature in Japan and creating a synergistic joint force to roam globalized markets. Goldman was perfectly willing to accept the terms that gave Komatsu what he most wanted: on-the-job training for Japanese investment bankers in New York and London.

Later that year the deal was cemented: Sumitomo would pay nearly $500 million for a 12.5 percent stake in Goldman that could grow to 25 percent over time. Rohatyn walked away from months of negotiations deeply impressed. The Japanese "did their homework on the deal so well, they knew things about me even my children didn't know," he observed. "The Japanese take a long time to build an internal consensus, but once they do, their ability to implement it is awesome. If you combine that capacity for execution with the scale of financial resources they are accumulating, you begin to get a sense of how important they're going to be in our markets and all over the world."

The $500 million itself was not a terribly great sum for Sumitomo, whose own market capitalization was then approaching $40 billion. But the deal was a pathbreaker. John Gutfreund, the chief of Salomon, accurately assessed its real significance: "This delivers a $500 million message. The most important part of the deal is what it says about the Japanese; it acknowledges that their long-range strategy is to be major participants in our markets and our infrastructure. Goldman won't be unique in selling to a Japanese institution, only the first."[15]

American regulators, however, were taken aback by the underlying implications of a bank like Sumitomo tying up with a securities company like Goldman, even if one of the deal's conditions was that Sumitomo obtain no voting rights on Goldman's board. Glass-Steagall, after all, was still on the books. In principle, regulations prohibited commercial banks from owning more than a fractional share of securities houses. Tremendous political pressure was brought to bear on the Federal Reserve Board to approve the deal, not so much by lobbyists for Sumitomo or Goldman as by those who saw in this bold alliance a golden opportunity to force a new precedent in Washington's deregulatory path.

After careful scrutiny the Fed decided to approve the deal but added seven restrictions that resulted in making Sumitomo little more than a rentier, clipping its dividend coupons from Goldman's profits. The two clauses Komatsu most cherished—apprenticing Sumitomo's would-be investment bankers to Goldman for training and establishing a shared investment banking operation in London—were specifically proscribed. The Fed gave Sumitomo twenty-four hours to decide if it wanted to proceed. Komatsu refused to back down, arguing that judged simply as a passive investment, the deal would still pass muster. If the anticipated added value didn't come in the short run, it would come in the long run.

Less than a year later, however, the Japanese business press was calling Komatsu a "wounded tiger" and reporting that he had "lost face" because he couldn't deliver what he'd promised his colleagues: a direct vein for Sumitomo to enter the global investment banking bloodstream alongside Goldman's masters. Eventually the internal criticism became so intense, Komatsu was forced to accept a lesser position as the bank's deputy chairman.

Komatsu still expects events will vindicate him. An ethereal-looking man with a Buddha-like face, he fanned himself in Tokyo's summer heat and urged patience before judging the Goldman investment. Glass-Steagall will fall, he predicted. The Fed will no longer be able to curtail Sumitomo's involvement with Goldman. Sumitomo will get the investment banking expertise it desires. Eventually Goldman will need more capital. Sumitomo will be there to provide it, and in so doing, it will renegotiate the terms of the arrangement for the twenty-first century. It's all just a question of time, and of history. Even defeats are only temporary. . . .

As Komatsu suggests, the verdict on the Sumitomo-Goldman deal isn't yet in. But the experience suggests a few tentative conclusions.

- The Japanese *do* lack skills that are essential to functioning in the U.S. marketplace, especially at the high end. That's why Sumitomo was so eager to buy into a house like Goldman.
- On its own, Goldman appeared willing to give Sumitomo exactly what it wanted—training, expertise, network access—just as

America's great innovators in high technology were always willing to license their breakthroughs to the Japanese for small fees. Americans tend to look on these deals as money in the bank now; they never believe the Japanese they are training will become serious competitors.

- The Fed made the right decision but for the wrong reasons. U.S. regulatory authorities remain committed to a policy of "national treatment." This means that foreign financial firms operating in the United States are accorded all the rights and privileges of American firms—no more, no less. National treatment is in opposition to *reciprocity*, under which foreign firms would only be allowed to do in the United States what American firms are allowed to do in their countries. The Fed caveated the Sumitomo-Goldman deal not because Sumitomo was Japanese or because Citicorp would be barred from taking an equity stake in a Japanese securities house of Goldman's stature.[16] Rather, the Fed's ruling was based primarily on the tattered remnants of U.S. regulations separating the banking and securities businesses.

- If and when those U.S. regulations fall, Japanese giants like Sumitomo will be the first to step into the breach. Currently, when Americans debate the merits of abolishing Glass-Steagall, the arguments tend to be provincial considering the new global realities. So long as Washington maintains a policy of national treatment, any decision that encourages banks to enter the securities business will also mean allowing *Japanese* banks into the securities business.

Home Boys in Tokyo

Brian Kelly looks like Michael J. Fox. Handsome, fresh-faced, and full of energy, the young Morgan Stanley man stands out boldly from the crowd of frenzied traders on the floor of the Tokyo Stock Exchange. Flashing the hand signs for Japanese stocks (four fingers pointing up to suggest sun rays for Hitachi, which means rising sun; a two-handed pantomime of enlarged breasts to connote Meiji Milk), Kelly is the lone *gaijin* in the hubbub of two thousand floor traders.

On the symbolic level, Kelly's existence proves Americans *can* make it in Tokyo's financial markets. Few tasks could be more difficult than managing the high-pressured nitty-gritty details of floor trading in a foreign language and a foreign business culture, replete not only with obscure hand signs but dozens of other secret rituals and hidden nuances on which billions of yen ride at any given second. Kelly is proof positive that Americans can compete, regardless of the challenge.

But the fact that he is a solitary American in a sea of two thousand Japanese also reminds those watching the spectacle that even when the very best American companies do things right in Tokyo, they are still up against enormous and overwhelming odds.

"Morgan Stanley is a very important company in the United States," says Kelly philosophically. "Here in Tokyo, even though we're number one among foreign firms, we don't count for much." Two years after obtaining its seat on the TSE, Morgan Stanley's trading volume places it at number thirty-eight among Japanese firms—comparable in size to a very small, localized Japanese brokerage house.

Since 1984, when barriers to foreign entry first began to fall, American financial firms have rushed into Tokyo. They do business on behalf of their American and international clientele and claw fiercely for bits and pieces of the domestic Japanese market. At Ark Hills—a recently constructed office, hotel, restaurant, and shopping complex that resembles Century City in Los Angeles—the lobby directories read like a *Who's Who* of international finance. Here one can buy David's Cookies, goodies from New York's Silver Palate, and Hobson's Ice Cream from Santa Barbara and have lunch at a California-style salad bar before stopping by for a business meeting with Salomon Brothers, Goldman Sachs, or a flock of other American companies paying well over $100 per square foot to be headquartered in Ark Hills.

American financial firms now employ about six thousand people in Japan. The vast majority are Japanese, and the firms themselves have begun to resemble Japanese companies, even putting new recruits through Japanese-style boot camps.

Considering how xenophobic Tokyo was before 1984, some of the recent events are nothing short of miraculous:

• Salomon committed $300 million in capital to its Tokyo operation, becoming fifth only to the Big Four in total capital. It is using those funds to build an aggressive American-style bond trading operation, focusing on Japanese government issues. After intense lobbying efforts, Salomon and some other foreign houses were at last given an increased allotment in the bellwether ten-year bond syndicates, up from the microscopic .07 percent to the faintly visible 1 percent. In a two-year government note sale early in 1987, Salomon stunned the Tokyo investment community by flexing its muscles the way the Japanese do in the U.S. government bond market—buying 45 percent of the entire issue, well ahead of Nomura's 30 percent share. Over the last few years Salomon has actually succeeded in showing a profit in Japan—$11 million in 1986–87.

- Merrill Lynch has opened an Osaka branch to complement its long-standing Tokyo operation and plans to expand to four other Japanese cities. It is developing a clientele of wealthy Japanese individuals interested in U.S. style investment strategy and has built a research team capable of following one hundred Japanese stocks regularly.

- Foreign banks, allowed to enter the trust banking business in 1985, now outnumber indigenous Japanese trust banks nine to eight. Taken together, the foreign trust banks do less than one percent of total Japanese trust banking, but they have made some significant breakthroughs. The Japanese arm of Bankers Trust, for example, won management of a portfolio for a Japanese government welfare fund.

- New American financial techniques are being seeded in Japan. Goldman Sachs, for example, helped Shaklee spin off its Japanese subsidiary in a public stock offering designed for the domestic Japanese market.

- American brokers are attracting a small but prestigious following among Japanese institutional clients. Sometimes this is based on the independence and forthrightness of American research, sometimes it is part of larger global relationship-building efforts. Morgan Stanley reports that 40 percent of its trading on the TSE now represents orders from Japanese institutional clients.

- Some of Japan's most famous corporations, eager to demonstrate they are "international-minded," have put their underwritings out for highly competitive bidding. American firms able to master the intricate details of doing things the Japanese way—and add value with an American perspective—are winning some of this business. Goldman Sachs, for example, served as lead manager of an NTT "Yankee bond" issue.

• Foreign banks, led by Citibank, Morgan Guaranty, and Chemical, have garnered an impressive 45 percent share of the transaction volume in Tokyo's $4 trillion foreign currency trading market. Their success has been based at least in part on out-competing domestic banks by offering better service, lower fees, and more innovative financial products to Japanese corporations with mammoth currency trading needs.

Despite these inroads, however, the broader experience of Americans in the Japanese financial market indicates that they are *not* carving out a particularly integral role. Americans handle a statistically insignificant share of transaction volume in stocks, bonds, and bank lending. Most firms are only marginally profitable, if at all. Their activities are highly visible because of political considerations attached to questions about their market access. This tends to make a news event out of every small triumph. But in point of fact, the American presence in Tokyo is several orders of magnitude less significant than the Japanese presence in U.S. markets.

Salomon is perhaps the most successful. But it has taken a $300 million capital commitment and a staff of four hundred people to obtain what can at best be described as a toehold in Tokyo. How many other American firms can realistically afford to make that kind of commitment? And of the ones that do, how many will be able to maintain it through the period ahead of shakeout and retrenchment on Wall Street? Faced with eroding profits at home and cutback-minded management committees, how many U.S. firms will be able to continue doing whatever it takes to expand their capabilities in the world's most expensive city?

Even successful Salomon is not immune to such pressure. Reeling under the weight of management mistakes, plunging profits, and the scourges of Black Monday, it began 1988 by pulling back from a number of foreign markets. CEO John Gutfreund, "a man who once spoke ambitiously about Salomon's global expansion," according to *The New York Times,* "now speaks of a world of limits." Gutfreund himself says, "We won't be so arrogant as to think we can become a factor in their indigenous markets. We had been seduced into thinking we could do that."[17] Meanwhile Gutfreund's opposite numbers in Japan—Tabuchi, Chino, and the rest—still believe it is a world without limits. Should Salomon falter again, as it did in 1987 when it almost fell victim to a hostile takeover, more than one Japanese company will be waiting in the wings to buy all or part of it.

Contraction in the domestic U.S. financial services industry "will provide a real test of our capital markets firms and whether they will sustain themselves as major players overseas even if they have lower profits in the short term," observes Harvard's Samuel L. Hayes III, academia's foremost expert on investment banking. "If we don't understand this and hold our share of the international financial markets, the financial industry is bound to go the way of some of the others where we've been losing the battle. . . . The genius of an investment bank was always its flexibility, its ability to exploit change. You wonder now if they have created a monster, if they can react when they need to."[18]

Part of the monster faced by Americans in Tokyo today is indeed of their own making. Aggressive, "Type-A" American executives—the kind who do so well at the upper levels of the securities industry at home—have failed miserably in trying to run Tokyo operations, owing to their lack of patience and humility in a financial culture that requires newcomers to exhibit those virtues in massive doses. Some observers attribute the success of Salomon and Morgan Stanley to the fact that their Tokyo operations aren't headed by "typical" Americans. The driving force at Salomon is Deryck Maughan (British), while at Morgan it is David Philipps (ethnically Japanese).

No matter who the top man is at an American house in Tokyo, the Japanese know that he is *not* one of the very top people in the parent organization at home. "It is very hard for the Japanese to respect a company that doesn't send one of its most important executives to Tokyo," observes a *Nihon Keizai Shimbun* journalist. "Japanese securities companies will send a very important man to New York, but it doesn't work the other way around." Several heads of American operations in Tokyo complain privately that they have trouble getting direct access to the chief executive of their company back at home to discuss matters pertaining to Japan; their Japanese clients and business partners often suspect as much.

The language barrier is also formidable. How successful can a brain-intensive service business be if top executives are unilingual in English, their Japanese staff speaks only rudimentary English, and bilingual American staff are more likely to have a background in Japanese literature than in the securities business?

Even Americans well suited for work in Tokyo won't stay long enough to learn the language and dig the kind of personal roots mandatory to compete successfully in Japan. Underlying all Japanese business dealings is an intricately woven fabric of personal connections—going to school together, drinking together, golfing together, doing long-remembered favors for each other. These relationships are built up over a lifetime. Most Americans, however, will stay only two or three years, viewing Tokyo as a pit stop on their fast-lane résumés. Few stay longer than five years, when the Japanese government begins to tax expatriates like citizens. "Five years is nothing in Japan," says Merrill Lynch's Tokyo chief, Jack Williams, who himself plans to leave at the end of his fifth year. "It can take five years of persistent effort in this culture just to arrange the right introduction to someone you want to meet."

American-style recruitment is a double-edged sword. While U.S. companies have lured talent away from leading Japanese companies with financial incentives, this inducement appeals chiefly to the most open-minded and entrepreneurial types, not to those in the mainstream. The good news is that American companies have hired a lot of brilliant Japanese. The bad news is that not a few of those individuals are perceived as mavericks and misfits by the business world to which they are supposed to provide liaison.

American companies have also been some of the biggest employers of talented, career-oriented Japanese women. But the sad reality here too is that even though the women have important titles with the *gaijin* firms, they command little respect from the mostly male Japanese financial community.

When American companies finally succeed in recruiting the right kind of Japanese employees, the battle still isn't over. Goldman Sachs found an excellent rising star in Hideki Mitani at Sumitomo Bank and succeeded in wooing him away. Mitani's mentors at Sumitomo did everything but commit hara-kiri to keep him. He was forced to endure months of pressure sessions with high-ranking executives before they finally let him go. In another situation, three hard-won Japanese recruits showed up for work in the morning but never came back after lunch. Like Soviet defectors who glimpse life in the United States and decide to redefect even though they will be ruined when they return to Mother Russia, this trio chose to return to their Japanese employer, even though their brief morning fling would taint them the rest of their professional lives.

The age of limits is now descending on what was once the strongest

American trump card. "The Americans won't be able to offer such high salaries forever," says Daiwa's chief of equities, Koichi Kimura, who also believes there will be "some sort of salary arbitrage" under which Japanese salaries will rise to keep talent in the fold, and American salaries will decline due to pressure on profitability. "At some point, foreign firms that have expanded too fast will have to reduce their staff. As soon as they do that, they will scare many Japanese. Lifetime employment is practiced in the Japanese securities business. If the Americans can't offer stable employment, it doesn't matter how much they pay."

Barriers to Entry

Regardless of the strengths or weaknesses of any particular American firm, they are all up against the reality that Japan has agreed only to tolerate foreigners in the financial system—nothing more. And that is not enough. Like other fronts of U.S.-Japan economic competition, the formal, legal barriers to American participation are falling by the wayside, but the informal, "nontariff" cultural barriers remain in force.

A good example is the Japanese system of cross-shareholding. Ownership of "relationship shares" is an integral factor in determining who does business with whom. According to Larry Zoglin, an attorney with Paul, Weiss, Rifkind who studied informal barriers in the Japanese securities market, Americans standing outside that system are not likely to be successful in cracking either the Japanese pension fund management business or Japanese equity underwriting regardless of their skills. "The primary reason for their lack of success is clear: they do not hold sizable blocks of the shares of their potential Japanese corporate clients." As part of the system of quid pro quo on which business in Japan is based, "firms competing for the domestic financial business of Japan's major corporations are evaluated in large part on their willingness to hold their corporate clients' shares on a long-term basis. Thus, for example, a Japanese company expects the bank or insurance company that manages its pension fund to hold a sizable block, up to 5 percent, of the company's outstanding shares. It expects the same of other providers of financial services." Obviously few head offices of American banks would approve of their Tokyo branch manager deciding to buy 5 percent of XYZ Corp.'s shares just to bid for its pension management account. Unable to establish that sort of bond, the American banks are "effectively closed out from the majority of the pension fund management business in Japan."[19]

The deck is stacked in innumerable ways. When Goldman Sachs teamed up with Nomura to take Japanese companies like Canon and TDK to the U.S. equity market in public offerings, the deal was split fifty-fifty between the two underwriters. But when Goldman teamed up with Nikko to spin off Shaklee's Japan subsidiary as a public offering, Nikko got 85 percent of the deal, even though the idea originated with Goldman. With the U.S. market relatively open and the Japanese market relatively closed, the Americans have little leverage in these kinds of situations. An American underwriter trying to insist on more than 50 percent of the deal in the United States could be easily pushed aside by the Japanese in favor of another American partner. But the reverse isn't true.

Asked what would have happened if he had refused to accept only 15 percent of the Shaklee underwriting and had sought another Japanese partner instead, Goldman's Gene Atkinson says, "The deal just wouldn't have been done, because the head of Shaklee Japan had a long personal relationship with Nikko." Despite the fierce competition that exists among Japanese firms, they maintain a collective "Us against Them" mentality, Atkinson says, which prevents foreigners from capitalizing on splits in their ranks. "They all row together in the same boat," says Atkinson. "It's not in American culture for Americans to do that."

Having watched the Goldman office in Tokyo grow from two people in 1974 to over three hundred today, Atkinson is proud of the firm's successes but recognizes the limitations. "The Japanese have control of more of what we want here than we have of what they want back home. They've got the money; they're in the driver's seat."

Even some of the most celebrated "victories" won by Americans in opening the Tokyo market may prove dubious over time. Take the demand to allow foreign firms to join the TSE. This was an issue Donald Regan had raised when he was with Merrill Lynch and later as treasury secretary. From 1982 to 1985, MoF and the TSE played good cop, bad cop. MoF declared the TSE was a nongovernmental organization beyond its control. The TSE claimed first that foreigners didn't meet the criteria for membership. Later its argument shifted. No seats were available, and foreigners would have to wait until some of the smaller Japanese firms decided to sell their seats. Next, TSE scolded foreigners for waiting so long to express interest in membership. A modern new headquarters had been built that wouldn't have enough physical room for foreign members. Finally, in 1985, the TSE acceded to intensifying foreign pressure and agreed to allow Merrill Lynch, Goldman Sachs, Morgan Stanley, Vickers Da Costa, S. G. Warburg, and Jardine Fleming to join. Two years later sixteen more foreign members were admitted.

As symbol, the foreign entry *was* undoubtedly a victory. As substance, however, it is still an open question. The most concrete benefit to foreigners is that member firms are entitled to 100 percent of the commissions earned on trades generated by their clients, instead of sharing 27 percent with a Japanese brokerage house. When the cost of a seat is factored into that equation ($8 million in 1988), plus the additional overhead of maintaining a TSE floor-trading capability (ten to fifteen employees), one foreigner calculates his firm will need five years of brisk business to break even.

All this is a small price to pay for those companies desiring to be perceived as one of the megafirms of the future operating universally across the London-New York-Tokyo axis. But just how brisk foreigners will find the Tokyo business remains to be seen. Even after Merrill Lynch's twenty-five years in Japan, Jack Williams observes with resignation, "The hardest thing for foreigners to do is attract yen-to-yen business. You've got to try, especially when you're paying your rent in yen, but it ain't easy." (Sometimes overzealous foreigners trying to attract yen business become the first targets of Japanese charlatans. Shortly after Merrill gained its seat on the TSE, a Japanese client began accumulating millions of shares in Nankai Railway through Merrill and another foreign firm. When Nankai's stock price plunged, the client suddenly refused to meet its margin requirements, forcing Merrill to sell off the shares at a $17.3 million loss.)

Membership in the TSE is a prerequisite for a securities company to be considered by talented Japanese as a potential employer or by customers as a potential broker. But membership alone doesn't even solve all the problems at the level of symbol. For tax reasons and other legal considerations, foreign securities firms still face difficulty getting "KK" status—meaning incorporating their subsidiaries as Japanese entities. As a result most of them operate as branches of U.S. organizations. Merrill Lynch operates in Japan as a branch of a company that is *called* Merrill Lynch Japan but is actually incorporated in

Delaware. According to Merrill's Tetsundo Iwakuni, the Japanese securities industry doesn't believe that Merrill's "president" is a real
"president" since the company doesn't have KK status. "The president of a major Japanese corporation will wonder whether it is appropriate to meet the president of Merrill Lynch Japan, since our
president only has the technical status of branch manager," reports
Iwakuni.

As a native Japanese who hails from the same town as Prime Minister Takeshita, and as a veteran of eighteen years with Nikko Securities, Iwakuni doesn't partake in the often naive American enthusiasm
about business prospects in Tokyo. In an extraordinary speech to a
1987 symposium on international securities, Iwakuni synopsized the
competitive situation in terms far blunter than any native-born American financial executive would have dared:

> The Japanese Finance Ministry has recently agreed to modify certain
> regulations which have inhibited participation by foreign financial firms in
> the Tokyo capital market. This move has been welcomed in the United
> States and Europe in the belief that Japan is finally discarding its protec-
> tionist stance. Unfortunately . . . that is not the case. In fact, no new laws,
> no modification of regulatory barriers, will change Japanese society
> overnight. . . . Japanese will only give rhetorical support to the new regula-
> tions while continuing a way of doing business among themselves that has
> existed for hundreds of years. . . . Although it is true the American firms
> such as Merrill Lynch will make inroads into the Japanese financial mar-
> kets, it is equally true that, as in the past, their gains will not be achieved
> without great difficulty. . . .
>
> It is so easy for Japanese companies to become established in the
> United States that today twelve have fully operational U.S. subsidiaries
> versus no American companies in Japan. In this context, the Japanese
> Ministry of Finance is effectively controlling the two largest capital mar-
> kets in the world. If this were a baseball game, the score would now be
> Japan twelve, the U.S. nothing. A game that one-sided, where one team is
> so handicapped by the rules as to be noncompetitive, is unacceptable to
> us.[20]

Change in Japan, Iwakuni warned, comes only grudgingly, only
after prolonged negotiations, and even then, tends to be more appearance than substance.

For whatever optimistic expectations foreign firms had when they first gained access to Tokyo, those that survived the arduous process of lobbying for TSE seats now realize that their business will rely chiefly on handling the trades of foreign investors—usually less than 5 percent of Tokyo's volume. The irony is that in giving foreigners the seats they wanted, the TSE ushered in a debilitating situation where twenty-two foreign firms now compete for 5 percent of the market. Aron Viner, a former Yamaichi vice president, sees a certain calculating plan at work. "It is in Japan's best interest to permit *all,* rather than just a few, qualified foreign institutions into the business. . . . This process is the most likely way to prevent several foreign institutions from consolidating a significant share of the market under one roof."[21]

In a few notable areas, deregulation has actually meant a *loss* of profitable business for foreigners. In the old days even *gaijin* were allowed a few protected niches of their own. One important area was "impact loans" of foreign currency to Japanese corporations. Foreign banks in Tokyo had an advantage in that they could engage in unlimited currency trading, while locals were subject to quotas. Bank of America, Chase, Citibank, and others earned up to 40 percent of their profits in Japan from this one function. Today, however, deregulation has opened the field to domestic competition. The foreign share has slipped to one-third of what it was in 1982. Meanwhile the foreign slice of total bank lending in Japan has shrunk from 4.2 percent to 2.2 percent.

Clearly the Japanese side is getting the better part of the bargain in the process of deregulation and globalization. A few politicians have tried to galvanize domestic U.S. sentiment around this issue, but to little avail. Congressman Schumer believes inaction on reciprocity will result in Japanese firms ending up as the only players capable of participating in all corners of the globalized market. "That's a recipe for losing American leadership in financial services," he notes.

Theoretically the constituency for Schumer's crusade should be American financial firms. His effort to deny Japanese institutions U.S. primary dealerships until greater market-opening measures are taken by Tokyo was written into the 1988 trade bill passed by Congress. But he has yet to receive the public endorsement of a single prominent U.S. financial company. For one thing, no self-respecting Wall Street house is ready to admit failure in the global game or appeal for what most oppose in principle—government backing.

Some Americans are simply resigned to the situation. "It doesn't look like we'll get banking reciprocity with Japan," says Joseph Pinola, CEO of First Interstate. "Our banks operating over there are limited in what they can do, while their banks operating here can function like any American bank. The Japanese will talk about giving us reciprocity, but they will stonewall us."[22]

Privately a few of Wall Street's leading lights express support for Schumer-style legislation as a way of calling attention to the problem. But even those who see symbolic value in a "get tough" stance on reciprocity recognize financial protectionism as fatally flawed. As long as the U.S. budget deficit remains large, Washington will continue to favor the most active Japanese participation possible in the U.S. government bond market. The more active Japanese investors are, the cheaper and easier is the financing of the deficit. Those close to the issue understand that restricting Japanese involvement without cutting the deficit would be tantamount to the American government shooting itself in the foot.

The imbalance of power between Japanese and American financial services firms that has now arisen—and is rapidly worsening—is dictated by the macroeconomics of Japan's strength as an investor nation and America's weakness as a debtor nation. But the macro picture was unnecessarily duplicated and reinforced on the micro level by the Reagan administration's laissez-faire policies combined with Wall Street's own overconfidence. Nomura became a full member of the New York Stock Exchange in 1981 with little difficulty, while the case of Merrill Lynch trying to gain a seat on the Tokyo Stock Exchange became an epic international political battle that went unresolved until the end of 1985. Nomura and Daiwa became primary dealers in U.S. government securities in 1986, even though American firms in 1988 are still complaining of getting no more than crumbs from Tokyo's government bond syndicates.

The ideal time for fighting over reciprocity has come and gone. Had Americans insisted at the beginning of the 1980s on genuine symmetry in U.S.-Japan financial market access—before Japan had the wherewithal to penetrate the U.S. market directly and before Japanese financial companies had yet become world leaders—today's gross inbalances might have been minimized.

It is hard now to attempt to reverse that framework. The Japanese have entered the United States so deeply that attempting to curtail their activities now skirts a confrontation with extreme economic instability. Opportunities still exist to press the cause of reciprocity when *new* deregulatory steps are considered, as well as to link financial issues to negotiations over wider aspects of U.S.-Japan relations. But trying to take back what the Japanese have already obtained is an invitation to financial brinksmanship the United States is ill-prepared to manage.

After the Buzzwords Are Gone: Four Riddles for the Future

Only a handful of executives have been high enough inside the ranks of both a Japanese and an American securities firm to make a studied comparison of the inner workings of the two financial cultures. One of those who has answers questions about Japanese global trust with these four riddles:

As New York, London, and Tokyo become one integrated global market, who stands to gain more: Japanese companies like Nomura and Daiwa, which begin from a domestic market in Tokyo that they monopolize and are entering American and British markets that are wide open, or American companies like Merrill Lynch, Morgan Stanley, and Salomon, which begin from a domestic market in New York where they are important but by no means dominant and are trying to enter a highly restrictive Tokyo market?

If the evolution of a single international financial market implies that financial services will become more similar everywhere, then companies will have to compete more and more on price. Which institutions are more likely to provide financial services at the lowest cost—American or Japanese?

It is said that technology follows the marketplace. If Tokyo continues to grow as the biggest financial market, and if companies like Nomura continue to sink a high percentage of their enormous income into R&D, where is it more likely to assume the next generation of financial technology will arise—New York or Tokyo?

If we believe that the world in the year 2000 will be dominated by a small group of mega–financial institutions, we must assume there will be many mergers and acquisitions along the way. Nomura's market capitalization is more than $50 billion. It could buy the top ten American investment banks for that. Daiwa's is also very big. So are the market capitalizations of the Japanese city banks. These Japanese companies have the resources to buy what they lack. Do American companies?

These, of course, are rhetorical riddles. The answers are obvious. The energy of today's American financial community is wrapped up in the thrill of the processes represented by hot buzzwords like "globalization," "deregulation," "integration," and "securitization." For the most part, however, American financial companies fail to see the new buzzword that all the others add up to: *commoditization*. And in a commoditized financial world, the big winners will surely be the Japanese.

9

Foreign Correspondence: Japanese in London, Frankfurt, Hong Kong, Beijing, Moscow, and Everywhere Else but Africa

> Most of us should expect to see Japan as the dominent influ-
> ence in the financial markets for the rest of our working lives.
> —Thomas Chandos, director for
> international capital markets,
> Kleinwort, Benson Ltd., London[1]

Big Winners in the Big Bang

No event typifies the global wave of financial deregulation better than London's Big Bang of October 27, 1986. The City, as London's financial district is known, was turned overnight into the freest of the world's leading financial markets. As barriers and regulations were hauled down with abandon, Americans, Europeans, and Japanese rushed to set up shop, bringing with them mountains of global capital and a frenetic babble of international excitement. Employment in the City's financial services sector zoomed up to four hundred thousand. As an industry, finance suddenly began contributing more to Britain's revival than North Sea oil. Brokerage houses (and the human talent within them) were bought, sold, and combined by foreigners like pieces on a chessboard, cheered on by Margaret Thatcher's social Darwinists.

The markets rose, crested, and ultimately crashed in the wake of Black Monday. Porsche sales to the newly rich skyrocketed and then plummeted as so many potential customers became the newly unemployed. For better or for worse, the twenty-four-hour electronic trading day became a new global reality, and London played an important role in making it so.

Most American firms that expanded in London based on expectations of vast profits were severely disappointed. Almost from the first, the new opportunities presented by the City's return engagement at the pinnacle of global finance turned to cutthroat competition, making profits elusive and cutbacks inevitable. Even before jobs began to be slashed in the aftermath of Black Monday, one witty observer noted that only three kinds of players remained in the City: "the bruised, the badly bloodied, and those in a body bag."[2] There was, however, a fourth type as well: the Japanese. For them none of the above "B words" applied.

As Americans, Europeans, and the British themselves retrenched, most of the numerous Japanese banks, securities firms, insurance companies, and financial arms of giant *sogo shoshas* (trading companies) headquartered in the City simply proceeded along the path they had earlier charted, utilizing London's unregulated environment as a forward position for their global strategies. By the beginning of 1988, Japanese banks controlled over one-third of London's international banking business—somewhat more than the British themselves and three times the American share.

"When Japanese financial institutions in the city of London declare their intention of becoming number one in the key areas of international capital market activity, they do so with an air of almost clinical detachment rather than bravado," observed financial journalist Anthony Rowley. "It is as though they were revealing manifest destiny or historical inevitability."[3] London's experience offered compelling evidence that the freer the markets are in today's world, the easier it is for Japanese money to exert a hegemonic influence.

When the smoke of the Big Bang cleared, the Japanese suddenly dominated the City's most important business line—the underwriting of Eurobonds. Nearly $200 billion worth of these obligations are launched annually by corporate, sovereign, and supranational issuers from all over the world. For General Motors as for Toyota, for the Canadian government as for the Chinese government, the Euromarkets have become a fast, efficient, inexpensive way to raise capital.

The evolution of the Eurobond market over the last twenty years provided the impetus toward what would become a worldwide trend of "securitization," replacing traditional bank borrowing. The London Euromarket's phenomenal 400 percent growth between 1983 and

1986 convinced skeptics around the world that deregulation was indeed the inescapable wave of the future. The globalism that it embodied—American corporations going to London to issue bonds underwritten by Swiss banks to be purchased by investors in twenty other countries, for example—offered the most concentrated expression of investment banking's dream: a single market bringing together the world's biggest users and suppliers of capital, free from the meddling of governments.

Rather than laws or regulations, the Eurobond business relies on the international credibility of the financial institutions that participate in it. For most of Eurohistory, underwriting was therefore dominated by the crème de la crème of Western investment banking, such as Morgan Stanley, Morgan Guaranty, Union Bank of Switzerland, Merrill Lynch, Deutsche Bank, and Salomon Brothers. Credit Suisse First Boston (CSFB) in particular—a hybrid venture marrying the most hallowed companies of the old world and the new—was thought to own a permanent grip on Euroleadership in the 1980s.

As recently as 1982, Japanese institutions were absent from the annual "top ten" lists of London's Eurobond underwriters. In 1987, however, Nomura unseated CSFB as number one. Daiwa, Yamaichi, and Nikko were also in the top six; IBJ wasn't far behind. Between 1984 and 1987 the American share of the Eurobond business was cut in half, while the Japanese share tripled. Today Japanese houses underwrite more Eurobond issues than American and Swiss firms put together. Although Nomura and Deutsche Bank continue to duel for the top position and CSFB remains up there, Eurobonds have become a Japanese-dominated industry.

The Japanese presence has transformed the nature of the business. Traditionally high margins have become wafer thin. Several American companies have dropped out or greatly reduced involvement. Even CSFB began a major staff reduction in the wake of being unseated by Nomura. An exclusively dollar-based market has become a multicurrency market. The use of Euroyen has shot up from 1 percent of total offerings to 19 percent in just four years. In one typical 1988 case, the Swedish government, a frequent Euromarket borrower, decided to bypass its usual dollar-based offerings in favor of a 50 billion yen issue handled by Nomura. A dollar issue that size, Swedish officials feared, simply wouldn't be smoothly accepted by the marketplace.

The vast placement power of the Japanese enables them to know in advance that no matter how many hundreds of millions of dollars or hundreds of billions of yen worth of debt from the Danish government or Dow Chemical they underwrite, it will all be placed in the hands of Japanese customers in short order. Some Eurobond activity has actually become an all-Japanese affair. In Tokyo Japanese corporate issuers must post collateral and endure long lead times to float their bonds, whereas in London they face neither restriction. Thus Japanese underwriters bring Japanese issues to the London market, ultimately distributing them to Japanese investors back in Japan. Circuitous as this path is, it allows Japanese business the benefits of a deregulated market without having to deal with its problems at home.

"The Japanese Big Four have more capital than the Americans," observes Minoru Mori, general manager of Daiwa Europe in London. "And we have the greatest access to the largest market—Japanese investors."[4] Backed by such reservoirs of strength, the Japanese can sacrifice profit to the god of market share, while many American and European companies are eliminated by a corporate culture that seeks to post a profit on every deal. "We decided not to participate in that craziness," noted J. Nelson Abanto, a partner in Goldman Sachs's London office. "The money involved and potential losses were so great that we decided to . . . focus on other areas."[5] The Japanese, however, are undaunted by the lack of profitability in Eurobonds.

"We can afford the cost of publicity," says Daiwa's Mori in explaining the Japanese propensity to take on loss-leader business for the sake of building relationships with important customers.[6] What Mori euphemistically calls the "cost of publicity" is seen as outright dumping of financial services by others.

"The Euromarket is the place where cries of 'dumping' are most frequently heard: in particular that Japanese houses 'bought' the Euroyen market in 1985 by offering swap terms so cheap as to be sure loss-makers for the issue manager," noted the *Far Eastern Economic Review*. Americans and Europeans can say what they like about the Japanese strategy, but apparently it works. "A big corporate borrower does not shop round 30–40 Euromarket banks for terms on a deal. It looks to five or six big players, and leaves these lead managers to decide which smaller fry should be brought into the underwriting syndicate."[7]

Having conquered Eurobond markets, Japanese houses have moved on to the increasingly important spin-offs—Euroequities, Eurowarrants, and Eurocommercial paper. Nomura has declared its ambition to gain the number-one spot in the fast-developing Euroequity sector, where many American and European firms fled after being bested by the Japanese in bond underwritings. To better fulfill all these ambitious goals, Nomura reportedly hires more new graduates from Oxford and Cambridge than the Foreign Office, traditionally the leading employer of Britain's best and brightest.

Using the solid international infrastructure they have built up to handle the Eurobusiness in London, Japanese firms have tended to expand in two directions: vertically, by burrowing deeper into the domestic British financial markets; and horizontally, in a headlong rush to establish a presence in every major Western financial outpost —Frankfurt, Amsterdam, Paris, Zurich, Geneva, Lugano, Milan, Brussels, Toronto, and Sydney to name but a few.

Getting situated in Amsterdam and Toronto has been eased by "little bangs" of deregulation; in Paris a *petit* bang is imminent, which will also widen the scope of Japanese activity. The biggest problem in many of these investment markets, however, is that they are simply too small to sustain the sudden interest of what is usually all of the Big Four houses at once.

On the Toronto Stock Exchange, where Japanese houses bid up seats on the "other TSE" to a record $361,000 before the 1987 "Little Bang," a Canadian central banker telephoned the governor of BoJ to complain that investment from Japan was distorting Canada's financial and exchange markets.[8] At about the same time, *Business Week* reported that "the Japanese urge for German equities is rapidly propelling Frankfurt into one of the hot markets."[9]

After the Big Four set up branches in Milan during 1986–87, Nomura's representative expressed disappointment that stock exchange volume is "peanuts for Japanese institutional buyers. They are used to dealing in blocks of 50 billion yen, but a purchase order for the equivalent of 500 million yen is considered large by Milan standards."[10]

In Australia a Japanese property investor warned out loud that "Japanese capital represents a danger to the Australian market because the market is so small."[11] Indeed, Japanese buying pressure helped drive up real estate prices on Sydney's north shore by 50 percent in just a few months during 1987. Despite heavy currency losses in Australian dollar bonds, yen continue to flood into Australia's largely open markets. Daiwa has set up its own Australia fund, contributing to the $3 billion total Japanese investment in stocks and bonds. Another $2 billion has poured into hotels, golf courses, and shopping centers.

Even these and other diversification ventures throughout the world can't begin to satisfy the Japanese global investment appetite. Britain and the United States still remain the areas that can best absorb capital while offering the security and strategic benefits Japanese investors desire.

As a result, many Japanese houses have now decided to sink deeper roots in domestic British banking as well as local activity on London's International Stock Exchange and in trading gilts (British government bonds). For their Japanese customers alone they now buy about $4 billion worth of British stocks annually and three times that in gilts. These are businesses where the greatest deregulatory impact of the Big Bang has been felt. It is in these areas too where the biggest shoot-outs took place between the Americans, Europeans, and the British themselves. Now, just as bloodied competitors are trimming their staffs or quitting altogether, the Japanese have begun to replace them as local market makers and dealers.

Japanese commercial banks already hold a sizable chunk of the British retail banking market, and Sumitomo Bank has even entered the home mortgage market. "The Japanese banks are filling in their gaps of ignorance, and gaining an entry into such areas as leasing, credit cards, venture capital, and factoring," reports *The Economist*. "With the yen so strong, acquisitions look cheap to the Japanese. They use joint ventures when they need to learn new tricks. . . . Their methods will not surprise anybody familiar with Japanese business strategy in cars, chips, or cameras: begin with a standardized product; sell it cheaply and sell it in bulk."[12]

Japanese investors have become major players in London real estate—buying famous old buildings like the *Financial Times* headquarters. And Japanese industrialists are direct investors from small electronics outposts in Scotland's "Silicon Glen" to Nissan's factory at Sunderland, which will soon be building two hundred thousand cars annually. Fifty miles northeast of London, the town of Milton Keynes has been turned into a miniature Japan, hosting more than twenty Japanese companies and featuring amenities such as a local Japanese school for the children of executives.[13]

The growth of Japanese finance inside Britain was so rapid (while corresponding to the snail's-pace access for British firms to Tokyo's markets) that the normally free-trading Thatcher government became the first in the West to officially attempt to put teeth into a demand for greater reciprocity. On a 1987 visit to Tokyo, trade official Michael Howard threatened to revoke banking and securities licenses for Japanese firms if more British firms didn't get seats on the Tokyo Stock Exchange and if Japan didn't open its telecommunications market to greater British participation. Within a few days, however, Britain was backpedaling fast. Economists expressed worries over the thousands of financial jobs that would be lost in the City if the Japanese were forced out. Executives of financial houses warned that the Japanese would simply move to Amsterdam or another European city and turn it into London's rival. Sensing their great power over world finance, the Japanese called Britain's bluff, and the clamor died down. (Months later, however, a new crop of British-based firms did gain TSE membership, with many analysts crediting the Thatcher government's earlier saber-rattling as the catalytic force.)

To most Japanese, London is not important as an end in itself, but more for the strategic battle that will be played out there. On this topic they speak in terms drawn from military strategy. London, predicts Daiwa's chairman Yoshitoki Chino, is "going to be like the Battle of Waterloo."[14] The Japanese are cast in the role of Wellington and the Americans as Napoleon.

Most Japanese executives have read and assimilated the lessons of the classical Chinese sage of military strategy, Sun Tzu. "To be certain to take what you attack is to attack a place the enemy does not protect," Sun Tzu cautioned 2,400 years ago.[15] London, with its relatively weak domestic firms and its overextended American firms, is thus the Japanese battleground of choice.

The Pacific Vision

The large-scale wars the United States has fought over the last half century have been overwhelmingly Pacific wars: the Asia theater of World War II, Korea, and then Vietnam. America clearly perceives itself as a Pacific power with vital Pacific interests. During the last twenty-five years of phenomenal economic growth throughout east Asia, the United States was the region's leading investor, trade partner, and military protector. Today it still plays the military role but has been overtaken by Japan economically.

Japan is deeply involved in the economic life of almost every country in the Asia/Pacific region. Many of these nations were occupied by Japanese forces during World War II and retain deep emotional scars from those days. Even so, they want and need Japanese investment and have little choice but to welcome Tokyo's new economic expansionism. A few barometers of this trend:

- In booming South Korea, for example, new Japanese direct investment is now twice as great as new U.S. investment on an annual basis.
- In Singapore, a high-growth economy with traditionally strong economic ties to the United States, new Japanese investment exceeded new American investment in 1987. Nomura expects to introduce $50 million worth of new Japanese money annually to the Singapore stock market—a commanding sum in such a small market.
- Accumulated Japanese investment in the ASEAN group (Indonesia, Malaysia, Thailand, Singapore, Philippines, and Brunei) currently stands at 150 percent of the U.S. total.
- Even in the face of the yen's continuous rise over the last few years, the Japanese currency has begun to assume the role of Asia's coin of the realm. Foreign debt denominated in yen in Indonesia is about 40 percent; in Thailand it's closer to 45 percent.
- The assets of twenty-five Japanese banks in Hong Kong have doubled in the last two years to $125 billion. "By the time China takes over, Japan may own the joint," remarked *Business Week,* extrapolating toward the 1997 Chinese takeover based on current trends in Japanese real estate, stock, and manufacturing investments.[16]
- With almost one-third of Malaysia's new investment coming from Japan, the government of Prime Minister Mahathir bin Mohamad has openly appealed to American corporations to help counterbalance the Japanese presence. By and large, however, American companies have been scaling back operations in Malaysia.
- In Seoul, where foreign investors are currently excluded from direct trading in stock market shares, Japanese financial companies have begun to establish a strong behind-the-scenes participation in anticipation of the time when the market will be opened. The most active investors in Korean equity funds listed in New York and London are Japanese.

- Japanese investment in Thailand is widely credited with turning the local economy around. In 1987 more than two hundred new Japanese ventures were launched that will ultimately employ eighty thousand Thai workers. But recognizing the profound impact Japanese investment will have on Thailand's future, Bangkok businessmen are already complaining that Japan invests in a neocolonialist way, exploiting labor and only grudgingly transferring technology and managerial responsibilities.[17]
- In Australia, which is increasingly identifying itself as a Pacific nation, MITI, together with a host of Japanese technology, trading, and construction companies, has proposed developing a "city for the 21st century." Designed to house research centers as well as living quarters for a population of Japanese and foreign engineers that could reach 250,000, the new city would be underwritten from scratch by Tokyo just like two dozen "technopolises" now slated inside Japan. Plans call for ultramodern conveniences from high-speed "linear motor car" transportation to a database facility conceived as one of the world's largest repositories of on-line knowledge. Australians are intrigued with the potential benefits in this arrangement. Top political officials expect it will succeed in some form. But many have also expressed fears that it will tie Australia's destiny too closely with Japan in the future.

Nowhere is Japan's long-term Pacific vision more evident than in China. Of all Asian countries, China retains the deepest memories of Japan's brutal wartime occupation. Even today Chinese newspapers routinely editorialize against the dangers of a Japanese military revival. Despite the many shared features of the two cultures, most Chinese view Japanese business with skepticism. "We would much rather do business with Americans than with Japanese," says the director of a Chinese semiconductor factory. "The Japanese are very stingy. They extract very hard terms. They never share technology the way the Americans do. They keep to themselves and have an arrogant and superior attitude. But we have no choice. They are the ones who are willing to do business here."

The great promise of the China market has been a subject of fanfare in the United States for much of the last decade. Leading American corporations have hurried to Beijing to get in on the ground floor of what everyone knows will eventually be one of the world's most important markets. Yet the costs, complexities, and slow pace of negotiations in the People's Republic have also exasperated Americans, leading to a significant slowdown in new U.S. business activity. The Japanese, meanwhile, have not diminished their drive into China at all.

Japan, in fact, is beginning to crack the China market in a deep and fundamental way, while U.S. exports remain only on the surface. Japanese goods account for almost a third of total Chinese imports—far more than those from any other country and three times as much as the American share. Japanese companies have more offices in more cities than American companies. Their employees are committed to longer tours of duty with fewer perks. While most American companies will try to house American staff in hotels and apartments that conform to international living standards—and will often assume the cost of moving a whole executive family—Japanese companies expect most of their employees to grin and bear substandard amenities and to live in China without their families. Most notable of all, Japanese companies continue to practice the now patented Japanese approach of building market share at the expense of profits.

"By outworking and often outsmarting their American and European rivals, Japanese companies have taken such a lead in doing business in China that other countries have only a meager chance of catching up," concluded Nicholas Kristof of *The New York Times* after investigating the race for the China market.[18]

In the area of finance, Japanese institutions are building even more fearsome leadership than in trade. They lend to China at rates below the world-standard LIBOR (London Interbank Offered Rates) benchmark, whereas American bankers insist on at least a fraction of a point above LIBOR. "For now, Japanese banks commit hara-kiri," noted a representative of Mitsubishi Trust and Banking Corp. in Beijing. "Later we will recover a profit."[19] Sanwa Bank will soon have six offices in China; Citibank has only three. Most of Sanwa's Japanese staff in China speaks Chinese; few of Citibank's American staff in China are bilingual. Even a spokesman for Bank of America predicts that by 1990 "almost all American banks and most European banks will be wiped out of the credit market."[20]

All Big Four Japanese securities houses have built "China departments," and all are actively helping China develop its financial infrastructure. Nomura served as the lead underwriter for the powerful

China International Trust and Investment Corporation (CITIC) when it became the first contemporary Chinese institution to tap global bond markets. Masanori Ito, a former Nomura executive, now advises Beijing on experimental efforts to create debt and equity markets. Nomuramen are also involved in ventures ranging from hotel and office building construction to underwriting yen bonds for the Bank of China. "To be realistic, we should not expect big profits for a long time," says Tetsuo Koyama, who oversees Nomura's China campaign from Tokyo and makes visits to Beijing every three weeks or so. "But China will develop a stock market and a bond market and other kinds of financial activities. Nomura is not afraid to be patient."

In addition to patience, Japan's new wealth is allowing its companies greater risk-taking capabilities. At a time when the American oil industry is almost uniformly disappointed with exploration efforts in China's coastal waters, Beijing's Ministry of Petroleum found itself approached by C. Itoh & Co., a giant Japanese *sogo shosha*, with a proposal to supply $6 billion to finance development of an oil site in the Takla Makan Desert. Just the initial stage of the project will take twelve years and include building a twelve-hundred-mile pipeline through some of the world's most remote areas. A Western geologist cautioned, "The risk is enormous. You could drill for years and find nothing."[21] But cash-rich C. Itoh is ready to ante up for a shot at what might be the world's largest supply of untapped oil reserves.

The Japanese fully expect to be rewarded both for their patience as well as the risks they take, not just in China, but throughout Asia. Rather than viewing the "new Japans" arising around them as potential competitors, they see them as new investment opportunities instead. Labor is cheap in these countries. Work forces tend to be sufficiently skilled, educated, and pliant to function well in Japanese-managed organizations. The land and raw materials Japan needs so badly are in abundant supply. Japan can now export its low-end industries to production sites throughout the region and, in doing so, help Asia/Pacific economies develop to the point where they become active buyers of Japan's high-technology products and high-end financial services.

"The Pacific era is an inevitability," Prime Minister Nakasone once said, and many economic experts throughout the world agree with him.[22] The record of double-digit GNP growth exhibited by many Asia/Pacific countries over the last generation is, in a sense, only the beginning. Much of the region is deeply influenced by the same cultural forces that have helped make Japan so successful. If one adds to this mix the potentially catalytic role of Japanese capital in seeding new industries and accessing remote raw materials, the prospects increase for a Japan-led, Pacific-driven world economy of the future.

For the present, the focus of Japanese investment strategy remains outside Asia in the developed markets of North America and Europe. But that will change, and some of the investments cited above augur such a shift. Indeed, it could well turn out that Japan's greatest competitive advantage in the twenty-first century will be its superior ability to interconnect with and benefit from the rise of the rest of this region—an ability that the Japanese are now cultivating, even as the United States allows its former Pacific prowess to wane.

Money without Morals

An executive of a Japanese securities house explains the global nature of his firm this way: "We have offices in every world financial capital. Our company is doing business on every continent . . . except, of course, Africa." Then he laughs as if he has just told a great joke. The idea of a Japanese securities house finding any business to do amid the impoverishment of black Africa is simply preposterous to him.

Actually Japan does a great deal of business with Africa—South Africa, that is. With annual two-way volume more than $4 billion, Japan has surpassed the United States as South Africa's leading trade partner. Although Tokyo maintains some apartheid-related sanctions, vital areas like coal are not covered. Presented with an opportunity to capitalize on a vacuum left by withdrawing Americans and Europeans, Japanese businessmen have seized it.

Much of Japanese industry supports an Arab economic boycott of Israel, not out of political opposition to Zionism, but because Japan's national interests are overwhelmingly on the side of Mideast oil suppliers. When the Reagan administration denounced the "narco-terrorism" of Panama's Manuel Antonio Noriega and tried to force him from office, Tokyo announced it would continue supporting him—at least as long as he controlled the canal through which so many Japanese trading ships must pass.

In these cases, Americans tend to see a moral deficiency on Japan's part—a culture governed by an infuriating streak of mercantile self-interest. Internationally minded Japanese sometimes confirm that judgment, such as the Foreign Ministry official who, when asked about Japan's enthusiasm for doing business with South Africa, confided that "frankly speaking, the moral consciousness is not that keen."[23]

In reality, however, the problem is not bad moral values but different ones. Although there may be considerable racism in Japan, the Japanese relationship with South Africa is not motivated by racism as such.[24] Intensely concerned with what they perceive as right and wrong within their own borders, the Japanese are much less focused on such questions far from home. Japan's trade with the outside world originated as a matter of survival, not as a matter of preference. To put moral or ideological issues in a foreign country ahead of pragmatic matters involving trade makes little sense to Japanese businessmen.

Rich countries of the modern world—notably Britain and the United States—have historically been Christian countries. The political expression of their wealth has been accompanied by a Judeo-Christian–influenced moral agenda, albeit often hypocritical, on questions ranging from charity for poor nations to human rights. As wealth passes to Japan, a different set of moral values is coming to the fore, lacking both the impulse to global charity as well as the attendant hypocrisy characteristic of the American order of things. In a culture whose ethical basis does not assume that we are all God's children, and whose interest in brotherhood falls within its own borders rather than the world's, the primacy of national self-interest is a virtue, not a vice.

Thus Japan has developed a reputation for selfishness in foreign aid, even though it has become one of the world's largest donors. About 70 percent of its aid goes to China and other Asian countries where Japanese businesses are expanding. Programs with direct strings attached—once the mainstay of Japanese aid—have been mostly jettisoned. But as Ezra Vogel observes, "Although officially strings are no longer attached, terms are generally not attractive, feasibility studies often lead to delays or postponements, and locals often feel compelled to purchase products from Japanese companies attempting to expand local markets. Some cynics have charged that Japanese foreign aid is given less from genuine human compassion for the needy than from a desire not to appear overly selfish compared to other countries."[25]

Indochinese refugees adrift in Japan's own sea-lanes, let alone more distant African famine victims, have received what can only be described as paltry assistance from a nation that is the world's leading creditor. While Japan has announced that it hopes to assist developing countries with debt problems, it has taken few concrete actions. With nearly twice the assets of American banks, the Japanese banking industry's exposure to Third World debt is only half as large. In a sense, therefore, it faces only one-quarter the problem. Practically speaking, Japanese bankers see no need to take the lead in diffusing the crisis, even though their institutions have the resources to do so.

"In truth we have not done nearly enough to help the Third World," says Saburo Okita, a former Japanese foreign minister noted for a liberal humanitarianism that is rare in Japanese political circles. Okita, like a number of American economists, believes that to truly solve the global crisis of unbalanced trade and capital flows, Japan should be investing more heavily in less developed countries. If Japan could ease the Latin debt problem and help turn the economies of Mexico, Argentina, and Brazil around, the United States would rediscover large export markets in its own hemisphere. By reviving debt-drained Third World economies, Japan could promote global economic growth that would not require deficit-driven American stimulation for sustenance.

The "Okita Plan" calls for recycling $125 billion from Japan's trade surplus over the next five years toward the goal of aiding developing nations. That figure is three times more than what the Japanese government is now planning to spend even in its grandest programs. In spite of Okita's prestige—and the fact that the plan makes macroeconomic sense—it has found only amorphous political support. Okita himself says, "We Japanese have no experience with philanthropy. We must learn."

On a broad range of issues, Japanese business is distinguishable by its blatant economic self-interest. This was seen most clearly in the lax export controls that permitted Toshiba Machine to engage in its now infamous sale of strategic submarine-silencing equipment to the Soviets. To the executives of the Toshiba unit, the Soviet Union was simply another customer.

The same sentiment allows Japanese trading companies to set up shop in Hanoi and turn Japan into Vietnam's number-two trade partner, second only to the Soviet Union—even while the United States and Southeast Asian countries are trying to keep economic pressure on Vietnam to force a troop withdrawal from Cambodia. Similarly, Japan has become the biggest non–Soviet bloc trading partner with both Cuba and Nicaragua. "We've become dependent on Japanese technology the way we used to be dependent on American technology," a Sandinista official gladly points out in an effort to illustrate the folly of the U.S.-imposed trade embargo against his country.[26]

The realpolitik of the Sandinistas is quite accurate. Whether one approves of U.S. policy in these situations is not the question. What is important to note is that while America continues to act as if it were still the unchallenged leader of industrial world, Japan is not following. To be more precise, Japan's approach gives it a significant competitive advantage by allowing it to monopolize trade in countries where Washington has called American business home. The Japanese willingness to subordinate other questions to the imperative of trade is, in a sense, a more advanced outlook better suited to the new world environment than America's parochial moralism.

The next phase in the development of this issue will be played out in the 1990s over the Japanese relationship with the Soviet Union itself. Mikhail Gorbachev has repeatedly hinted that he would like to trade Soviet oil, gas, minerals, and timber for Japanese investment and technological know-how in opening up Siberia's vast reaches and retooling backward Soviet industry. The Siberian seaport of Nakhodka already has far more contact with Yokohama than with Moscow. At nearby Vostochny, a facility for what is expected to become the Soviet Union's leading port of the twenty-first century has been built with Japanese assistance. So far, Japan has increased trade with the Soviet Union without committing to a fundamental change in what has been an icy relationship. A Japan-Soviet rapprochement must first clear the hurdle of Tokyo's demand for the return of four islands in the Kurile chain occupied since the war. Gorbachev may offer to return at least two islands sometime in the near future.

There are those who believe Japan will use such an opportunity to play the Soviet card, thereby trumping American pressure and protectionist threats.

Part IV

FINAL RECKONING

10

Glimpses of the U.S. Economy in a Nipponized World

The Japanese feel victimized, the Americans feel exploited, and resentment is reciprocal.... If history is any guide, there can only be three outcomes to the emerging financial dilemma: war, bankruptcy or inflation

—Zbigniew Brzezinski, former assistant to the president for national security[1]

A Bloody Shakeout in Financial Services

Most of this book has focused on events of the recent past. Occasionally the discussion has detoured briefly to contemplate what lies ahead. Now the time has come to focus more closely on that question. Consideration of the future is speculative by definition, yet only by trying to look in that direction can we understand the magnitude of the changes taking place today and attempt to confront them sensibly.

Intuitively most Americans find something ominous about the thought of Japanese banks and securities firms dominating world finance. Yet we are reassured by many learned economists, business leaders, and politicians that there is nothing wrong with what is happening. Foreigners may own $1.5 trillion worth of U.S. assets, but that astounding sum is only a small fraction of total national wealth. While a few prime bits of America are sold off to Tokyo investors, the country as a whole is in no immediate danger of surrendering to a hostile takeover bid. In a paid advertising campaign, the Japanese

257

Chamber of Commerce in New York attempts to reassure those "worried that the Japanese presence may become so strong that it leads to economic domination" by suggesting that even when Japanese companies employ a million U.S. workers, their role in the U.S. economy will be "marginal rather than mainstream."[2] Anyone thinking carefully about Japanese involvement in the U.S. economy as a whole, or the financial services sector in particular, will be able to identify potential repercussions that are both positive and negative, although determining which will be more prevalent in the years ahead is a subject of intense debate.

Does it really matter, then, if Japanese financial firms exert a predominant role in the world financial economy? If the man in the street gets his car loan from Sumitomo Bank instead of Bank of America, or if his pension fund buys stocks from Nomura instead of Merrill Lynch, or if Daiwa's London operation proves more successful than Salomon's—will the impact be felt beyond the elite group of financial executives whose careers understandably rise and fall over such issues?

Between this year and next, the answer is no. Over time, the answer is that the impact will be very significant—not so much because Japanese financial services companies are gaining power while American companies are losing it, but because of the process that underlies that change: the enrichment of Japan and the erosion of American economic strength.

It is in the financial services area, however, that the change will be most sharply felt at first. As the pattern of growing Japanese influence unfolds, a bloody shakeout is likely to transpire. Jobs will be lost at American firms, profits narrowed, opportunities for growth lost, companies folded. The worst-case scenario for coming events could be similar to what happened in the U.S. auto industry in the 1970s, when several hundred thousand jobs were lost to Japanese competition, the profits of the most successful corporations in American history were squeezed to the bone, Chrysler nearly disappeared altogether, world markets that once provided a constant stream of surplus revenue dried up, and the ripple effect of closed plants and shuttered neighborhoods helped sound the death knell for smokestack America.

The U.S. financial services industry will lose a smaller percentage of jobs initially than the auto industry, since most Japanese financial companies operating in the United States tend to employ large American staffs. Instead the job losses will come over time as the field itself is commoditized and as the center of gravity in international transactions moves to the locus of investment capital—Tokyo.

The meaning of shrinkage in the financial sector will have no less impact on the U.S. economy as a whole than the contraction of the auto industry, however. In fact, it is likely to have a deeper influence, because the financial sector in recent times has generated a disproportionately large share of American wealth. The jobs lost will be higher paying and higher skilled; the companies whose power will be compromised, curtailed, or bankrupted are companies that have served as locomotives in the shift to a high value-added, information-intensive American service economy.

The weakening of the financial sector's health and profitability will be immediately echoed in telecommunications and in the computer industry, two growth businesses that for the last decade have consistently found strong demand for new products among bankers and brokers. Leadership positions now held by American companies in information age services such as databases, newsletters, and global information systems will be relinquished as Japanese financiers become the largest global users of such utilities and begin to buy them from Japanese suppliers.[3]

Downtown skylines of major U.S. cities, reshaped largely by booming financial services in the 1980s, will lose some of their vibrancy. Whatever excessive "wealth effect" remains in the wake of Black Monday is likely to disappear from Wall Street under the burden of competing with the Japanese. The psychological damage of losing still more ground to foreign competition—especially in a field as identified with the future as global finance—cannot be underestimated.

By itself, however, a weakened financial sector is not necessarily cataclysmic. After all, even the Big Three automakers are still alive and kicking, humbled as they may be, and the U.S. economy has managed to endure the body blows of the Japanese industrial challenge and still survive. In this sense the growth of Nomura and Sumitomo at the expense of Bank of America or Merrill Lynch is about as significant as the growth of Toyota at the expense of General Motors. The change is important, it will have severe economic repercussions, and it raises a host of other questions alongside it. But the American economy can still manage to absorb it.

What is potentially far more devastating to American interests is the accumulation of financial resources in Japan that is merely *symbolized* by the rise of Japanese financial services companies. Companies like Nomura or Sumitomo are really just intermediaries in the process, albeit extremely powerful in their own right. Questions about who profits from the commissions on trading stock, who makes the point spread on bank lending, or who gets a percentage of a merger deal are vital to those working in the financial sector. But they pale in comparison with the question of who has the money to invest in the first place and what the strategies for those investments will be. It is in those areas where the most far-reaching transition will take place.

The Coming Decline of American Living Standards

The most arresting implication of Japan's growing wealth and America's growing debt is the pressure this situation puts on American living standards—both absolute and relative. U.S. economic growth, hamstrung by foreign debt service costs, could actually turn to negative real numbers in the years ahead, with direct downward consequences for personal income and household purchasing power. Today Americans are annually consuming about 3 percent more than they produce. As the invisible macroeconomic hand begins to force the nation to live within its means instead of beyond them, the belt tightening will be painful. Even with a lift from weak dollar exports, American economic benchmarks are almost certain to show a sharp relative decline when compared with their Japanese equivalents. It is worth noting that should the dollar fall below one hundred yen (a distinct possibility even in the short run), Japan, with half the population, could wind up enjoying a GNP larger than that of the United States measured in dollar terms.

Japanese investment patterns, of course, won't be responsible for the dramatic changes ahead. Deep structural problems of the U.S. economy, as well as economic competition from many foreign quarters, are parts of the mix. But the Japanese role will very likely be the most visible force. Part of the public perception will be derived from firsthand encounters with the growing presence of powerful Japanese companies and individuals on U.S. soil and in American daily life. In addition, as technology shrinks the global village still further in the next decade, the media will keep millions of people constantly aware of the chasm between Japanese progress and American decline.

Some of the ways that chasm could reveal itself include the following:

- *The world will go off the dollar standard.* The combination of America's debtor status, a volatile dollar, and Japan's new role as leading creditor will almost certainly mean the demise of the U.S. dollar as the world's key currency. After years of shunning an international role for the yen, the Japanese are now ready. "The yen undoubtedly should take over part of the role now played by the dollar," says Yusuke Kashiwagi, the chairman of the Bank of Tokyo and one of Japan's most influential financiers.[4] It is unlikely that the dollar will be immediately replaced by the yen. A joint dollar-yen-mark standard or other currency "basket" is more probable. But the loss of the dollar standard, as suggested in chapter 1, will translate into higher international business costs, greater borrowing burdens for the U.S. government and business community, and far greater inflationary pressures from changing world currency and commodity prices. Meanwhile, Japan's continued economic growth, combined with its well-controlled financial system, its locomotive role in world investment and trade, and its prominent position in the Pacific Rim, could lead to a yen standard in Asia. Eventually, as a volatile world economy seeks a tangible common currency, the yen *could* well assume that function—enhancing Japan's competitive position and undermining the United States still further.

- *U.S. domestic manufacturing will be squeezed.* The growing Japanese-owned sector of American industry, driven to manufacture in the United States by the politics of the trade deficit and able to do so easily because of the yen's strength, will exert an extreme new competitive pressure on many businesses. Some American companies will simply not be able to survive with Japanese competitors down the interstate introducing new manufacturing systems, expanding facilities at a lower cost of capital, and buying market share inside the United States through ruthless price cutting. Meanwhile, although Japanese companies will pay taxes and provide jobs, at least some of the profits they earn will be repatriated to Japan to further stoke the engines of Japanese global expansion. This will create a new kind of capital drain out of the U.S. economy.

- *American companies will lose profits from abroad.* Some American manufacturers will gain greater export revenues over the next few years because of the weak dollar, but their ability to make new investments in international manufacturing operations will be hampered by strong foreign currencies. While Japanese companies in the 1990s pursue a strategy designed to ensure their proficiency at sourcing components, manufacturing, and marketing in all corners of the globe simultaneously, American companies won't be able to afford such worldwide integration. Over time the result will be a marked loss of efficiency and hence profitability for American participants in an increasingly unified world marketplace. Profits from foreign investments, invisible as they tend to be, have historically buoyed the American standard of living well beyond its domestically generated level. In 1987 Americans became net debtors for the first time in the "invisible income" account—paying out more in interest and dividends than the economy received from abroad. This trend presages a "double whammy" for per capita income: not only will Americans be increasingly burdened by foreign debts in the future, but traditionally high contributions to the economy from foreign investment income will begin to dry up.

- *American and Japanese workers will "trade places."* The erosion of corporate profitability will hinder American industry's expansion, especially into costly development of new products, processes, and technologies. The debt-burdened federal budget will not be able to play the role required in spearheading a drive toward new industries. As a result the U.S. economy will be redirected backward toward competing in traditional industries based on a moderate cost of labor, rather than forward into new areas of added value that can sustain higher labor costs. Japan, meanwhile, by exporting low- and moderate-skilled jobs to foreign countries, will be forced to move its own domestic production farther up the ladder of technology and skill. Since it has both the necessary capital resources and the planning capabilities, it is likely to be successful. The result could be a substantial role reversal involving incomes, quality of work, and quality of life. Japanese workers will come to dominate more of the world's brain industries, while American competitiveness will rely heavily on keeping hourly wages down in "brawn" industries.

- *The consumer society will consume less as prices rise.* Price increases of Japanese and other foreign goods were held to a minimum during the fall of the dollar from 1985 to 1987. But by fighting tooth and nail to maintain market share during those years, the Japanese staved off a resurgence of U.S. industry and won a renewed capacity to set the pricing agenda. What's more, now that demand is growing in the domestic Japanese market, manufacturers there are less reliant on foreign sales and therefore freer to raise export prices. Much of the appearance of abundance in American homes is a direct outgrowth of years of importing cheap, high-quality consumer items from Japan and other countries. As those items continue to rise in price, consumption will eventually be curtailed. As Lester Thurow puts it, Americans "will have become workers for the rest of the world, while the rest of the world will have become the owners of America."[5]

- *Japan will extract better competitive terms from the United States.* As America becomes increasingly reliant on Japanese capital, and as Japanese industry becomes an increasingly important force in U.S. economic life, the political ground will shift: instead of emphasis on American demands for market access in Japan, the Japanese will be arguing their agenda for changes they desire abroad. Already, Japanese business groups have made it known they want key personnel associated with companies investing in America to be able to travel without U.S. visas. They are also pushing for a limit on product liability awards to consumers injured by defective Japanese products, an end to unitary tax laws whereby states tax foreign companies on their worldwide profits, and an end to regulations that require corporations traded on U.S. stock exchanges to give detailed sector-by-sector breakdowns of their business. Japanese lobbyists are leading the fight against new legislation to require foreigners to disclose large-scale holdings of American assets. Early in 1988, Keidanren, the leading Japanese business organization, announced an initiative to bring two hundred corporations together to coordinate U.S. investment strategy with the ostensible purpose of reducing friction and calming American anxiety about growing Japanese investments. The very thought of two hundred giant Japanese corporations meeting together to collectively address strategic issues about American investment was hardly reassuring, even if the group's goal was well intentioned. The intention, however, was somewhat in doubt. The first specific proposed by Keidanren—repeal of Alaska's unitary tax—certainly sounded more like a demand for concessions to Japanese interests than a method for easing American fears. Such demands are just the tip of the iceberg. Noting that Japanese leaders vowed to block an economic summit if Washington didn't take stronger budget-cutting action, *Business Week* observes, "Americans had better get used to tough talk, because a major restructuring of U.S.-Japanese relations is under way."[6]

- *U.S.-Japan financial brinksmanship will be punishing.* Bearing in mind that the recent frenzy of Japan bashing has taken place in a period of relative *boom* for the U.S. economy, one can only guess how emotionally charged the situation could become in the next period of economic *contraction.* But if the United States takes retaliatory actions against Japan, the Japanese are likely to respond in kind. Threats and counterthreats could lead to concerted efforts to withdraw Japanese support from the U.S. bond market, the dollar, and the stock market. The fallout might include sudden interest rate jolts, stock market spikes, gyrating real estate values, and bankruptcies of large-scale financial institutions.

- *Inflation will take a heavy toll.* Apart from any concerted political move by Japanese investors out of the U.S. bond market, a natural dwindling of their enthusiasm for U.S. government bonds is inevitable. The more American debt obligations they accumulate (especially in the absence of real deficit-cutting measures in Washington), the riskier their portfolio becomes. The worldwide expansion of Japanese financial services companies now offers Tokyo investors a much wider choice of attractive options. The Japanese won't desert the American bond market altogether, except in a political skirmish. But as they move more money into equity, real estate, and acquisition of American businesses, they will reduce their bond buying accordingly. Even a small reduction in Japanese support for Treasury bonds will push interest rates up dramatically and rekindle inflation. Hyperinflation and the "Argentina syndrome" can't be ruled out as the Japanese press U.S. borrowers to denominate more debt in yen.

The spiral of economic decline inherent in the above-cited trends —even if all of them don't come about together, and even if some of them are mitigated by improvements in other areas—could bring about severe, sustained depression. At the very least, America will stop generating the quantity of newly affluent citizens witnessed in the 1980s. The accepted norms of middle-class life (home ownership, college education for children, an abundance of consumer goods) could move beyond the means of many. Even in that scenario, America will remain a relatively rich country. But like Britain in its period of decline, the sense of limits imposed from outside will be tangible. Much that was once possible in America will simply no longer be feasible.

The *Nichibei* Economy, G-2, and the U.S.-Japan Divorce

History teaches that wealth is never judged in absolute terms, only in relative terms.[7] Americans in the 1990s will undoubtedly own more material goods than Americans in the 1950s at the height of U.S. power in the world, but they will perceive themselves as living *less* well than Japanese in the 1990s. And that is what the popular mind will focus on. For mirroring America's economic decline will be Japan's continued rise, as its financial assets are turned into investments in new technologies and the complete renovation of its domestic infrastructure.

Two alternatives are likely to present themselves as this contradiction intensifies. Either the United States will be forced to develop a much closer cooperative relationship with Japan, based on a more clearly defined shared agenda, or else the United States will be pushed into sharper conflict and rivalry with Japan.

As to the first alternative, some strategists and economists both in the United States and Japan see salvation in the so-called *nichibei* economy—a merged symbiosis of Japan and the United States. The word itself is made up of two Japanese characters signifying sun and rice—Japan, the land of the rising sun, and America, land of amber waves of grain—*rice,* in the Japanese mind. The *nichibei* economy is already a reality in broad strokes: the United States provides Japan's defense, Japan enjoys access to American markets and invests its trade surpluses back in the United States to help keep the economy going. But as economic imbalances grow, this "deal" no longer suffices. On the brainstorming list of an upgraded *nichibei* accommodation are ideas like a transpacific common market, a joint U.S.-Japan currency, joint industries, and shared defense burdens.

Thinking along these lines, former National Security Adviser Zbigniew Brzezinski has called for "a new global bargain" and the evolution of his own version of *nichibei,* which he dubs "Amerippon." In Brzezinski's view this would take the form of "an informal complex of overlapping elites, corporate structures, and increasingly joint political planning" with the United States and Japan effectively "commingling . . . business and financial institutions."[8]

C. Fred Bergsten, another former Carter administration official, has suggested the formation of "G-2"—a joint U.S.-Japan approach to world leadership that would replace the unwieldy "G-7" and "G-5" groups that include other major Western powers. Crumbling American hegemony, Bergsten has suggested, could feasibly be replaced with the "bigemony" of the United States and Japan leading the global economy together.[9]

Nichibei, G-2, and similar ideas offer much food for thought but are also fraught with dangers. From the strategic perspective, "bigemony" is not likely to be appreciated either by American allies in Europe or by American friends in Asia worried by Japan's growing strength. More relevant, perhaps, is the danger that in drawing Japan so close to the United States, dropping all barriers to its participation in the U.S. economy and commingling industries, the American grip will slip, and Japan will gain its best opportunity yet to seize the advantage, just as the United States wrested the balance of power from the Anglo-American alliance.

Despite the pitfalls, a carefully crafted *nichibei* solution is preferable to the more likely outcome of the intensified financial imbalances: *the U.S.-Japan divorce.* Faced with a blighted American economy whose problems can easily be blamed on Japan, the populism of protectionism is apt to hold much more appeal for politicians than a further deepening of the U.S.-Japan partnership. Here again the financial question poses a startling new wrinkle. The American financial services business is more powerful and better connected politically than the auto industry was over the last two decades. Today, leaders of American finance harbor the dream of dominating the globalized money game. As they begin to wake up to the nightmare that they have not only lost on a global scale, but lost significant ground to the Japanese right inside the United States, they could become as fiercely protectionist as they are now globalist. Nor will they have a difficult time making their case. The independence and stability of the U.S. financial system is certainly perceived as something much more strategic to defend than the auto or steel industries. And once politicians begin to think along such lines, the recognition that Japanese investments are mostly scraps of paper and blips on computer screens will make them tempting targets for debt repudiation or protectionist taxes.

Could such a mood set in among Americans who pride themselves on an open economy and open society? David Hale, chief economist for Kemper Financial Services, reminds us:

> Although it may seem hard to believe today, during America's previous incarnation as a debtor nation in the nineteenth century, there was intense hostility to British financial power because populist politicians convinced millions of Americans that the Bank of England had bribed the U.S. Congress into pegging the dollar to the gold standard in order to produce large profits for foreign bondholders.
>
> In 1896, William Jennings Bryan won the Democratic presidential nomination with a spellbinding oration denouncing British monetary policy and the "financial servitude to London" resulting from the gold standard.

According to Hale, a "similar sense of outrage" could arise when contemporary Americans realize the degree to which today's politicians are allowing foreign investors to influence the U.S. economy. Hale suggests American television should incorporate into its election coverage "a panel of Japanese life insurance portfolio managers to address the American people on the policy changes they will demand before putting new funds into the U.S. securities markets next year. Such a program probably would give American voters more information about the direction of economic policy after 1988 than they appear likely to get from the candidates themselves."[10]

Although it is important to recall the William Jennings Bryan experience, it is also important to remember that, despite his abilities as a "great communicator," he was *not* elected. Thus, although financial protectionism may be inevitable as a trend in debtor America, victory for those subscribing to it is far from certain. But if it does gain momentum, its consequences could be more perilous than simply erecting trade barriers on imported goods. To attempt to curtail Japanese production or to attempt to reduce the power of Japanese banks and investors a decade from now—when Japanese companies will already be manufacturing most of their output for the U.S. market inside the United States and when Japanese institutions will occupy a commanding position in the financial structure—will not be possible without risking the fundamental stability and guarantees of American capitalism. To levy special quotas or taxes on foreign-owned companies at a point when they will be fully integrated with the rest of the U.S. economy—or to take even more extreme measures, such as defaulting on Japanese-owned American bonds and loans or nationalizing Japanese holdings—would thrust a highly globalized world economy into lethal rounds of market closings and retaliation. An all-out financial war could be started that way. It could escalate very rapidly toward the total collapse of a world financial system that is, at bottom, an incredibly fragile set of promises, beliefs, and confidences underwriting trillions upon trillions of dollars' and yen worth of value.

Nor should Americans allow themselves the luxury of believing that only the American side has the power or the potential inclination to initiate a rupture in the U.S.-Japan relationship. Even while investment in the United States is booming, MITI has initiated a high-powered research effort designed to "seek ways for Japan to move from heavy reliance on the United States to develop the ability to survive independently," according to one Japanese press report. The report says a "rapidly growing" number of executives agree with the president of a high-tech company who declares, "Perhaps we have been suffering a grand illusion about the United States. The belief that Japan cannot exist without a close relationship with America may simply have been a fantasy."[11]

History holds many examples of how the scales of economic balance tip and new global leaders emerge. From ancient Egypt, Greece, and Rome through the days of Spanish, Dutch, British, and American empires, each experience has been different. Yet there has been one constant. No new empire has replaced another without the attendant circumstances of international chaos, economic crisis, and war.

"The great wars of history . . . are the outcome, direct or indirect, of the unequal growth of nations," asserted Halford John Mackinder, a founding father of modern geopolitical thought.[12] The experience of the twentieth century reinforces that generalization. After World War I, Britain could no longer exert the stabilizing influence it once had.

The United States, like Japan today, was obviously a rising power but lacked the global leadership tools to step immediately into Britain's shoes. Between the wars, protectionism choked off world trade, economies stagnated, and the fascist Axis formed. All these factors helped ignite the conflagration of World War II.

To some astute historians, the critical factor that exacerbated all the others was the global disequilibrium ushered in by Britain's decline. Those same historians would look at present circumstances and conclude that we are about to enter a remarkably similar period of time.

11

Money, Power, and Guns: The Birth of the Japanese Empire

Today, the basis of the world's wealth is shifting from natural resources to advanced technology. The natural resource superpowers are watching the relative worth of their assets dwindle while nations with intelligent human resources are expanding their trade and accumulating surpluses.... The population of the United States is now twice that of Japan, but both have a roughly equal number of engineers. The United States has a higher illiteracy rate and more citizens on welfare.... In America it is apparently possible to earn a high school or even college diploma and still not be able to read a map or a menu....

Japan's new supercreditor status, its recent technological surpluses, and its continuing general trade surpluses are just precursors to what may come in the future.... As we approach the twenty-first century, Japan's reserves of highly trained and educated workers will be the asset most fundamental to our ability to create wealth.

—Kenichi Ohmae, managing director, McKinsey & Co., Tokyo[1]

The Revenge of the *Ronin*

General MacArthur's occupation staff made thousands of changes in Japan after the war, but one of the most intriguing was banning performances of *Chushingura,* the great Kabuki play.

Known in English as *The Tale of the 47 Ronin,* this work is adapted

from an episode in early eighteenth-century history in which a certain
Lord Asano plotted the murder of another nobleman, Lord Kira.
Asano's attack on Kira failed; he succeeded only in wounding him.
When the shogun learned of Asano's incredible breach of feudal
ethics, he ordered Asano to commit *seppuku* (ritual suicide).

The suicide of Asano meant that his loyal samurai retainers became
masterless, wandering *ronin*. For years they plotted revenge. In a
daring mission they finally burst into Kira's house on a snowy winter
night and murdered him. Impressed with the unswerving loyalty the
ronin had shown to their master by fulfilling his wish to murder Kira,
the shogun allowed the forty-seven murderers to die honorably by
committing *seppuku* as well.

The *ronin* became instant folk heroes. It wasn't long before the
drama was written down, immortalizing them forever. The themes of
loyalty and revenge that underlie the story have turned it into one of
the central shared myths of Japanese culture. After World War II, "the
Allies did not want the Japanese to entertain the idea of vengeance for
their total defeat," according to one Japanese commentator.[2] And so
the evocative force of *Chushingura* was banished from the stage.

In today's Kabuki repertoires, *Chushingura* is back. It is also celebrated in puppet theaters, comic books, movies, and ballets. "One
just cannot avoid *Chushingura*," Ian Buruma has written. "Rarely, if
ever, has one story captured the imagination of an entire nation to this
degree."[3]

As theater, *Chushingura* is a rich work, layered with meaning and
implication. But at its heart it is a story about the virtue to be demonstrated by fulfilling a master's interrupted mission, regardless of how
ignoble the mission itself might have been to begin with. It is, in
short, about the glory to be gained in seeking and obtaining revenge.

In a country where *Chushingura* is the quintessential cultural work,
the idea of Japan's imperial destiny cannot be assumed to have van-
ished simply because the war was lost. A great and proud society that
endured not only the humiliation of military defeat and foreign occupation four decades ago, but continues in 1988 to be forced to listen
to American admonishments as if the United States still occupied
Japan, will not go on practicing the alien method of "turning the other
cheek" forever.

At the moment, it is fashionable in America to believe that the
Japanese—clever, self-effacing, consensus-building souls we know

them to be—have made the crafty decision to preserve all the blessings of their powerful industrial and financial economy without subjecting themselves to the costs and burdens of maintaining an empire. Scholars commenting on the causes of contemporary global instability note that while U.S. hegemony is breaking up, the Japanese, Germans, and other new economic powers are reluctant to fill the vacuum. America, it is said, is a debtor nation with the impulse to leadership that emanates from the habit of having been a creditor for so long; Japan, although it has become a supercreditor, still maintains the outlook of frugal insularity rooted in its past.

Harvard's Edwin O. Reischauer, dean of American Japan specialists and former U.S. ambassador to Tokyo, insists that the process of becoming a superpower requires belief in a global mission—something akin to the American zeal exhibited in "making the world safe for democracy." This, he says, the Japanese lack. "The Japanese have none of this sense of empire. They have trouble even joining a United Nations peacekeeping force."[4]

The relatively comforting image of a Japan that doesn't want to challenge the United States directly for world leadership is reinforced by public comments of Japanese spokesmen themselves. "We hope the United States can recover and Japan will be the second fiddle. Being number two is really quite pleasant," Yutaka Kosai, president of Japan Economic Research Center, told *The New York Times*.[5]

Such sentiments are genuine—for now. The Japanese economic machine may already be number one in that it works better and more productively than its American counterpart and is accumulating greater wealth as a result. But Japan still has far to go before it eclipses the United States in an overall sense. It must complete a massive restructuring of the domestic economy, insert itself more deeply into the international political structure, give its breakthrough scientific projects a chance to achieve critical mass, develop the Tokyo financial center further, and establish an independent military force capable of providing most of its own defense. In doing all this, Japanese businessmen must be careful that their expansionary verve continues to be tempered with restraint (as it has been up until now) so that their power rises gradually and quietly without triggering too severe a backlash.

Consciously or unconsciously, Japan is already embarked on these goals. As the Japanese pursue them in the 1990s, their interests are well served by a United States that continues to lead, however problematically. If, for example, American banks absorb most of the burden for Third World debt, developing countries will become safer havens for Japanese investment down the road. If, in its waning days as global hegemon, the United States can manage to keep the sealanes open for another decade, Japan will gain time to reduce its dependence on Mideast oil. If an American president can conclude a disarmament agreement with Moscow, Japan will become less vulnerable to attack from its Soviet neighbor. Perhaps even more important, superpower disarmament lowers the threshold Japan will need to match to become a major military power itself.

Japanese who harbor grand ambitions also must prepare the subjective ground. Asia's fears of a militarist revival in Tokyo, whipped to hysterical levels by the mere publication of Japanese textbooks whitewashing events of fifty years ago, must be significantly neutralized. The Japanese people's own instincts toward isolationism and pacifism must be realigned.

Neither of those tasks is quite the obstacle some experts have suggested. As Japan becomes Asia's main investor, trade partner, source of technology, and purveyor of development aid, even the countries with bitter World War II memories will be forced to accept the politics of Japanese expansionism. This is already happening in the Philippines, for example, where Japan backs the fragile Aquino government with half a billion dollars a year in aid. A recent poll showed that even though Filipinos more than almost any other group of Asians believe Japan will inevitably become a military giant again, 91 percent approve of Japan's role in Asia just the same.[6]

As for the Japanese people themselves, they are already being inundated with the concept of *kokusaika* (internationalization). No important business meeting or political speech is complete without the requisite appeals to dispense with insular horizons. Internationalizing Japan was the single most often expressed theme of 1987 Japanese newspaper editorials. In the West it is assumed that this talk is a healthy trend, making the Japanese more open-minded, open-hearted, and open-marketed. In reality it is a double-edged sword. By breaking down the last vestiges of the postwar Yoshida Doctrine, under which Japan deliberately shunned global politics and deliberately forswore ambitions beyond its borders, the climate for revival of an imperial thrust is fostered.

To assume that because Japan doesn't *yet* articulate or manifest a clear vision of global empire implies such a trend won't emerge in the future would be a dangerous miscalculation. Today, the *ronin* are still wandering. Their moment is yet to come.

From Financial Power to Superpower

No categoric rules exist to differentiate an ordinary great power from a superpower. Taiwan has accumulated over $70 billion in foreign currency reserves—about as much as Japan—but nobody thinks this makes Taiwan a superpower. Dutch investors own more U.S. assets than the Japanese, yet because the Dutch haven't been a great power for several hundred years—and perhaps also because the racial issue is not present—the "Dutch invasion" is scarcely noticed in the U.S. business community. Meanwhile, the Soviet Union, strapped for hard currency, owning no U.S. assets worth speaking of, and notable among industrial nations chiefly for its economic backwardness, is without question a superpower.

The inquiry by historians, geographers, and political economists into how empires rise and fall reached its high point in the period of Pax Britannica. The British were unafraid to admit that theirs *was* an empire; indeed, they reveled in its glory and created a prodigious body of literature to explain and justify what they had built. In the period of Pax Americana, however, democracy-conscious Americans have shunned the notion that an American empire even exists. We prefer to believe that the postwar world has followed our baton chiefly out of its desire to emulate our unique democratic institutions, our freewheeling life-style, and our standard of living. These subjective factors do, of course, exert a powerful pull. But the real basis of American power has more to do with the way the United States has monopolized the Western world's military and economic muscle and, since World War II, created a nexus of international relationships to reinforce that situation.

Oxford historian Paul Streeten has advanced a list of characteristics that permitted the United States to dominate the postwar world order: an export surplus with which to influence the flow of trade, the ability to supply long-term capital to spark world development, industrial supremacy, technological leadership, and the military strength to secure peace.[7] These factors offer useful starting points for considering whether Japan has the potential to create an empire that could supplant America as a dominant force in world affairs.

As to export surpluses and the supply of long-term capital to meet global development needs, little needs to be said here. In this book we have seen that Japanese statistics in these areas are huge positive numbers, while the comparable American statistics are huge negatives. Japan's trade surplus and global investment surplus, moreover, are greater than the surpluses of America in its prime.

Turning to industrial strength, Japan has already attained rough parity with the United States in per capita output—something economists didn't anticipate for another decade or more. A combination of the yen's strength, the current restructuring of Japan's domestic economy, and a consistently higher rate of growth than the United States's now makes possible an idea that a few years ago was absolutely unthinkable: Japan, with half America's population, could approach the United States not just in per capita output, but in absolute size of GNP.

In the textbook view, Japanese industry should now be drawing increased profit down from its huge prior investment in technology and manufacturing systems. But because Japanese industrial companies are so capital rich, they have actually increased their rate of investment in new technology. This is true even in fields where they already lead the world, even where the investment is extravagantly costly, and even when it offers only small enhancements over systems in place. The Japanese know full well that it is now exactly those small steps that will make the difference. They can afford to take them, despite what might be viewed as prohibitive costs in other industrial countries.

Automobile production provides a clear picture of this trend. The Japanese automotive industry's widespread deployment of robotic systems brought the average number of man-hours needed to build a car down to 100 in 1987, compared with 150 in the United States. The American auto industry, meanwhile, finally launched a desperately needed campaign of modernization, retooling, and rationalization in the mid-1980s. These changes are expected to be paying off fully by the early 1990s, when the number of man-hours needed to produce a car in the United States is expected to fall to the current Japanese level of one hundred. But the Japanese aren't standing still. They are continuing to invest heavily in incremental modifications to plants that are already state of the art. By the time one-hundred-hour cars are a reality in the United States, eighty-hour cars will be rolling off Japanese assembly lines.[8]

In computer chips, the cost of a world-class fabrication facility has already pushed over $200 million, leaving many entrepreneurial American companies in this business with no choice but to ship designs to Japanese "fabs" for production. When X-ray lithography and other advanced production methods become standard early in the 1990s, building a fab will cost $500 million to $1 billion. Big Japanese electronics companies are prepared to make those investments, but most surviving U.S. chipmakers are not.

Other aspects of the computer industry are undergoing a similar rapid escalation in the cost to compete. Even in basic desktop workstations and peripherals, "the main weight of the cost structure is shifting toward the front end of the product cycle," notes former IBMer Charles Ferguson, now MIT's resident expert on technology policy. "Architecture and design are now more capital intensive, using large computer and software systems to increase the complexity and productivity of the design process." Thinly capitalized companies born out of Silicon Valley's gold rush years are ill-suited to this environment. Ferguson's conclusion: "The Japanese are moving toward control of semiconductors and computers. This will be a watershed in geopolitical relations as well as in Japanese industrial power. For the first time, the U.S. no longer will dominate the critical technologies needed for military power and future industrial development."[9]

Aptitude for developing new manufacturing technology—and the availability of investment capital to permit industrywide introduction of new processes—is increasingly recognized in the United States as a supercompetitive mix of strengths in the Japanese system. What Americans once regarded with some disdain as a mere proclivity for "adaptation" by Japanese engineers is now recognized, at least in the professional engineering community, as a potent form of innovation. American science continues to make world-shaking breakthroughs. But the route to commercializing them as often as not now passes through Japan, where cost-effective, quality-controlled productive processes make the difference between brilliant ideas and real-life products. As a result, the United States now suffers a trade deficit with Japan in high-tech electronics.[10]

In the race to commercialize the hottest of all new technologies—

the ever-warmer superconductor—Japan moved into the lead almost overnight. Four days after the fateful February 1987 announcement at the University of Houston that American researcher Ching-Wu Paul Chu had broken the barrier to liquid nitrogen (a key experiment accentuating the near-term commercial viability of the technology), a superconductivity research consortium was launched in Japan made up of the country's leading electronics companies and university and government labs. "The objective is to organize industry to get the jump on the West in applications and commercialization for a huge new market," reported the *Nihon Keizai Shimbun*.[11]

Houston's Chu worries that Japan's approach, spearheaded by MITI, could lead to victory. "We cannot afford not to move the same way as the Japanese," he warns.[12] Yet the Japanese lead is growing in financial support for superconductivity research, in government-level coordination, and in patents applied for.

Japan will continue to use its capital advantage to gain greater dominance on the applied side of science. But it is also beginning to fund programs with the potential to wrest leadership away from the great reserve of U.S. strength—basic research.

The proverbial notion of "knowledge as power" has taken on a new meaning in the information age. The most productive and wealthy societies of the future are likely to be those that best cultivate the conditions necessary to gain economic advantage from the new frontiers of science. It is quite possible that tomorrow's breakthroughs in superconductivity, artificial intelligence, recombinant DNA, new materials, space exploration, or robotics could reshape the world's power balance more profoundly than the computer revolution or the development of nuclear energy.

Nearly one-third of all patents awarded by the U.S. patent office go to Japanese nationals and the top three recipients of *American* patents in 1987 were all Japanese—Canon, Hitachi, and Toshiba. A new method for quantifying progress in science suggests that Japanese patents are actually more important and innovative than American patents, based on the number of times other inventors cite Japanese patent applications in their own work.[13]

Only in this decade has Japan publicly enunciated the goal of becoming a world leader in basic science. But the change has already proven remarkable. "Japan is transforming itself from a nation of imitators into one of innovators," reported science writer Walter Sullivan after a 1987 visit. He saw dramatic evidence of advances in studying materials under high pressure, probing the aging process, and developing rockets for space exploration.[14] At the Tsukuba Science City, researchers are using the most powerful particle accelerator of its kind to chase the elusive top quark; elsewhere, Japanese scientists have played a key role in capturing data about neutrinos and other obscure bits of matter.

MITI's project to develop a "fifth generation" approach to computer languages and artificial intelligence has made modest progress. A still-hazy Japanese government–sponsored "sixth generation" project promises to bring together exotic software concepts with new hardware designs and biologically synthesized materials to reproduce human sensory functions on a chip. In building costly synchrotrons (the devices necessary to produce X rays capable of etching chips with one thousand times more circuitry than today), Tokyo is financially committed to world leadership. In areas from ceramic engines to magnetically levitated trains to protein engineering, Japanese research sets the global standards.

The popular American stereotype of Japan's hierarchy-conscious society as one that fails to promote the right atmosphere for creative individuals has historic validity—aptly summarized by Susumu Tonegawa, the MIT researcher who, on winning the Nobel Prize for Medicine in 1987, declared, "Had I stayed in a Japanese university, I may not have been able to do this kind of work."[15] But the situation is changing, in part because Japan's needs are changing. For the last forty years a mother lode of American research lay unexploited—just waiting for the Japanese to mine it, refine it, and come up with useful products based on it. Today, however, a Japanese expert on science policy explains, "As Japan becomes more competitive, it becomes increasingly difficult to find superior technology in the rest of the world."[16] The Japanese have no choice but to become pioneers.

The relationship between finance and science has undergone a momentous shift. The scale of scientific research today makes it a capital-intensive field. Scientists working in many areas know where they want to go, they can see how to get there, but they can't raise the capital to do it. Genetic engineers, for example, are in general agreement that it is possible to "map" the entire human genome, releasing a tremendous amount of information about the basic fabric of life in the process. But it will cost billions of dollars to do the work, and the commercial value of the results is uncertain. Should it be done?

It is likely that future Japanese answers to questions like that will be yes, while future American answers will be equivocal. The financial resources will be available in Japan and unavailable elsewhere. This pattern is already emerging in biotechnology.

"Biotech research consumes much time and money, with payback far in the future," observes *The Wall Street Journal*. "This isn't a problem for most of the Japanese players, because they tend to be huge corporations loaded with cash from their other operations. But many of the most promising American biotechnology firms are small and don't have any profitable businesses to sustain them. . . .

"Most perilously, large Japanese corporations are bankrolling some hard-pressed American start-up firms in exchange for a look at their best scientific secrets. 'The American R&D companies . . . need the money,' says Yaichi Ayukawa, a prominent Japanese venture capitalist with an American doctorate. 'They're really hungry. They make a deal with the Japanese. But then the Japanese tap you, strip you down. And three or four years later, the American side doesn't know what's going on.' "[17]

Japan's financial advantages are never far from the surface in the competition to unlock the secrets of science. While the U.S., European, and Soviet space programs dwarf Japan's beginning efforts, Tokyo's National Space Development Agency (NASDA) has mapped plans for a space shuttle in the not-too-distant future. NASDA's twenty-first-century program calls for building space stations, factories, and colonies to capitalize on the special properties of the orbiting environment for manufacturing pharmaceutical products, semiconductors, alloys, ceramics, and new materials.

Just when the American NASA program faces huge political hurdles in securing appropriate funding for continued U.S. leadership in space, Japanese space scientists find themselves in a golden age, with Tokyo earmarking $40 billion for space research over the next thirteen years. Public enthusiasm is so high that even a tax-soaked citizenry appears ready to pay more for Japanese advances. The current per capita taxpayer contribution to the space program is $6.66 per year, but "people tell me they would gladly spend $20 or $30," claims the director of Japan's space center.[18]

The list of scientific fronts on which Japan is likely to rival or even outperform the United States in the twenty-first century could go on at length. But perhaps just as important to future technological leadership is Japan's human interface with the advances in technology now being made. The Japanese educational system, while it fails the Western test of inculcating "creativity" and "individuality," far outstrips American public education in the goal of delivering high school graduates who are literate and knowledgeable in the areas deemed essential by their society. If one assumes that widespread literacy—technological as well as linguistic—will be a prerequisite of a successful information age economy, then one must expect Japan will hold a powerful advantage.

The fact that Japan's population is half America's is far less relevant than that both countries graduate almost the same number of engineers annually. Or that a large number of Japanese scientists can read American publications in English, while only an obscure handful of American scientists can follow the Japanese literature. Or that thirteen thousand Japanese are studying the best of what America has to offer in U.S. universities, while only eight hundred Americans are now studying in Japan. Or that Japanese companies routinely endow chairs at leading U.S. universities and have first access to some of the best new American research, while only the most visionary American companies have any means of benefiting from Japan's expanding research efforts.

A chilling metaphor for what may lie ahead comes from the classroom: only half the students at a California state college can locate Japan on a map.[19] At a working-class Tokyo junior high school, however, 100 percent of students know exactly where to find the United States.

Style of the Empire

In the above discussion, we have touched on most of Streeten's characteristics of hegemonic power, and we shall return in a moment to military power. But first it might be appropriate to examine another superpower characteristic: the ability to inspire a global following based on the relevance of a particular national culture to the period of history in which it rises. This is by no means the primary building block of empire. As suggested before, American observers tend to excessively overweight such subjective issues in trying to understand the eminent place of the United States in the postwar world. Nevertheless it is an important secondary factor.

British leadership in the period of Pax Britannica was accepted in distant corners of the world not only because of the presence of British gunboats, but also because the fruits of the Industrial Revolution, the parliamentary political system, and the ideology of free trade had a resonant appeal in their day, just as American democracy, technology, and popular culture have more recently. Even the Soviet empire draws a certain portion of its strength from the fact that people in the countries aligned with it still believe Moscow to be their Mecca.

In looking at Japan's unique, inward-directed culture, many in the West assume that the "Japanese way" could never exert the kind of universal appeal of the "American way." And yet all around us it is beginning to do just that. The vogue of "Japanese management theory" in the late seventies and early eighties indicated that even zealous American patriots at the top of big corporations could come under the spell of Japan's highly rational approach to industrial organization.

Infatuation with Japanese management theory has died down, but ideas derived from the Japanese model have become deeply rooted in some American businesses. At NUMMI, the General Motors–Toyota joint venture on the site of a failed former GM plant in California, productivity and quality standards above the American auto industry's norm are attributed to the Japanese influence. Sematech, the Austin-based consortium of leading American chipmakers funded by the U.S. government, is a direct attempt to compete with the Japanese on their own terms by replicating the shared-interest approach of Japan's electronics companies and government ministries.

In Britain, where Japanese manufacturing and management methods have allowed Nissan's new plant to outcompete more established manufacturers, the main issue in a bitter 1988 strike at Ford had to do with Ford's desire to introduce Japanese-style work rules. Even union negotiators admitted that some form of emulation of the Japanese was necessary to keep British manufacturers competitive. The strike centered on how much and how soon. In France 20 percent of the $1 billion budget for a new Peugeot factory is designated for "training workers in Japanese-style assembly techniques."[20]

The number of sushi bars in New York shot up by 1,000 percent during the 1980s; New York's municipal officials regularly visit Japan on study tours to learn about Tokyo's success at mass transit, garbage collection, road repair, and other urban ills. Even some of the most idiosyncratic Japanese traditions like sumo wrestling, *karaoke* bars (where patrons get up and sing popular songs, usually badly), and *manga* (adult comic books) are now finding small audiences in the United States, Europe, and Asia. In Hong Kong, the world's largest nightclub is modeled on the Japanese "hostess bar" concept, complete with hundreds of Japanese-speaking Chinese girls ready to entertain visiting businessmen.

Nowhere is the Japanese cultural influence stronger than in the West's visual arts. Whatever is new and rising in fashion, design, architecture, packaging, and performance art owes a debt to Japanese innovators. This is particularly true on the Pacific Coast of the United States, where trend-setting areas like Los Angeles's Melrose Avenue are brimming with Japanese shops, fashions, restaurants, and visual imagery. *Time* declares that Japan's "new architecture and graphics lead the world."[21] Getting bluntly to the point, *Forbes* notes, "Over the centuries, art has gone where the money is."[22] And with the money in Japan, artists from all over the world are going there to work and to be inspired. Jay McInerney, one of the leading new American writers of the 1980s, lived in Kyoto for two years and set one of his novels in Japan. "Europeans and Americans look to Japan for tradition and structure that are almost totally lacking in our culture," he observes.[23]

In other parts of the world, people look to Japan not so much for artistic ideas as for economic and political inspiration. Japan has created a middle-ground model previously unavailable to developing Asian countries trying to choose between socialism and capitalism. Long-term planning, the search for social cohesion and consensus, a mix of protected and competitive sectors of the economy, attention to detail and quality, emphasis on education, the ability to mobilize a society to study, sacrifice, and save—all these are perceived as virtues of the Japanese system that countries such as Korea, Malaysia, and Singapore are trying to incorporate into their own nation building.

Certainly the Japanese will face giant problems adjusting to the twenty-first century, manacled as they are in many ways by age-old traditions. It is still possible that America's great social assets in the departments of creativity, diversity, openness, and responsiveness to change will continue to provide the world's most dynamic model of leadership. Yet even though Japan currently trails in these attributes, its ability to create, diversify, and open in a more controlled way, and to assimilate change more deeply and evenly, are likely to prove the preferable set of characteristics in a world becoming constantly more volatile and chaotic. Just as the American system appeared uniquely well tailored to the conditions of this century, the Japanese system may prove itself better adapted to the probable environment of the next.

One of the mental roadblocks in trying to think of Japan as a true superpower is that it is hard to imagine the Japanese acting like Americans politically—fomenting insurgencies in Central America, staring down the Russians at the bargaining table, lavishing foreign aid on obscure countries, whipping allies into line, and creating grand regional economic initiatives. The point, however, is that the Japanese empire is unlikely to be run that way. The essence of its thrust internationally will remain closely tied to trade, technology, and finance. Financial power is a razor-sharp tool that cuts the shortest distance between the wishes of those who have it and their fulfillment. The Japanese trading company, says analyst Ronald Morse, "is their equivalent of the British navy."[24]

True to the minimalist aesthetic, Japan is likely to exert influence without either of the two baroque structures of responsibility and intervention typical of Pax Americana—the desire to export liberal humanitarianism to the rest of the world on the one hand or the desire to contain communism on the other.

In Tokyo brainstorming is already under way about what the value system of the Japanese-led future ought to be and how best to articulate it. Nomura's report on the world economy in 1995 takes a pointed historical look back at the way America elevated itself to a position of global intellectual and moral leadership prior to overtaking Great Britain. Japan, says the report, must now do the same. Just as pragmatism and other American-spawned ideas brought "an American culture . . . into bloom, which helped the United States gain trust and influence around the world," Japan must now "win the trust of other countries" by developing "an intellectual value system worthy of its new role as a leader of the world."[25]

The ideology of the Japanese empire, in short, is still in the R&D phase. But it is soon to be revealed.

The Remilitarization of Japan

The world has come far down the road of human progress, yet it has made relatively little headway in diminishing the influence of armaments and armies as bastions of power or of warfare as the ultimate arbiter of conflict. One of Japan's contributions to history may be that it demonstrates the possibility of constructing a vast global empire with comparatively less reliance on military force than other great powers have deemed necessary in history. Yet that possibility does not mean Japan won't become a military power. Japan is already more militarized than most Americans think. By the beginning of the twenty-first century, it may well be a military superpower.

The relevance of Japanese finance to military developments is threefold. In the first place, the increasing extent of investment abroad creates a compelling new reason for Tokyo to rethink its lack of forward military capability. Second, Japan's wealth in general, and low cost-of-capital structure in particular, provides it with the means to build one of the world's most technologically advanced arms industries in a comparatively short period of time. Third, as Japan becomes richer and America poorer, the antagonism is heightened between the protected and the protector, exacerbating the very real Japanese fear of American unwillingness to meaningfully defend Japan.

The coming together of these factors against the backdrop of a hostile world at large (and a situation in north Asia less stable than is generally acknowledged[26]) makes the remilitarization of Japan not only possible but virtually inevitable. American strategists don't seem to believe that Japan could ever again be a threat outside its own borders, but other governments, especially those close to the scene in Asia, are uneasy about what is happening.

China's leaders are outspoken critics of Japanese military expansion. Having witnessed the rapid militarization of Japan once before in this century—and its dire consequences—China is keenly aware that neither Japan's small size nor its smaller population preclude it from becoming an aggressive threat. "To be candid, the Chinese people are nervous about Japanese defense expenditure," Deng Xiaoping told Noboru Takeshita during the Japanese leader's 1987 visit to Beijing.[27] The official Chinese press has taken the position that Tokyo's current plan to expand maritime air defenses throughout Asia's sea-lanes constitute a "grand defense program [that] far exceeds Japan's need to defend its territory."[28]

Lee Kuan Yew, prime minister of Singapore, says his number-one fear for Asia is of Japanese rearmament. "The most terrifying thought for me is a fundamental shift in the belief of the Japanese that the world that they have known since 1945"—that is, the world of Pax Americana in Asia—"is at an end and that they have to either depend on themselves or come to some understanding with China or the Soviet Union."[29]

Leaders of other ASEAN countries are also growing increasingly uncomfortable with Japan's future military role—so much so that when Takeshita addressed their Manila summit, the main theme of his speech was his determination to "reject the path to military power." Even though Takeshita used the occasion to offer $2 billion in aid to the region, his audience was hardly reassured. A correspondent covering the summit noted widespread fear among ASEAN leaders "that the U.S. may be about to abandon its world-policeman role in the area, effectively handing it over to Japan."[30]

Deng Xiaoping, Lee Kuan Yew, and other ASEAN leaders have vivid personal memories of Japan as a military power. Most of today's Americans, on the other hand, do not. To Americans looking at military affairs, the facts seem to speak for themselves: the United States remains incredibly strong, while Japan, by its Constitution and by the antimilitarist bent of its postwar culture, appears weak. But this seemingly institutionalized balance is about to undergo a shift.

Article IX of Japan's Constitution, drafted by MacArthur's occupation staff, states, "The Japanese people forever renounce war as a sovereign right of the nation and the threat or use of force as means of settling international disputes. . . . Land, sea, and air forces, as well as other war potential, will never be maintained."

Specific as this language appears, it has been subject to constant interpretation ever since it went into effect. Its original meaning was strict. Japan was to have no armed forces of any kind; the U.S.-Japan Mutual Security Treaty guaranteed American protection of Japan in case of enemy attack. With the advent of the cold war, the Chinese Revolution, and the Korean War, John Foster Dulles and others in Washington decided Japan should have a limited military defense of its own. Dulles compelled the pacifist Japanese to accept an interpretation of the Constitution as banning only the use of *aggressive* troops. Thus, the "Self-Defense Force" was born—an army that today numbers nearly three hundred thousand troops and utilizes some of the world's best tanks, state-of-the-art fighter aircraft, and antimissile equipment.

In 1976 the Diet decided to cap military spending at one percent of GNP in response to public sentiment within Japan and throughout Asia that feared the beginnings of a trend toward rearmament. One percent of the world's second largest GNP is still a huge sum—$30 billion in 1988. Depending on the currency conversion rate used, "pacifist" Japan can now be considered the world's third largest military spender after the USSR and the United States, spending roughly as much as unpacifist Britain, which maintains nuclear forces, is an integral part of NATO, fights a quasi-civil war in Northern Ireland, and still mans colonial garrisons in far-flung outposts.

Like so many other things in Japan, the 1976 budget cap of one percent is flexible. Nakasone deliberately exceeded the one percent rule by a hair's breadth in 1987 (1.004 percent), largely to demonstrate that it could be done without a political showdown. Among other things the current $30 billion budget buys: 14 new naval vessels, including destroyers, submarines, and minesweepers; an extensive array of surface-to-air missiles; 108 new aircraft including fighter planes and antitank and antisubmarine helicopters; and an assortment of 203mm self-propelled howitzers, tanks, armored personnel carriers, and antichemical weapons vehicles.[31]

A good chunk of Japanese spending is also hidden in nonmilitary budgets, including much of the cost of hosting American bases and troops. The U.S. embassy in Tokyo estimates that real Japanese military spending is already 1.8 percent, but even that figure doesn't include research on strategic areas of technology that in America would be the province of the Department of Defense.

Japanese consumer technology is so studded with military applications that a majority of all new *American* military hardware systems use at least some components made in Japan. Carbon-fiber composites originally developed in Japan for tennis rackets are now used in U.S. jet fighter frames. Electro-optics breakthroughs in Toshiba's home video equipment are used in the Pentagon's most advanced missile guidance systems. A high-tech shoulder-fired antiaircraft missile developed by Japan's Defense Agency using a number of consumer electronics innovations is reportedly more accurate than the much publicized U.S.-made Stinger.[32]

Step by step, domestic political groundwork is being subtly prepared for greater military activity in the future.

- At the height of Iranian attacks on foreign oil tankers in 1987, Nakasone asserted that Japan had a right to send minesweepers into the Persian Gulf. Although he didn't actually dispatch any, he insisted there was no difference from a legal viewpoint whether maritime Self-Defense Forces removed mines from the Sea of Japan or the Persian Gulf. This was the first time a postwar leader had suggested Japan's "self-defense" extended beyond east Asia.
- Soviet aircraft, which have routinely violated Japanese airspace over the years, were fired upon for the first time in December 1987.
- The Information Research Office (Japan's low-level equivalent of the CIA) began publicly lobbying in 1987 for a greatly expanded global intelligence-gathering capability.
- The launch of a Japanese satellite was scrubbed in early 1988, with great accusatory fanfare devoted to U.S.-made computer chips that failed to function properly. The incident provided more ammunition for those who have argued that Japan can no longer afford to depend on "shoddy" American goods in an area as strategic as the nation's defense.

The debate over reliance on American military technology reached its height over the question of whether Japan should build its own next-generation FSX fighter planes or import them from the United States. At stake was a $6 billion plan to thoroughly renovate Japanese air defenses with upward of 130 planes. Top White House officials pushed Tokyo hard to buy American. But Mitsubishi Heavy Industries argued that it could build a better airplane more suitable to Japanese needs. Mitsubishi Heavy cited evidence that it already produces better-quality F-15s than McDonnell-Douglas, the American licenser of the F-15 design. Nor was quality the only issue. A consistent undercurrent of the debate was whether Japan could count on the United States for sensitive military equipment at a time when "Japan bashing" was becoming the favorite pastime of American politicians.

In the end, the FSX issue yielded a typical Japanese compromise.

In name, Japan will "lightly modify" the General Dynamics—designed F-16. In reality, as much as 80 percent of the new FSX will end up Japanese-designed, with most of the technology developed in Japan and most of the production taking place there as well. The Pentagon was reduced to pleading with Tokyo's Defense Agency to arrange for 30 percent of the assembly work to be given to American companies.[33] The cost of domestic design and production will be considerably higher than if Japan had chosen to import the planes whole from the United States. But the benefits—stimulation of the aircraft and military industries—will be even greater.

Executives at Mitsubishi Heavy and the rest of Japan's once-and-future military industrial complex have the technological sophistication and industrial capacity to be leading manufacturers of military equipment. These defense contractors are already lobbying for an end to the existing political ban on developing the arms trade as an export industry. Knowing that it is only a matter of time before the ban is dropped, they are also looking to ramp up domestic business to a level where they will be internationally competitive as arms manufacturers.

Japan's coming rearmament, however, will not be determined by the business plans of the military-industrial complex alone. At bottom it is a political question. And Japanese businessmen long unconcerned with international politics have suddenly begun to ask themselves questions as they export capital abroad. "We are not so comfortable with the idea that we have no means to protect our investments in some foreign countries," says one Tokyo banker. "If the government wants us to invest more in the developing countries, then we need to know what we can do if our holdings there are suddenly nationalized or our businessmen taken hostage."

This sentiment is only the beginning. As Japan moves toward a trillion dollars' worth of external assets in the next decade, the argument in favor of developing a basic projection-of-power mechanism will grow more fervent. The generation with painful memories of how militarism nearly destroyed the nation is moving aside. Many of those coming into power have lived in a world characterized by Japanese success, pride, and even arrogance.

Henry Scott Stokes, a veteran Tokyo correspondent and biographer of Mishima (the famous Japanese novelist known for his espousal of rearmament), says that younger Japanese "regard the world as a 'tabula rasa' upon which they will write a large design. That design is the Japanese flag. . . . They see the center of gravity of the world economy moving to their part of the world. They say, 'Hooray, the world is ours. . . .' They are very international in their thinking, which is a point we concentrate on in business writing from Japan. But we fail to note, at the same time, that they are very serious nationalists."[34] As such they have no fundamental reason to oppose the development of Japan's military potential.

A surprise move in the U.S. Congress to try to block the sale to Japan of the $500 million Aegis—the U.S. Navy's most sophisticated air defense system—gave Japanese proponents of greater military self-reliance exactly the kind of grist they need from their mill. That Japan could be denied the right to buy a defense system from the United States simply because some congressmen wanted to pressure Tokyo for more concessions on trade is perceived in Japan as blackmail. If American attempts to link trade issues to defense persist, there is little doubt Japan will move more rapidly to build its own systems.

The real strategists of remilitarization are watching and waiting. They are counting on *gaiatsu* to literally force the government's hand. If Japanese military renewal is perceived as an unfortunate but necessary accommodation to American pressure, rather than as Tokyo's initiative, it stands a better chance of being tolerated both in Japan and throughout Asia.

Washington has already made it quite clear that it wants the Japanese and European allies to share more of the burden for the free world's defense. That general idea will soon crystallize into specific initiatives. One bill actually passed by the House calls on Japan to increase defense spending from one percent of GNP to 3 percent as a way of relieving U.S. military commitments and allowing the Pentagon's budget to be cut. Several congressmen and a few former top navy brass have proposed that Japan pay a "user's fee" for protection of its oil routes. Informal estimates put Japan's share of the cost now borne entirely by the United States at $14 billion per year.

The populist appeal of this issue was amply demonstrated in a series of full-page ads placed by billionaire (and would-be presidential candidate) Donald Trump in *The New York Times, The Wall Street Journal,* and other leading newspapers. In the wake of Reagan's decision to dispatch American forces to keep the Persian Gulf open,

Trump wrote, "For decades Japan and other nations have been taking advantage of the United States. . . . The world is laughing at America's politicians as we protect ships we don't own, carrying oil we don't need, destined for allies who won't help. . . . It's time for us to end our vast deficits by making Japan . . . pay. Let's help our farmers, our sick, our homeless . . . and let America's economy grow unencumbered by the cost of defending those who can easily pay us for the defense of their freedom."[35]

Trump, whose entrepreneurial instincts bring him far closer to the popular mind than most Washington politicians, has his finger clearly on the pulse of what may become the biggest American domestic political issue of the 1990s: Is global military leadership worth the cost of a crumbling domestic economy?

In the short run, Japan may be willing to subsidize certain American military operations. In the long run, however, if the Japanese are going to spend the billions now being discussed, they will certainly want to see that money provide jobs in Japan and stimulate the development of Japanese industries. Most important, if Japan is going to end up bearing the financial burden for military power it has largely avoided up until now, it will want to be the master of its own destiny in terms of how that power is developed and deployed.

While Japan may be fully cognizant of the benefit it has gained from undercommitment to the military sector (relative to other industrial countries), and while it may try to prolong its innocence in this regard as long as possible, modern geopolitics present certain objective limits. The pressure on Japan to pick up the slack from a declining United States will be great. The very fact that the United States is in decline, moreover, is also forcing Japan to reassess its military dependency.

Although a Soviet attack against Japan is highly unlikely, those entrusted with Japan's defense must ask themselves what they could expect from the United States if such an event were indeed to transpire. Looking at Washington on days when congressmen are smashing Toshiba boom boxes or expressing the desire for Truman to have bombed Japan more heavily—or even just looking at Washington in the midst of hearings over the bungled Iran-contra quagmire— thoughtful Japanese can hardly be faulted for concluding they would be better off in charge of their own defense.

In trying to envision Japan's potential as a military power, one must be careful not to set things in the context of the world as it has been, but to think instead of the world as it may be in the future. Unlike past and current military superpowers, Japan is unlikely to seek to lead a multinational military alliance, to recklessly dispatch troops to foreign territories, or to serve as supply sergeant to surrogates fighting in numerous low-intensity conflicts on several continents simultaneously.

For the foreseeable future, Japan's military buildup *is* likely to be defensive, with the exception of small-scale strike forces applicable to specific local situations where vital Japanese interests are subject to threats. But as students of military history know, the line that divides defensive and offensive military power is an extremely fine one, and it grows finer all the time in light of modern technology.

Over the next few decades Japan will probably evolve a new generation of military technology easily convertible from defense to offense. A "Star Wars"–type system is one possibility. Having brought Japan into the initial stages of Star Wars research, the United States may at some point abandon the program as too costly or unworkable. Japan, with its combination of high-tech proficiencies and financial resources, may be quite willing to develop and perfect such a system. Jack Donegan, the director of phase one development for the Strategic Defense Initiative, says the toughest technological problems he faces have to do with "miniaturizing the sensor design" and perfecting a manufacturing process to make sensors "in enormous quantity and cheaply enough."[36] Both are areas where Japanese industry excels.

In fact, Japan may well be the only country in the world capable of sustaining the long-term commitment necessary to make Star Wars work. But as the Soviets have often pointed out, the defensive appearance of Star Wars also carries an inherent offensive connotation. The nation that first absents itself from the threat of nuclear retaliation gains the freedom to act in newly aggressive ways abroad.

A workable Star Wars, whatever nation designs it, is still quite far off. But the day when Japan gains effective control over its own defense with existing state-of-the-art weapons systems is not. Indeed, such an eventuality now seems to be the logical outgrowth of current U.S. policy.

A Japan given the green light to embark on assuring its own defense means the rapid development of a very powerful Japanese military force. Quality conscious as they are, the Japanese are not about to settle for a defense program that doesn't fully protect them or one that doesn't define defense in the broadest possible way. Even if this new Japanese military force never fires a single missile at a foreign target, its very existence will alter the world balance of political and economic power in profound ways.

A militarily self-sufficient Japan will put U.S.-Japan relations on an entirely new footing. Today Japan needs the United States both for its markets and for its military protection. It still must back down on some issues, much as it doesn't want to, to avoid pushing the United States too far. Tomorrow, when Japan no longer needs protection, it will be free to be even more ruthless in its economic competition.

A Japan decoupled from the U.S. military umbrella implies a Japan free to redesign its own relationships with the Soviet Union, China, and Europe in a way that suits its own interests first. Since those interests are increasingly divergent from American interests, a re-drawing of the world's alliances and power relationships is a likely concomitant of Japan's remilitarization.

Finally, as the strategy of "decoupling" gains credence (West Europe looks after European security, Japan looks after Asia, and the United States maintains its current level of military commitment only in the Western Hemisphere), Japan might become a hegemonic power not on a world scale, but "just" in Asia, which also "just" happens to be the most important region of the world for the next century.

Considering the way the conflict of U.S. and Japanese interests in the world was once pushed over the brink to actual war, and consider-ing the ferocity of recent economic antagonisms, it is not out of the realm of possibility that the process of Japanese remilitarization could begin within the context of American global strategy, gradually di-verge (as France under de Gaulle separated itself from NATO), sepa-rate completely (based on a reconfiguration of Japan's alliances), and end up with American and Japanese missiles pointed at each other.

It is not a prospect Americans ought to take lightly. The remilitari-zation of Japan has all the hallmarks of becoming an issue like others, where, for shortsighted reasons, Washington takes policy initiatives whose long-term consequences enhance Japan's strength and speed America's decline.

The world is unstable enough. It surely does not need yet another military superpower. The United States, which has lost virtually every competitive conflict with Japan in recent years, certainly does not need to set in motion the twenty-first-century possibility of an ulti-mate, final showdown with Japan.

12

Hard Choices for Americans

> More than two hundred years after the Declaration of Independence, the United States has lost its position as an independent power. . . . Our increasing dependence on foreign capital is not just an economic issue. It is also a security issue, as well as a political issue with major implications for foreign and domestic policy. . . . This country will not be able to deal politically with its economic problems until a simple, basic requirement is recognized: to recapture our lost financial independence.
>
> —Felix Rohatyn, managing director,
> Lazard Frères & Co.[1]

Toward a New American Consensus

This book has sketched out large forces at work reconfiguring the global map of wealth and power, triggering the rise of Japan's empire, and draining America of its economic vitality. The dangers of foreigners dictating American interest rates, practicing competitive trade policies that effectively undermine the solvency of large sectors of corporate America, and gaining disproportionate influence over strategic elements of American life from the banking system to the political process on Capitol Hill are not remote nightmares of the future, but increasingly visible realities of the present. As Felix Rohatyn suggests, America in 1988 has already ceased to be an independent economic power.

Economists may argue that all nations are losing some of their independence as the world melds into a single globalized economic

293

realm. But as we have seen, what Japan needs from the United States is diminishing in importance; what the United States needs from Japan is growing in importance. The Japanese, moreover, are far more cautious than Americans when it comes to discarding systems that protect national interests. The result is a process of interpenetration that is actually working to make Japan stronger economically and the United States weaker. Globalization, in a sense, has become a code word for Japanese expansion at the expense of vested interests in the world, mostly American.

The irony is that the enemy is not without, but very much within. The problem is not so much that the Japanese are conspiring to buy America, but that Americans are so gleefully selling it off. The solutions, therefore, must lie not so much in restricting foreign activity in the United States (although more prudent and strategic policies in that regard are necessary), but in changing the systemic flaws that have brought us to this precipice.

If the trends depicted in this volume are allowed to develop unchecked, the curtain will go up on a twenty-first-century America outmaneuvered and outgunned by Japan in the battle for control of world financial resources. It will be an America of remarkably lower living standards and far greater social polarization; one that is severely constrained from capitalizing on its own intellectual and technological assets, even with the information age economy in full flower. It will be an America awkwardly beholden to its allies and trading partners and isolated from the benefits of the global markets its companies pioneered.

Like postwar Europeans, twenty-first-century Americans will have to come to grips with a world that is no longer theirs—a world in which U.S. currency, institutions, corporations, and culture are no longer de facto international standards. True, the U.S. economy is inherently too diverse, its market too large, and its military superiority too far ahead for American power to evaporate as rapidly as Britain's did after World War II. But at least Britain had the luxury of declining into an American-dominated order with which it shared both a cultural affinity and a special political relationship. In the twenty-first century, the United States faces the possibility of declining into a fiercely competitive and potentially hostile Japanese- and Pacific-influenced world order.

The problems posed by Japan's rise and America's decline are neither moral nor racial—although it is inevitable that they will be increasingly posed in those emotion-charged terms. For some, the thought of a newly powerful Japan will conjure up images of the Rape of Nanking or the Bataan death march. But in fairness, those images need to be balanced by the scenes of Japanese-American citizens marched off to California's concentration camps and the nuclear annihilation of Hiroshima and Nagasaki.

To say that there are no moral distinctions between the American order the world has known and the Japanese order now evolving would be idealistic; yet to read too much into those distinctions would be equally fallacious. When today's events are viewed several centuries hence, neither East nor West is likely to have any greater claim to the moral high road. From the safety of that distant perspective, apocalyptic issues involved with the U.S.-Japan rivalry will surely appear somewhat quaint, just as England's great battles with France two centuries ago appear now. Today, we know that the fiery antagonisms whipped up in London and Paris were a small part of a much more wrenching process of global change that culminated in the Industrial Revolution. Tomorrow, our twenty-second-century progeny may be taught that the Tokyo-Washington invective of the 1980s and 1990s was a small, albeit central phase of an even more wrenching global transformation culminating in the Postindustrial Revolution.

But we don't have the luxury of centuries of retrospect. The experience we are about to live through may be only one among many similar episodes in history, but the fact that it is happening to *us*—not to people in a book about rising and falling empires—will make the issues seem outsized, overwhelming, and all-embracing. The Japanese challenge to American power is therefore an incendiary one. No matter how sophisticated we think ourselves, no matter how cosmopolitan our outlook, the question of which nation wields greater influence on the world will have a direct impact on our pocketbooks, our way of life, our self-image, and our security.

That prospect should provide ample reason to reexamine the many mindless follies of Washington and Wall Street alike in the 1980s and to question the narrow, short-term policies of deficits, deregulation, devaluation, disinvestment, and dissavings that characterized the Roaring Eighties. Whether Americans would like to face the facts now or later will soon no longer be a choice. The decade of decoupling the desire for consumption, wealth, and weapons systems from the consequent burdens of paying for such extravagance is over. The future is here, the bills have begun to arrive, and decisions will have to be made fast.

We Americans pride ourselves on our resilience, adaptability, and willingness to rise to challenges. Our history in these areas is vividly demonstrable. Yet in rising to the challenge posed by the declining American economy, we have unfortunately departed from our previous path. Americans are known for facing problems squarely and coming up with bold solutions. But in the Reagan years we exhibited an uncharacteristic collective tendency toward denial and dissembling about what was happening to us.

The first step in trying to reverse current trends, therefore, is to get rid of the rose-colored glasses and adopt a more accurate assessment of what must be done. Part of that assessment is to recognize that the problems run so deep and are complicated by so many factors, both domestic and international, that a program seeking solutions must, by definition, be comprehensive and of a long duration. Somehow Americans have to be convinced that the stakes warrant doing away with our traditionally short time horizons and our expectations for instant solutions. Somehow the election-year cycles, partisan politics, and combative, contradictory special-interest groups must be held in abeyance long enough to deal effectively with these issues.

Another facet of the reality we must recognize is that America cannot compete as a nation in the world without a shared vision of our interests, purpose, priorities, and values—and at least a modicum of public willingness to contribute to and sacrifice for those goals. We are currently witnessing what happens when the vast majority of the 125 million Japanese row in the same direction, while the vast majority of the 250 million Americans row in a wide variety of conflicting directions. To compete with Japan and other rising economic powers, we must develop a national consensus of our own. The consensus we adopt need not be focused in as narrow a range as theirs, but it must have *some* common focus. There must be some general level of agreement about what constitutes the public interest and the public good. That agreement, moreover, must not be based in idle political demagoguery, but in grass-roots reality.

Only with such a consensus can government accomplish the work that needs to be done without incurring either a prohibitive financial cost or a stifling bureaucratic burden. In education, for example, no matter how much the government spends, the United States will not obtain literacy rates comparable to Japan's if parents are not willing to assume a responsible role in their children's schooling. When it comes to foreign trade, no tariffs, threats, or retaliatory action can accomplish what the private sector could if it became genuinely concerned not only with this quarter's bottom line, but with larger issues of keeping jobs in the United States and finding ways to promote domestic industrial productivity and growth. In government, no conflict-of-interest laws can substitute for the development of a cadre of dedicated public servants who find merit, satisfaction, and glory in serving their country. Similarly, in finance, not even $100 million fines can deter corruption if the financial community itself pretends not to know the difference between right and wrong and continues to do business with those who regularly overstep the line.

The 1980s have been characterized by Ronald Reagan's view that the greatest thing about America is that it is a land where anyone can get rich. While that is certainly a fundamental pillar of the American dream, we cannot allow it to be the basic definition of national purpose. The Reagan years helped cultivate a group of entrepreneurs and billionaires whose role in igniting economic excitement cannot be denied. Yet the shift toward personal wealth as the chief motivating factor in American life is actually antithetical to national prosperity as a whole. A nation where the best and brightest all want to be investment bankers is a nation that gets rich at the top and rots at the bottom.

Just as our values must undergo change, we must also be willing to question some of our long-held economic beliefs. "Free trade" is not one of the freedoms articulated in the Bill of Rights; it is an ideology and a business practice that served American interests well at one stage in history but now needs updating to new global realities. Similarly the idea that a national "industrial policy" is synonymous with some heinous form of socialism—or that it is improper for government to play a leadership role in managing America's economic development and foreign trade—must be cast aside if the United States is to continue to compete with other large capitalist economies where government is a conscious, skilled, and successful interventionist.

Shifting our priorities doesn't necessarily cost money—indeed, it saves money. What it takes, of course, is leadership. And at the moment, that part of the equation is missing.

To Be Specific

Developing the new American consensus is an extensive undertaking, requiring many minds and many constituencies working together. When elaborated, that consensus must cover a broad spectrum of issues that reach far afield of topics in this book. But having established the potent role of financial resources in tomorrow's world, and having illustrated how the fulcrum of U.S.-Japan relations is tipping on that question, it is appropriate here to highlight examples of steps that, if taken soon, could begin to counter the current flow toward dangerous imbalance and restore a semblance of economic equilibrium:

1. **The Budget Deficit Must Be Cut and Reliance on Foreign Capital Must Be Reduced.** Everyone knows that the budget problem underlies much of what is wrong with the U.S. economy; most know too that huge deficits and high debt service costs are the forces that directly compromise American independence. Experts have gone through the budget monster and found billions that could be sliced and barely missed. Obviously such efforts should be endorsed and the knives put to work with greater vigor than either the White House or the Congress has so far shown.

Real reductions of government-spending levels, however, will take years to achieve. Some reforms—like the idea of a national youth service program to reduce government expenditure in human resource–intensive undertakings such as education, health, and infrastructure building—require a whole new philosophical approach to the role of government and its citizens. Other changes—such as meaningful disarmament negotiations with the Soviets—are worthy goals with uncertain schedules.

In the meantime Washington must raise new funds in order to reduce indebtedness. The ideas below, while representing a significant level of personal sacrifice on the part of individual Americans, could go a long way toward wiping out the deficit. Combined with substantive budget cuts, they could actually begin to reduce the U.S. national debt itself, exert a powerful downward force on interest rates, and, most important, eliminate American reliance on foreign capital:

- *Gasoline Tax.* One often proposed and workable idea is a gasoline tax. At fifty cents a gallon some experts say this one tax could raise up to $50 billion a year without pushing fuel prices higher than Americans became accustomed to paying in the late 1970s and early 1980s. Remembering that global competitiveness is what this battle is about—and that people throughout the industrial world pay an average of nearly $4.00 a gallon for gasoline because it is so heavily taxed in other countries—asking Americans to pay $1.50 instead of $1.00 a gallon doesn't seem to be too far out of line.

  Apart from an across-the-board tax at the pump, an additional surcharge on imported oil is also warranted, given the fact that the United States has lost thousands of domestic oil-related jobs, expe- rienced the decimation of the once fast growing Sunbelt economy, and even put many domestic oil wells permanently out of service because of the sudden chimera of "cheap" foreign oil. An import surcharge would not only help reduce the budget deficit and stimu- late Sunbelt economies, it could curb America's new and growing reliance on foreign oil *before* the next oil shock hits.

  All monies raised from gasoline and imported oil taxes must go directly into a fund that pays down the U.S. government debt. With the right educational effort, the American public could be won to accepting this form of sacrifice, especially if they could see the money actually going to solve the debt problem instead of being pork-barreled into new government spending.

- *War Bonds.* Americans across a broad range of socioeconomic strata are deeply worried about the country's economic future. Yet there are few ways to do anything about their concerns on a practi- cal level. Washington should admit that the economic battle ahead is as vital to the national interest as any war the United States has ever fought. "War bonds" (perhaps more optimistically termed "American twenty-first-century bonds," should then be issued, yielding minimal interest—3 percent, for example. No effort should be spared to awaken the American people to the fact that each individual could make a difference by buying these below market rate bonds. The proceeds would go directly to reduce U.S. dependence on higher interest rate obligations and foreign borrow- ing.

- *Wealth Bonds.* Since upper-income Americans benefited dispropor- tionately from the Reaganomic tax cuts that in turn created much of the government's dependency on foreign capital—and since the current top bracket is currently lower by half than Japan's or most of Western Europe's—it is now appropriate to consider new taxes for upper-income individuals. One way to do this without incurring all the deleterious effects of added income taxes would be to create a new instrument to serve as a cross between a tax and a bond. Economist Robert Kuttner, for example, has suggested a temporary levy equal to a surcharge of 20 percent of federal tax due each year. This money would be placed in below market rate ten-year bonds, which would trade in financial markets at a steep discount, so that bondholders could recover some of their money at any point if they didn't want to hold the bonds to maturity. Once again, the proceeds from these bond issues would be steered directly toward deficit reduction and diminishing the government's foreign borrowing.[2]

2. **Strengthen the Dollar.** Improving U.S. fiscal health through the above measures ought to contribute significantly to shoring up the dollar's value. The Reagan administration's policy of deliberate depreciation of the dollar, especially against the yen, should be immediately halted in any event. In the period ahead, the Treasury and Federal Reserve Board should coordinate a policy of money supply and currency market intervention that would have as a goal restoration of the dollar's value to 200 yen. At that level, Japanese financial assets will no longer threaten to drown the world in quite the deluge as before, while American exports could still be priced competitively. This policy should be carried out in coordination with American manufacturers, so that they can adjust accordingly their balance of output for domestic and international markets. Ultimately a new long-term currency agreement among the world's major economies is needed. In that context the dollar should be pegged to a trading range somewhere between the extreme highs and lows created by Reaganomics.

3. **End the Free Trade Charade.** Whether we like to admit it or not, the United States is no longer a free-trading nation. Numerous kinds of protectionist influences are at work—from relying on Japan's "voluntary" auto export quotas to new tariffs, quotas, and penalties that have been assessed on other countries. Existing protectionism is already so pervasive that it costs American consumers at least $66 billion annually.[3] Yet it is a cost devoid of strategy, shaped

by special-interest lobbies into a crazy quilt of conflicting measures, often without justification in terms of strengthening American industry.

While continuing to promote the aims of global trade, Washington should cease the hypocrisy inherent in arguing for free trade without fully practicing it. We should admit we need a policy of managed trade and, for the first time, carefully enumerate the areas of business we seek to protect fully, why, and for how long; which areas need only modest forms of protection; and which are crucial to keep completely free and open. Domestic industries should be awarded measures of protection principally on the basis of their strategic relevance to the economy's future. Any degree of insulation from foreign competition so gained should be maintained only if protected industries can regularly show progress toward becoming more competitive.

Clyde Prestowitz, Jr., one of the Reagan administration's former top trade negotiators with Japan, has masterfully demonstrated the Keystone Cops-quality of recent U.S. trade policy in his incisive book, *Trading Places: How We Allowed Japan to Take the Lead*. Striking the right balance between the extremes of free trade and protectionism and developing a realistic approach to managing American interests in global trade, says Prestowitz, are no less important for the next president than pursuing superpower disarmament issues.

4. **Freeze Financial Deregulation.** No further steps toward deregulation of the financial system should be taken until a greater body of evidence is accumulated on the net effects of deregulatory moves already made. Government policy should now focus on the issues of how best to curb excessive speculation and how to guarantee the stability of the financial system. We need to spur a reshaping of our financial culture toward long-term investment. Tax incentives could be used to make investors more patient and to end the mad scramble for quarter-to-quarter earnings that is turning strategic planning into a nonexistent business function. The separation of financial powers defined by the Glass-Steagall Act ought not to be abandoned—especially without a full study of the consequences in regard to Japanese banking activity in the United States.

5. **Reciprocity Must Become the Watchword of the Day; Even Demands for Affirmative Action Are in Order.** Once the United

States ceases to be reliant on foreign capital, we will regain some of our former bargaining leverage in dealing with Japan and our other financiers. At that point the current policy of "national treatment," which allows foreign and domestic financial institutions equal access to U.S. financial markets, should be rescinded in favor of an explicit policy of reciprocity prohibiting further expansion in the United States of financial institutions from countries whose financial markets are not sufficiently open to American institutions. In the case of Japan, the United States should press not just for formal, market-opening measures (many of which have already been taken), but for "affirmative action" goals to redress the current imbalances.

6. **Create a Procedure to Review Foreign Acquisitions in the United States Where Necessary.** The current sell-off of American assets to Japanese and other foreign buyers raises many troubling questions, especially in areas such as high technology and finance. Putting it plainly, Malcolm Forbes (about as free trading as American capitalists come), has suggested that "before Japan buys too much of the U.S.A., we must instantly legislate a presidentially appointed Board of Knowledgeables whose approval would be required before *any* foreign purchase of any significance would be allowed of *any* consequential U.S. company."⁴ Such mechanisms go without saying in Europe and Japan, but what passes for review procedures in America is inadequate, bureaucratic, and almost never used. Our friends and allies can hardly object to Americans being as circumspect about our national interests as they are of theirs. The vast majority of foreign acquisitions may well be harmless, but it is necessary to have a viable system in place to focus the debate on those that could become negative influences. Even more important, such a system needs to generate alternatives to foreign takeovers. Furthermore, since Japan seems to be evolving a concerted investment strategy vis-à-vis the United States, it would seem only sensible that Americans develop a concerted strategy for receiving those investments. The current spectacle of state governments frantically bidding against each other to attract Japanese factories, for example, is clearly not the most cost-effective way to benefit from the job-generating aspects of Japan's overseas push. Granted that foreign investment *can* play a positive economic role, a coordinated American policy ought to attempt to steer it in the most beneficial directions.

7. **End the "Tax Neutrality" Charade.** It is time to recognize that tax policy *is* a basic tool of social policy and wield it as such, based on the new American consensus.

- *Encourage Savings.* Tax policy ought to encourage rather than discourage savings. The original IRA concept, allowing most Americans to shelter up to $2,000 a year in long-term savings, worked incredibly well until the 1986 Tax Reform Act destroyed it. The original program should not only be restored, it should be expanded to $5,000 annual levels. A secondary program should be created to further strengthen the savings habit by allowing taxpayers to shelter another $5,000 annually in five-year CDs. Instead of having to wait for retirement, the tax-advantaged rewards of savings would pay off in just five years.
- *Encourage Investment.* Capital gains preferences should be restored that encourage R&D in specific areas of potential consequence to the economy as a whole. The investment tax credit should be brought back to encourage modernization of plant capacity and installation of process technology that makes manufacturing operations more efficient.
- *Encourage a Better Trade Balance.* Special tax incentives should be extended both to companies willing to produce products domestically that are now "endangered species" because of foreign competition and to companies trying to create new products for foreign export markets. In both cases the qualifying products should enjoy temporary, not permanent, exemptions.

Much of the tax revenue lost as a result of the above exemptions should be retrieved through a combination of "sin taxes" on liquor and cigarettes, sales taxes on luxury items, and ending interest deductions on mortgage indebtedness above the national median home price.

8. **Create a Cabinet-Level Department of Trade and Industry.** This department would be the key agency responsible for researching, developing, and implementing many of the initiatives necessary to restructure the U.S. economy. It should be small but influential. It should aim to recruit a brain trust of top economists and representatives of the private sector with proven commitments to the public

good. The department would hold the power to propose to Congress an annual tax-exemption list to stimulate development of trade and investment-related items described above. It would also have a budget of its own designed to seed investments for projects of special significance to the economy, such as the current Sematech venture.

The goal of this department should not be an industrial policy, but a *postindustrial policy*—one that consciously attempts to position the U.S. economy for maximum advantage in the world of the future. It would not allow its trade negotiators to get dragged into the swamp of arguing with the Japanese over economically backward, marginal issues—such as beef, citrus, and cigarettes—as has been the recent U.S. experience. Instead, it would focus on issues of equal access to the growth markets of the future, including financial services, computers, biosciences, and telecommunications.

Rather than relying on dollar-bashing to make American exports competitive, this department would take more innovative approaches. It might, for example, establish a venture capital arm to provide financing to the small R&D companies involved in new technologies that are now being compelled to mortgage their future export markets by taking in Japanese investors. It would also work to extend the still-provincial horizons of U.S. business by sponsoring extensive programs under which Americans could learn Japanese and other foreign languages and business cultures.

9. **Pressure Japan to Invest in the Developing World.** We must move away from tactical management of the U.S.-Japan relationship and begin to redefine its parameters strategically, based on a clear-headed assessment of how both nations are changing. A long list of issues falls under this heading, but one of the most urgent is to seek "burden-sharing" with the Japanese on matters of Third World economic development. Both the United States and the world economy would be far better served by a Japan that invested a goodly portion of its surplus capital in the developing world, especially Third World debtor nations. An economically revitalized Latin America would create new global markets for Japanese as well as American products and would help diffuse the credit crisis. If developing countries returned to the path of economic growth, the last decade's widening gulf between poor and rich nations would be reversed, and global security would be enhanced. Ultimately, stimulation of the rest of the

world's economy is really the only way to expand the total global pie, rather than continuing to intensify U.S.-Japanese-European competition over the saturated markets of the developed world.

The idea of a Japanese-sponsored "Marshall Plan" for the Third World already has some prominent Japanese adherents, such as former foreign minister Saburo Okita, who points out, "It is not very constructive from the viewpoint of global economic development for Japanese surpluses to be devoted so heavily to such unproductive investments as Treasury bills or Manhattan skyscrapers. It is much more productive for Japan to invest in the developing world's infrastructure." Takako Doi, chairman of the Japan Socialist party (Japan's largest opposition party), makes a good point when she says, "I am bewildered by the absence of U.S. criticism of the small scale of our foreign aid program relative to the size of our economy when your government has been so severely critical of our supposedly small military outlay."[5]

The above points are embryonic ideas for the larger platform needed to properly address the Japanese challenge. Can Americans do it? Can we turn back the enormous tide of history that now seems to be flowing against us?

Maybe.

We certainly cannot do it by defending yesterday's greatness. Nor can we do it by rushing to wall ourselves off in a cocoon of protectionist comforts. And we cannot do it simply by committing ourselves to working harder and consuming less. We can only do it if we are willing to make comprehensive changes in the American political and economic system that will allow us to compete at last on something that resembles a level playing field.

There is a new set of realities in the world, and the time has come for America to adapt to them. The need for those adaptations is urgent. Indeed, it is a relatively clear-cut case of "adapt or die."

Notes

Except where noted, quotations are from author interviews.

Part I

Prelude

1. Yuichi Takahashi, "Silent Tradition Mutes Modern Japanese Society," *Japan Economic Journal* (July 25, 1987).
2. Allan Dodds Frank, "We Better Keep Them Happy," *Forbes* (November 30, 1987).

Introduction

1. C. Fred Bergsten, "Economic Imbalances and World Politics," *Foreign Affairs* (Spring 1987).
2. Ambassador Mike Mansfield, America's elder statesman in Japan, used this phrase on many occasions, including in an interview with me in Tokyo in 1987. He had an excellent grasp of the issues, but the Reagan administration paid scant attention to him. "Nobody can help us but ourselves," he told me. "But we like to blame others. The problem isn't bilateral, it's global. We've been complacent, and the day of reckoning is coming."
3. Norman Jonas, "The Nichibei Economy Could Lead to Future Shock," *Business Week* (October 5, 1987).
4. George R. Packard, "The Coming U.S.-Japan Crisis," *Foreign Affairs* (Winter 1987/88).
5. Gerald L. Curtis, "Enough U.S.-Japan Poison," *New York Times* (June 17, 1987).
6. "You have a reduction of inventory costs due to just-in-time delivery, a new concept that we had, the Japs took, and now we're going to take it back," Secretary of Commerce William Verity said in a University of South Carolina speech, according to the *Asian Wall Street Journal Weekly* (October 26, 1987).
7. Jeff B. Copeland with Bradley Martin, "America-Bashing: A New Japanese Sport," *Newsweek* (April 13, 1987).
8. CBS Evening News, October 14, 1987, reported that 49 percent of Japanese children think they would fight the United States in a war, compared with 41 percent who named the USSR as their likely antagonist.
9. "Wake Up, America!" *Business Week* cover story (November 16, 1987).
10. Peter G. Peterson, "The Morning After," *Atlantic* (October 1987).
11. Paul A. Samuelson, "The U.S. Still Leads the Global Economic Race—But the Gap Narrows," *Christian Science Monitor* (August 18, 1987).

12. Paul Kennedy, *The Rise and Fall of the Great Powers: Economic Change and Military Conflict from 1500 to 2000* (New York: Random House, 1987), 515.
13. "Japan's Troubled Future," *Fortune* cover story (March 30, 1987).
14. Alan Murray and Ellen Hume, "Reagan's Fiscal Policy May Blight the Future Despite Current Gains," *Wall Street Journal* (November 17, 1987).

Chapter 1
 1. George Soros, "A Global New Deal," *New York Review of Books* (August 13, 1987).
 2. Gary Hector, "The Japanese Want to Be Your Bankers," *Fortune* (October 27, 1986).
 3. Igor Oganesoff, "Mr. Okada's Rise: It Points Up Gains of Japan's Workers, Nation's Auto Makers," *Wall Street Journal* (January 9, 1959).
 4. John Heins, "A Mixed Blessing," *Forbes* (February 22, 1988).
 5. Peter F. Drucker, "The Changed World Economy," *Foreign Affairs* (Spring 1986).
 6. Ezra F. Vogel, "Pax Nipponica?" *Foreign Affairs* (Spring 1986).
 7. Paul Kennedy, "The (Relative) Decline of America," *Atlantic* (August 1987).
 8. "Currency Clout," a business note in *The New York Times* (January 25, 1987).
 9. Walter S. Mossberg, "Cost of Paying the Foreign Piper," *Wall Street Journal* (January 18, 1988).
10. Bruce Nussbaum, "And Now the Bill Comes Due," *Business Week* (November 16, 1987).
11. Walter S. Mossberg, "Reagan Goes to Venice Hurt by U.S. Position as Top World Debtor," *Wall Street Journal* (June 4, 1987).
12. Betsy Morris, "Kirin Unit Buys Fifth Coke Bottler in New England," *Wall Street Journal* (January 12, 1988).
13. William J. Holstein, "Japan Is Winning Friends in the Rust Belt," *Business Week* (October 19, 1987).
14. Jonathan P. Hicks, "Bridgestone's New U.S. Challenge," *New York Times* (February 22, 1988).
15. Kenneth B. Noble, "A Clash of Styles: Japanese Companies in U.S. Under Fire for Cultural Bias," *New York Times* (January 25, 1988). Noble reports that former top-ranking American managers at NEC Electronics in California have resigned and filed suits contending that every aspect of the U.S. company's activities "from hiring to marketing and finances, is run with a dictatorial and arrogant hand from afar by its parent company, NEC Corporation of Tokyo."
16. Heins, op. cit.
17. Robert Lindsey, "Japanese Riding Hawaii's Real Estate Boom," *New York Times* (March 18, 1988).
18. Takashi Hosomi, "Why International Cooperation Does Not Work," *Tokyo Business Today* (April 1988).
19. *The World Economy and Financial Markets in 1955: Japan's Role and Challenges* (Tokyo: Nomura Research Institute, 1986), 3.

Chapter 2

1. "The Post-Hirohito Century: Where Will Wealth Propel Japan?" *The Economist* (October 17, 1987).
2. "Build Island in the Bay, Tokyo Architect Urges," *Wall Street Journal* (January 5, 1988).
3. Walter Sullivan, "Japan Shedding Role of Imitator, Is Emerging as Scientific Pioneer," *New York Times* (September 29, 1987).
4. Andrew Tanzer, "Land of the Rising Billionaires," *Forbes* (July 27, 1987).
5. "Japan Banking on Big Bucks, Sumo Power, in Pursuit of Yachting's America's Cup," report in the *Japan Times* (July 5, 1987).
6. Jennifer Colin, "Japanese Tourist Tsunami: Busing Through New York," *Manhattan inc.* (October 1987).
7. Susan Chira, "Some in Japan Feel U.S. Is Using It as a Scapegoat," *New York Times* (March 30, 1987).
8. John H. Makin, "Our Problem—and Japan's," *New York Times* (August 30, 1987).
9. "Japan's Global Role Great: Blue Book," *Asahi Evening News* (July 24, 1987).
10. American states are carrying out their own foreign industrial policy, trying to outdo each other with incentives to attract Japanese plants. The macro problems created by the micro focus of governors and state legislators is highlighted by Martin and Susan Tolchin in *Buying into America* (New York: Times Books, 1988).
11. Tadanobu Tsunoda, *The Japanese Brain: Uniqueness and Universality* (Tokyo: Taishukan Publishing Co., 1985).
12. John W. Dower, "The End of Innocence," *The Nation* (September 12, 1987).
13. Ian Buruma, "A New Japanese Nationalism," *New York Times Magazine* (April 12, 1987).
14. "Japanese Raises Jewish Question," *New York* magazine (April 27, 1987).
15. Clyde Haberman, "In Japan, Unsettling Ripple of Crime," *New York Times* (February 1, 1988).
16. *The New York Times* (September 24, 1986), translated Japanese reports of Nakasone's statement: "In a highly developed information society and a highly educated society such as Japan, the people require politics that bravely faces problems. In the United States, because there are a considerable number of blacks, Puerto Ricans, and Mexicans, the (intellectual) level is lower." Correspondent Susan Chira explained that Japanese newspapers put the word "intellectual" in parentheses, "implying that the reporter had supplemented a direct quote. This is common procedure in Japan because Japanese often leave out parts of sentences expecting their listeners will know what they mean."
17. Despite Nakasone's assertion that Japan is a "monoracial" society, the status of ethnic Koreans is sometimes compared with that of American blacks. The Ainu have fought for official recognition as a minority. Okinawans and Chinese say they face discrimination. Some one hundred thousand illegal immigrants from Asia's poorer countries are unprotected against employer abuses.
18. The IQ statistics are cited by Ezra Bowen, S. Chang, and John Edward Gal-

lagher, "Nakasone's World-Class Blunder," *Time* (October 6, 1986). Other comparative education data are from the *Business Week* cover story, "Can America Compete?" (April 20, 1987).

19. John W. Dower, *War Without Mercy: Race and Power in the Pacific War* (New York: Pantheon Books, 1986), *passim*.

20. Buruma, op. cit.

Chapter 3

1. Leonard Silk, "A Dependence on Foreigners," *New York Times* (May 20, 1987).

2. Default risk for U.S. government bonds has traditionally been calculated at zero in risk-weighting models used by technical analysts. The deficits of the Reagan years, however, have prompted a few analysts to question that assumption.

3. George Anders, "What Are the Japanese Up To?" *Wall Street Journal* special supplement on global finance (September 29, 1986).

4. *Bondweek* (May 26, 1986).

5. William Falloon, "Was It Nomura's Trading Clout?" *INTERMARKET* (August 1986).

6. Japanese securities companies have little trouble attracting distinguished American officials. They come cheaper than Wall Street veterans, and their Washington experience makes them more adaptable to the hierarchy and protocol of Japanese firms. But for American financial firms operating in Tokyo, recruiting career-track MoF officials is virtually impossible. "One guy from MoF could save us several man-years in time figuring out how to do our business here," says an American investment banker in Tokyo. The trend of American government officials going to work for Japanese companies is now so widespread that some call such lobbying Washington's "biggest growth industry." In a celebrated 1987 case, the U.S. Commerce Department's top negotiator on automotive affairs sent out job-seeking letters to Honda and Nissan *while he was a government official*.

7. Michael Brody, "Yellow Peril Politics," *Barron's* (July 6, 1987).

8. Japan now claims the lowest average tariffs of any major economy. Prohibitive tariffs do, however, remain in force in agriculture and certain other categories. Even if these barriers were lifted—on beef or citrus, for example—there's only so much American beef and citrus Japanese are likely to eat. Economists calculate that if all barriers were dropped simultaneously, Japan could absorb no more than $15 billion worth of additional U.S. imports. But if Japan relaxed *all* barriers, the United States would have to respond in kind, forgoing such prerogatives as voluntary Japanese quotas on auto exports. This would increase Japanese exports to the United States. A total "free trade" environment would therefore improve the $50+ billion U.S. deficit with Japan only by a net $10 billion.

9. "Trade Wars: The U.S. Gets Tough with Japan," *Time* magazine cover story (April 13, 1987).

10. Michael S. Malone, "Fear and Xenophobia in Silicon Valley," *Wall Street Journal* (February 23, 1987).

11. Stan Baker, "Brooks Blames Rivals for Bustup," *Electronic Engineering Times* (March 23, 1987).

12. Reflecting the fractious interests that make U.S. policy so inconsistent, Ameri-

cans dependent on Japanese products lobbied against the tariffs even before they were imposed. According to Andrew Pollack ("Many Seek Exemptions at Japan Tariff Hearings," *New York Times,* April 13, 1987), even law enforcement agencies from three states publicly opposed tariffs on the grounds they would add millions to their bill for Japanese-made equipment used to identify fingerprints. The mayor of Richmond, Indiana, complained that tariffs on imported compressors might cause Sanyo to lay off 190 Americans at its refrigerator plant.

13. Forcing the Japanese to raise their prices on chips was not in the best interests of American high technology. "If we have to build a box with more expensive chips in it because the semiconductor agreement has forced the Japanese to raise their prices, our retail price is going to have to go up, and we will become less competitive as a result," Scott McNealy, president of Sun Microsystems, told me. Japanese electronics companies were encouraged by the agreement to move up the ladder to challenge American leadership in areas not covered. "The Japanese feel the answer to the semiconductor agreement is to come up with technology the U.S. doesn't have," John P. Stern, Tokyo representative of the U.S. electronics industry, told *Business Week* (August 31, 1987).

14. David E. Sanger, "Chip Dispute: Reading Between the Lines," *New York Times* (March 30, 1987).

15. Damon Darlin, "Japan's Trade Negotiator Irks Americans," *Wall Street Journal* (April 3, 1987).

16. Gerald M. Boyd, "President Imposes Tariff on Imports Against Japanese," *New York Times* (April 18, 1987).

17. Andrew Pollack, "Cuts by Japan Now Spur Fears of Chip Shortage," *New York Times* (April 7, 1987).

18. Estimates by Japanese and American sources of Japanese bond purchases showed a disparity of nearly $50 billion for 1986.

19. "Now Hear This," *Fortune* (June 8, 1987).

20. *Tokyo Business Today* (July 1987). According to the report, Chief Secretary Masaharu Gotoda and MITI Minister Hajime Tamura made these comments just before the May 1987 U.S. Treasury refunding auction at an off-the-record meeting of the Tanaka faction's shadow cabinet.

21. Tom Herman, "Treasury Bond Prices Take Biggest Fall in 6 Months as Worry About Dollar Grows," *Wall Street Journal* (March 31, 1987).

22. James P. Miller and G. Christian Hill, "Mortgage Markets Turn Chaotic as Lenders Limit Commitments," *Wall Street Journal* (April 15, 1987).

23. Edwin A. Finn, Jr., "In Japan We (Must) Trust," *Forbes* (September 21, 1987).

24. Paul Blustein, "Dollar Looms Bigger in the Fed's Decisions at Risk of a Recession," *Wall Street Journal* (May 19, 1987).

25. *Wall Street Journal* lead news item (May 7, 1987).

26. Michael Quint, "Bonds Dive as Japanese Hold Back; Tension Builds," *New York Times* (May 7, 1987).

27. Jeff B. Copeland and Rich Thomas, "The U.S. Gets Foreign Aid," *Newsweek* (May 18, 1987).

Part II
Chapter 4

1. The sense of kinship between Japan and Britain is unmistakable. Britain, after all, is also a small island nation. Japan is of Asia but completely distinct from it, just as Britain is different from Continental Europe. The feudal past and residual monarchies of both nations have deep thematic resonances. The roaming knights of Arthurian Britain were not so different from Japan's samurai. In *Ran*, the great filmmaker Kurosawa had little trouble recasting the King Lear story in Japanese history; *noh* troupes have adapted Macbeth to Japanese settings. What the Japanese see most in British history is a trading and engineering nation that, despite its small size and scant resources, dominated the world economy.
2. David Halberstam, *The Reckoning* (New York: William Morrow & Co., 1986), 115.
3. Herman Kahn and Thomas Pepper, *The Japanese Challenge* (Tokyo: Charles E. Tuttle Co., 1980), 141.
4. Peter Drucker, "Japan's Choices," *Foreign Affairs* (Summer 1987).
5. One of the reasons Japan is able to implement the economic plans it espouses is that unlike the United States, the government's chief executive almost always has firsthand experience in economic, financial, and trade matters. Out of eleven prime ministers since 1956, eight previously headed MITI, seven headed MoF, and five played both roles.
6. Thomas K. McCraw, ed., *America versus Japan* (Boston: Harvard Business School Press, 1986), 8.
7. Jiro Tokuyama, "Macroeconomic Analysis and U.S.-Japan Trade Relations," speech given at the Japan Society of Boston Symposium (March 21, 1987).
8. This saying is attributed to Tokugawa philosopher Honda Rimei (1744–1821) and is cited at the beginning of Steven Schlosstein's *Trade War* (New York: Congdon & Weed, 1984).

Chapter 5

1. Paul A. Gigot, "Reagan Risks Being 'Hoovered' by Democrats," *Wall Street Journal* (October 23, 1987).
2. Jeffrey A. Frankel, *The Yen/Dollar Agreement: Liberalizing Japanese Capital Markets* (Institute for International Economics, Washington, D.C., 1984), 71–72.
3. Jeffrey E. Garten, "Japan Cashes in on Yen-Dollar Accord," *Asian Wall Street Journal* (March 28, 1985).
4. Karel G. van Wolferen, "The Japan Problem," *Foreign Affairs* (Winter 1986/87).
5. Frankel, op. cit., 3.
6. Garten, op. cit.
7. Peter T. Kilborn, "Reagan's Turnabout on the Dollar," *New York Times* (September 29, 1985).
8. David A. Stockman, *The Triumph of Politics* (New York: Avon, 1987), 447–58.
9. Peter G. Peterson, "The Morning After," *Atlantic* (October 1987).
10. Those changes included wiping out some of the only pro-growth, pro-savings

elements of U.S. tax law such as IRA savings deductions and preferential treatment for capital gains. The bill also had the effect of turning what little savings most Americans *had* built up in the form of home ownership into perilous tax-advantaged liquid credit cards known as "home equity loans."

11. A large trade deficit could be a sign of economic strength rather than weakness, Ronald Reagan told a Cleveland audience in January of 1988. To many people this utterance appeared to be one of the most outrageous of the president's career, but there is a surprising amount of truth in it. A strategy-conscious American leadership might have found real competitive advantage in keeping the dollar strong, continuing to source high-quality, low-priced components and consumer goods from Japan and other foreign countries *if,* in doing so, American industry could have been simultaneously shifted toward next-generation products and technologies that could continue to employ American workers in higher value-added areas. The trade deficit is, after all, fundamentally an employment problem. But the choice to solve the problem through weakening the dollar was backward-looking. It made the United States marginally more competitive in the industries of the past, at the expense of infusing Japan with the financial resources necessary to outcompete the United States in the future.

12. These statistics were cited in *Business Week* (August 18, 1986), from data supplied by Robert F. Graham and Hambrecht & Quist Inc.

13. These statistics were cited in *Fortune* (February 15, 1988) and reflect 1986 data. GM's labor costs reflect the fact that it makes more of its own parts than Toyota.

14. In an op-ed piece I wrote for *The New York Times* ("When the Yen Comes Down from the Sky It May Capture the Earth," September 3, 1986), I argued that American efforts to strengthen the yen would enhance Japan's long-term competitiveness. An American at a Japanese securities firm joked, "They'll never let you into Japan again—you're printing Japanese state secrets in *The New York Times!"*

15. Toyoo Gyohten's reminiscences of 1971 appeared in an article he contributed to *Institutional Investor* (June 1987).

16. J. Terence Gallagher, "Bank of Japan Playing Key Role in Global Economics," *Asian Wall Street Journal Weekly* (December 21, 1987).

17. Official White House statement from the president's office released by Press Secretary Marlin Fitzwater, October 19, 1987.

18. Susan F. Rasky, "Trade Deficit: Cheaper Dollar Not a Cure-All," *New York Times* (February 4, 1987).

19. The fact that Japan is consciously worried about the danger of "hollowing out" suggests this phenomenon will be less devastating there than in the United States. A collective effort by business, government, and labor is under way to design an approach to internationalizing Japanese business that doesn't wither the domestic base. Even the term "hollowing out," now accepted in American business parlance, reflects Japan's sensitivity to the problem. It was reportedly coined by Sony's Akio Morita, who observed the trend in the United States and worried about its implications for Japan.

20. Barnaby J. Feder, "What the Dollar's Drop Won't Do," *New York Times* (December 6, 1987).

21. German auto sales in Japan, for example (mostly BMW, Mercedes, Porsche, and Audi) shot up from 25,000 in 1983 to 68,000 in 1987. U.S. car sales remained consistently flat through that period at around 4,000 per year.

22. Charles P. Alexander, "The Declining Dollar: Not a Simple Cure," *Time* (November 16, 1987).

23. Kevin Kelly, "A Weakened Komatsu Tries to Come Back Swinging," *Business Week* (February 22, 1988).

24. Honda, along with at least twenty other Japanese companies, is currently reducing the U.S. trade deficit even further by taking advantage of cheap American labor to export a growing portion of its U.S. production back to Japan. Honda executives speak enthusiastically of developing worldwide production capabilities and switching freely between production sites as currency rates change. In tomorrow's world, will American manufacturers be as nimble in switching back and forth between U.S. and Japanese production sites? Will they be able to own their own Japanese production sites at all?

25. Martin and Susan Tolchin, "Foreign Money, U.S. Fears," *New York Times Magazine* (December 13, 1987).

26. Bill Powell, "Your Next Boss May Be Japanese," *Newsweek* (February 2, 1987).

27. Peter Gumbel and Douglas R. Sease, "Foreign Firms Find Resentment in the U.S.," *Asian Wall Street Journal* (July 27, 1987).

28. Robert B. Reich, *Tales of a New America* (New York: Times Books, 1987), 88.

29. Kenichi Ohmae, *Beyond National Borders: Reflections on Japan and the World* (Homewood, Ill.: Dow Jones-Irwin, 1987), 26.

30. Tolchins, op. cit.

31. Nathaniel C. Nash, "A New Urgency for Reforms in Policing Securities Trades," *New York Times* (December 17, 1987).

32. Clyde Haberman, "Tokyo Stocks Continue to Advance," *New York Times* (October 22, 1987).

33. Karl Schoenberger, "Tokyo Shares Recover Much of Record Loss," *Wall Street Journal* (October 22, 1987).

34. Advertorial appearing in *The Wall Street Journal* (December 17, 1987).

35. James Sterngold, "Infighting Is on the Rise at Troubled Firms After Stock Plunge," *New York Times* (February 4, 1988).

36. Thomas E. Ricks, "Task Force's Brady Says Japanese Sales of U.S. Bonds Touched Off Oct. 19 Crash," *Wall Street Journal* (April 22, 1988).

Part III

Chapter 6

1. *Beyond the Ivied Mountain: The Origin and Growth of a Japanese Securities House* (Tokyo: Nomura Securities, 1986), 16.

2. John Carson-Parker, "What Makes Nomura Really Different," advertising supplement to *Euromoney* (May 1986).

3. Kevin Rafferty, "Nomura Flexes Its Muscles," *Institutional Investor* (July 1986).

4. Bernard Wysocki, Jr., "Tough Japanese Firm Grows in Importance in Securities Market," *Wall Street Journal* (April 1, 1987).

5. David Fairlamb, "Nomura Securities' Global Ambitions," *Dun's Business Month* (November 1986).
6. Peter Hall, "Nomura Securities' Yoshihisa Tabuchi, *Financial World*'s Man of the Year," *Financial World* (December 23, 1986).
7. Rafferty, op. cit.
8. Wysocki, op. cit.
9. James B. Treece, "Mighty Nomura Tries to Muscle in on Wall Street," *Business Week* (December 16, 1985).
10. *Beyond the Ivied Mountain,* op. cit., 114.
11. Ibid., 113–15.
12. Michael R. Sesit, "Kurokawa Looks to Expand the Territory," *Wall Street Journal* (October 5, 1987).
13. Carson-Parker, op. cit.
14. Jack Lowenstein, "Nomura: Integrating Capital Markets on a Global Basis," *Euromoney* supplement.
15. Fukushima is not quite the diplomat Tabuchi is. He doesn't mind giving a Western interviewer the unvarnished party line as it is spoken inside the organization. Nomura's only weakness, he says, is that it is always the first to do things in Japan—and being first is costly. "But since we are so profitable, we can afford to spend this money." Americans are putting their companies at risk with new financial products, he believes, citing Salomon, which he says is overextended in futures. "I asked John Gutfreund if he could assure me that there would be no panic. His face just turned red. He could say nothing." For those hoping Nomura's arrogance may be curbed by a Tokyo stock market crash, Fukushima has bad news: company studies show that in the worst case, revenues would fall by no more than 40 percent. Nomura would still be far and away the world's biggest securities firm.

Chapter 7

1. Howard Rudnitsky, Allan Sloan, and Peter Fuhrman, "Land of the Rising Stocks," *Forbes* (May 18, 1987).
2. Paul Aron, "Japanese Price Earnings Multiples: Refined and Updated," Paul Aron Report #30, Daiwa Securities America (May 28, 1987).
3. These figures come from Goldman Sachs, International Research Japan, report, May 1987, based on share prices as of April 20, 1987. Goldman's reports on Japan like this one by Charles R. Elliott, Nicholas C. Akers, and Jeremy Hale represent some of the best research done by foreigners on the Tokyo market.
4. Kathryn Graven, "Japanese Stock Buyers Follow the Fads, Send Tokyo Prices Soaring," *Wall Street Journal* (May 29, 1987).
5. Everett Mattlin, "High Rolling in Japan," *Institutional Investor* (March 1987).
6. James Davidson, *Strategic Investment* (December 15, 1987).
7. Rudnitsky, et al., op cit.
8. Aron, op. cit.
9. Jeffrey M. Laderman, "Why New York's Eyes Are Glued to the Tokyo Market," *Business Week* (August 3, 1987).
10. Brochure advertising the newsletter *Strategic Investment*, whose editors referred

to the coming Tokyo market collapse as "Pearl Harbor II."

11. "The Meaning of October 1987," *Asset International* (January 4, 1988).
12. Lawrence J. De Maria, "Merrill Sees Volatility for 1988," *New York Times* (January 11, 1988).
13. It is useful to remember that the Japanese are accustomed to paying premiums for the quality of Japanese-ness. They buy Japanese-grown rice, their national staple, at a price eight times higher than world market. Fine women's kimonos can be more costly than the latest Paris original fashions. Entertaining guests at a dinner in Tokyo entails three times the expense of New York.
14. If a Japanese "salaryman" runs out of cash in a restaurant, he can usually leave his *meishi* (business card) and assume the proprietor will send the bill to him the next day. "My face is my credit card," a Japanese businessman says; the fact of being Japanese implies intrinsic virtue.
15. Unlike the United States, Japan's traditional companies are expected to be the big beneficiaries of the changing environment. While a few "hot" new companies have appeared, it is the old and powerful that have the resources needed to invest in major new industries. Ajinomoto, a traditional food-processing giant, has emerged as one of the leaders in Japanese biotechnology. Seed, the trendiest clothing boutique in Tokyo, is the brainchild of Seibu, Japan's biggest retailing group.
16. Japanese experts generally forecast an earlier introduction of commercial applications for superconductor technology than American sources. One report in the *Nihon Keizai Shimbun* predicted the first consumer applications of the technology by 1990.
17. Alvin Toffler, *Previews & Premises* (New York: William Morrow & Co., 1983), 62–63.
18. "The Japanese Strategy: MITI's Vision of the 1980s," *New Perspectives* (Fall 1985).
19. "Tokyo Land Prices Teeter," *The Economist* (January 9, 1988).
20. Jared Taylor, *Shadows of the Rising Sun: A Critical View of the "Japanese Miracle"* (New York: William Morrow & Co., 1983), 123.

Chapter 8

1. "Stocks Down 156.83 After Drop Abroad," *New York Times* (October 27, 1987).
2. During the recent bull market, Wall Street overhead grew even faster than burgeoning revenues. With 1987 salaries at the ten largest brokerage houses *averaging* $500,000 for stockbrokers and traders, $750,000 for bond brokers and traders, and nearly $1 million for merger bankers, the U.S. financial services industry is not quite the lean, mean, efficient machine it imagines itself.
3. Peter Fuhrman, "Comparative Disadvantage," *Forbes* (May 18, 1987).
4. Bernard Wysocki, Jr., "Tough Japanese Firm Grows in Importance in Securities Market," *Wall Street Journal* (April 1, 1987).
5. A stained-glass artwork presides over the entrance to the Sanyo executive suite in Tokyo. It depicts Halley's comet, first observed in 1910, when Sanyo was founded. The comet passed by again in 1986, when Tsuchiya assumed command of the company. Just in case the visitor misses the point of the work, Tsuchiya

makes it explicit: when the comet returns in 2062, "the Pacific Basin, not the Atlantic, will be the center of the world"—and Sanyo will be a global household name.

6. The "dividend arbitrage" strategy of the Japanese has attracted little attention despite awesome implications. As a statistical phenomenon it has been cited by Lawrence J. De Maria ("Tax Maneuver by Japanese," *New York Times,* August 26, 1987) and Phillip H. Wiggins ("42.94 Jump Puts Dow at 1,946.45," *New York Times,* January 26, 1988) among others.

7. Robert L. Rose and Scott McMurray, "Top 2 Futures Exchanges Investigate Pattern of Trading by Japanese Firms," *Wall Street Journal* (April 21, 1987).

8. Jan Wong, "Foreign Banks Grab a Market Segment," *Wall Street Journal* (December 15, 1986).

9. Advertisement in *Wall Street Journal* (April 30, 1987).

10. Fuhrman, op. cit.

11. Michael Schrage, "Financial Finesse: Size vs. Smarts," *Wall Street Journal* (January 28, 1988).

12. James Sterngold, "Is Wall Street Ready for Bad Times?" *New York Times* (May 17, 1987).

13. Richard B. Schmitt, "BankAmerica to Sell Stocks and Notes to Japanese Investors for $350 Million," *Wall Street Journal* (October 8, 1987).

14. Daniel F. Cuff, "Joint Mitsui Venture Draws Lease Experts," *New York Times* (February 8, 1988).

15. James Sterngold, "Goldman, Sachs May Sell Stake to Japan Bank," *New York Times* (August 7, 1986).

16. The last time Citicorp even tried to buy a small Japanese bank, the attempt was scuttled by MoF, which reportedly quickly arranged for Sumitomo to acquire the bank instead.

17. James Sterngold, "Too Far, Too Fast: Salomon Brothers' John Gutfreund," *New York Times Magazine* (January 10, 1988).

18. Sterngold, "Is Wall Street Ready for Bad Times?" loc. cit.

19. Larry Zoglin, "Japan's Informal Financial Barriers," *Asian Wall Street Journal* (July 15, 1987).

20. Tetsundo Iwakuni, "Laws May Change, But Japanese Society Does Not," speech to the International Securities Market Symposium, Berkeley, California, October 17, 1987.

21. Aron Viner, *Inside Japanese Financial Markets* (Homewood, Ill.: Dow Jones-Irwin, 1988), 48–49.

22. Joel Kurtzman, "What's in Store for Banks?" *New York Times* (January 24, 1988).

Chapter 9

1. Gary Hector, "The Japanese Want to Be Your Bankers," *Fortune* (October 27, 1986).

2. Craig Forman, "Britain's Deregulation Leaves a Casualty Trail in Securities Industry," *Wall Street Journal* (October 14, 1987).

3. Anthony Rowley, "Japan at the Top and Aiming to Remain There," *Far Eastern Economic Review* (December 17, 1987).

4. Steve Lohr, "Hard Times for the Euromarkets," *New York Times* (September 20, 1987).

5. Ibid.

6. Ibid.

7. Robert Cottrell, "Nomura Securities: World Brokers," cover story in the *Far Eastern Economic Review* (July 3, 1986).

8. "Playing with Surplus Yen Abroad," *Asahi Evening News* (July 22, 1987).

9. John E. Pluenneke, "The Japanese Are Firing up Frankfurt," *Business Week* (April 20, 1987).

10. Michael T. Kinnicutt, "Japanese Securities Firms Come to Italy, Looking for Investments—and Investors," *Wall Street Journal* (June 8, 1987).

11. Hamish McDonald, "Big Capital Danger in Small Market," *Far Eastern Economic Review* (December 3, 1987).

12. "Overweight, Over-rich and Over Here," *The Economist* (April 4, 1987).

13. Christopher McCooey, "Guest Traveller's Tales," *Far Eastern Economic Review* (August 6, 1987).

14. William Kay, "Why Daiwa Scares the City," *Business* (February 1987).

15. Sun Tzu, *The Art of War* (New York: Oxford University Press, 1971), 96. Samuel B. Griffith, trans.

16. Maria Shao, "By the Time China Takes Over, Japan May Own the Joint," *Business Week* (May 25, 1987).

17. Helen E. White, "Japanese Investment Encounters an Uneasy Welcome in Thailand," *Asian Wall Street Journal Weekly* (February 1, 1988).

18. Nicholas D. Kristof, "Japan Winning Race in China," *New York Times* (April 29, 1987).

19. Ibid.

20. Ibid.

21. "C. Itoh May Finance China Oil Exploration in Northwest Basin," *Asian Wall Street Journal Weekly* (January 18, 1988).

22. Staffan Burenstam Linder, *The Pacific Century: Economic and Political Consequences of Asian-Pacific Dynamism* (Stanford, Calif.: Stanford University Press, 1986), xiii.

23. Susan Chira, "South Africa Trade a New Issue in Japan," *New York Times* (January 26, 1988).

24. At least Japanese businessmen in South Africa are consistent. True to their mercantilist faith, they don't object to the apartheid government's repugnant designation of them as "honorary whites." Those who want to do business in foreign markets must accept the terms of the market, they say.

25. Ezra F. Vogel, "Pax Nipponica?" *Foreign Affairs* (Spring 1986).

26. Clifford Krauss, "Japan Replaces U.S. Trading with Nicaragua," *Asian Wall Street Journal* (June 15, 1987).

Part IV
Chapter 10

1. Zbigniew Brzezinski, "How About an Informal U.S.–Japan Inc.?" *New York Times* (April 28, 1987).

2. "Surprise, Made in America," special sponsored supplement produced in cooper-

ation with the Japanese Chamber of Commerce, New York, appearing in the *Atlantic Monthly* (February 1988).

3. The rivalry for financial services information systems is heating up, according to Bob Johnstone *(Far Eastern Economic Review,* December 17, 1987). Hitachi's trading room systems compete directly with Reuters; Quick, an on-line market data network owned partly by Nikkei and partly by a group of Japanese financial firms, enjoys preferential access to the first information feed out of the Tokyo Stock Exchange and competes with Quotron and Telerate.

4. Yusuke Kashiwagi, "The Emergence of Global Finance," Per Jacobsson lecture, 1986.

5. Lester C. Thurow, "Paradise Lost," *New York Times* (February 24, 1988).

6. Barbara Buell with Steven J. Dryden, "Strong, Silent Japan Starts to Speak Up," *Business Week* (November 30, 1987).

7. Paul Kennedy has argued this case eloquently in *The Rise and Fall of the Great Powers* (New York: Random House, 1987). He resurrected a three-hundred-year-old dictum from the German mercantilist writer von Hornigk, who put the issue squarely: "Whether a nation be today mighty and rich or not depends not on the abundance or security of its power and riches, but principally on whether its neighbors possess more or less of it."

8. Brzezinski, op. cit.

9. C. Fred Bergsten, "Economic Imbalances and World Politics," *Foreign Affairs* (Spring 1987).

10. David Hale, "Accounting for the Dollar Glut," *Wall Street Journal* (April 18, 1988).

11. "Kissing America Good-bye?" *Tokyo Business Today* (April 1988).

12. Kennedy, 537.

Chapter 11

1. Kenichi Ohmae, *Behind National Borders* (Homewood, Ill.: Dow Jones-Irwin, 1987), 4–6.

2. Kimitada Miwa, "Future of Pacific Relations," *Japan Times* (July 12, 1987).

3. Ian Buruma, *Behind the Mask* (New York: New American Library, 1984), 153. There are differing opinions about the origins of the *Chushingura* story in Japanese history; the facts in this chapter are based on Buruma's account.

4. Louis Uchitelle, "When the World Lacks a Leader," *New York Times* (January 31, 1988).

5. Ibid.

6. "ASEAN Expects More Help from Japan, Survey Shows," *Asahi Evening News* (July 13, 1987).

7. Paul Streeten, "Global Institutions for an Interdependent World," Discussion Paper 128, Boston University Department of Economics (August 1987).

8. Jim Schwartz, "Restoring the U.S. Spirit after Years of Bludgeoning," *International Management* (November 1987).

9. Norman Gall, "The Japanese Strategy for Computer Supremacy," *Forbes* (February 9, 1987). In a landmark article in the *Harvard Business Review,* "From the People Who Brought You Voodoo Economics," (May–June 1988), Charles Fer-

guson demonstrates that America's love affair with small high-tech companies may be a national liability rather than an asset in an age dominated by highly efficient Japanese technology giants.

10. In 1987 the United States posted a trade deficit with Japan not just in consumer electronics or memory chips, but in every single sector of electronics products, including a 37 percent increase in the computer deficit over 1986.
11. Stephen Kreider Yoder, "Japan Is Racing to Commercialize New Superconductors," *Wall Street Journal* (March 20, 1987).
12. Evert Clark, "The U.S. Has the Advances, But Japan May Have the Advantage," *Business Week* (April 6, 1987).
13. William J. Broad, "Novel Technique Shows Japanese Outpace Americans in Innovation," *New York Times* (March 7, 1988). It is also useful to bear in mind that the patent-filing process has become so expensive and time-consuming that small high-tech American companies no longer bother with it. Big Japanese corporations, on the other hand, have applied for such a range of patents on bits and pieces of new technologies like superconductivity that they are accused of trying to preempt the field. About fourteen thousand U.S. patents annually are now awarded to Japanese innovators.
14. Walter Sullivan, "Japan, Shedding Role of Imitator, Is Emerging as Scientific Pioneer," *New York Times* (September 29, 1987).
15. "Now Hear This," *Fortune* (November 9, 1987).
16. Joel Dreyfuss, "How Japan Picks America's Brains," *Fortune* (December 21, 1987).
17. Bernard Wysocki, Jr., "Japanese Now Target Another Field the U.S. Leads: Biotechnology," *Wall Street Journal* (December 17, 1987).
18. Barbara Buell, "Blast-Off: Japan Inc. Is Joining the Space Race," *Business Week* (August 24, 1987).
19. "First Find Japan," *The Economist* (May 16, 1987).
20. Richard A. Melcher, "What's Throwing a Wrench into Britain's Assembly Lines," *Business Week* (February 29, 1988).
21. Kurt Andersen, "Japan Is on the Go," *Time* (September 21, 1987).
22. Edwin A. Finn, Jr., with Hiroko Katayama, "Follow the Money," *Forbes* (December 29, 1986).
23. Ibid.
24. "The Pacific Century," *Newsweek* cover story (February 22, 1988).
25. *The World Economy and Financial Markets in 1995* (Tokyo: Nomura Research Institute, 1986), 12–13.
26. With the Sino-Soviet border still heavily militarized and the Korean peninsula an enduring tinderbox, north Asia's calm is superficial. A 1988 poll of career military men voted Korea the most likely setting for the beginning of the next global conflict.
27. Barry Kramer, "China's Stepped-Up Criticism of Japan Is Attributed to Hu's Ouster, Trade Gap," *Wall Street Journal* (April 22, 1987).
28. Liu Jun, "Military Budget a Blow to Peace," *Beijing Review* (January 18, 1988).
29. James Fallows, "The Bases Dilemma," *Atlantic* (February 1988).
30. Rodney Tasker, "No Call to Arms," *Far Eastern Economic Review* (December 31, 1987).

31. "Outline of Japan's Defense Budget for Fiscal 1987," Foreign Press Center, Tokyo, May 1987.
32. Eduardo Lachica and Masayoshi Kanabayashi, "Japanese Arms Builders Now Vie Openly for Orders After Long Pacifist Period," *Asian Wall Street Journal Weekly* (August 24, 1987).
33. The Pentagon also wants technology "flowback," meaning the right to share Japanese innovations. Mitsubishi Electric opposes any provision forcing it to share phased-array radar technology with Americans.
34. Henry Scott Stokes, "Japan's Disquieting Soul," *New Perspectives* (Fall 1985).
35. Donald J. Trump, open letter advertorial, *New York Times* (September 2, 1987).
36. Harry Anderson and John Barry, "A Start on Star Wars," *Newsweek* (February 8, 1988).

Chapter 12
1. Felix Rohatyn, "Restoring American Independence," *New York Review of Books* (February 18, 1988).
2. Robert Kuttner, "Against Austerity," *The New Republic* (December 28, 1987). Warning of the economic dangers inherent in cutting the budget to the point where it no longer stimulates the economy, Kuttner attributes the origins of this idea to a 1940 book by Keynes, *How to Pay for the War.*
3. This $66 billion is a figure cited by Georgetown economist Gary Hufbauer in "After Reagan," a *Business Week* cover story (February 1, 1988). The article quotes Treasury Secretary Baker acknowledging that Ronald Reagan granted "more import relief to U.S. industry than any of his predecessors in more than half a century." Yet much of the relief handed to industry owed more to political favoritism than strategic economic need.
4. Malcolm S. Forbes, "Facts and Comment," *Forbes* (January 25, 1988).
5. Takako Doi, "U.S.-Japan Relations: Some Alternative Approaches," address to the Japan Society of New York, September 17, 1987.

Acknowledgments

I am grateful to the many leading figures in the Japanese financial community who took time out from incredibly tight schedules to be interviewed for this book. Executives in both the Tokyo and New York offices of the major Japanese securities houses were extraordinarily open and candid in their discussions with me. They shared ideas and information even when they disagreed with my viewpoint. They made top management available and permitted me to go inside their organizations and see how things are done up and down the line. Special thanks to these individuals is in order: At Nomura, Yoshihisa Tabuchi, Masahiro Aozono, Yoshiji Fukushima, Koji Higashi, Nobumitsu Kagami, Michio Katsumata, Robin Koskinen, Tetsuo Koyama, Masaaki Kurokawa, Steven Looney, Don McKinnon, Hirohiko Okumura, Yoshio Terasawa, Mitsuya Tokumoto, and Kinya Tsubaki. At Daiwa, Yoshitoki Chino, Tomohiko Abe, Yasukazu Akamatsu, Paul Aron, Bill Brachfeld, Masahiro Dozen, Takuro Isoda, Koichi Kimura, Teizo Taya, and Jiro Yamana. At Nikko, Steve Axilrod, Yasuo Kanzaki, Toshio Mori, Jun Okano, and Susumu Yamazaki. At Yamaichi, Shiro Inoue, Tatsuo Okaya, Scott Pardee, and Masaaki Yoshida. At Sanyo, Yoichi Tsuchiya, Ruishiro Ninomiya, and Kenji Takagi. Presidents of leading Japanese banks —Nobuya Hagura of Dai-Ichi Kangyo, Taizo Hashida of Fuji, and Koh Komatsu of Sumitomo—all helped me better understand Japan's financial future.

A number of American and foreign companies operating in Japan were understandably reticent about discussing their experiences on the record. I still found outstanding sources in Jack Williams, John Heimann, Tetsundo Iwakuni, Hisashi Moriya, and Noboru Takesaka of Merrill Lynch; Gene Atkinson and Hideki Mitani of Goldman Sachs; Deryck Maughan of Salomon Brothers; Brian Kelly of Morgan Stanley; David Dible and Eric Feder of Hoare Govett; Mime Egami of Prudential-Bache; and Richard Greer of Baring Securities. Others provided invaluable help but asked that their names not be used; I wish to extend my thanks to them just the same.

Others in Tokyo whose perspective and cooperation proved particularly useful include Ambassador Mike Mansfield, Vice-Minister of Finance Toyoo

Gyohten, MITI Vice-Minister Makoto Kuroda, former Foreign Minister Saburo Okita, Naohiro Amaya, Mitsugi Chiba, Judith Connor, Kazuhiro Fuchi, Toshio Hara, Yujiro Hayashi, Nagayo Homma, Junji Ito, Mikio Kato, Shuichi Kato, Masakazu Kubota, Tetsuko Kuroyanagi, Fumihiko Maki, Seiichi Mizuno, Kay Nishi, Shijuro Ogata, Ken Ohmae, Keichi Oshima, Kirk Patterson, Barry and Jan Petersen, Eisuke Sakakibara, Mitsuko Shimomura, Hajime Shinohara, Bill Sterling, Yoshio Suzuki, Nobuo Takahara, Seiji Tsutsumi, and Koji Watanabe.

Hiroshi Ishikawa of the Foreign Press Center was indefatigable in helping me find my way through the Japanese bureaucracy. Ken Kishi, Toshio Kimoto, and their staff provided me with what can only be described as the world's best service at Tokyo's Akasaka Prince Hotel.

In the United States, I interviewed scores of people at financial services companies as well as economists, historians, and experts on Japan. All of this information was useful to me. Occasionally some of the people I spoke or corresponded with offered an idea or an insight that proved to be a critical turning point in the development of my own thinking. I would especially like to thank some of those people, who might otherwise be unaware of how vital their contributions were: former Governor Jerry Brown, Peter Drucker, Brian Fernandez, Jeffrey Frankel, Jeffrey Garten, Shafiqul Islam, Carl Kester, Perrin Long, Thomas McCraw, Thomas Pepper, Felix Rohatyn, Congressman Charles Schumer, Paul Streeten, and Lester Thurow.

Alvin and Heidi Toffler were a great inspiration. Our conversations about Japan and the future always left me with provocative food for thought; their advice on practical issues of writing and publishing helped me explore what otherwise would have been a daunting terra incognita.

A great many people assisted with the awesome array of logistical details that go into a book like this. I'd like to thank a few of them here: Jenny Cox, Bob Ferris, Hiroshi Furusawa, Hiroshi Kamura, Carl Kaplan, Masahiro Kawai, June Kinoshita, Shingo Kuribayashi, David MacEachron, Jim McFarland, Barry Messinger, Shinji Nagashima, Nick Palevsky, John Pitt, Kaye Ramsden, Luis Rinaldini, Jun Shimizu, Mary Testa, Itaru Umezu, and Steve Wechselblatt. Lyrics from "The Boy in the Bubble," copyright © 1986 by Paul Simon, used by permission. Special thanks to Micropro International, which supplied the latest versions of Wordstar software.

Certain editors at magazines and newspapers played a particularly supportive role by publishing my first attempts to define themes that have taken full shape in this book: Tamar Jacoby and Bob Semple at *The New York Times,* Bob Berger at the *Los Angeles Times,* Dick Babcock at *New York* magazine, Maggie Simmons and Harold Evans at Condé Nast's *Traveler,* Carl Burgen and Joan Ogden Freseman at *Global Finance,* Shigeki Hijino of *Newsweek/Japan,* and Fred Smith and Erla Zwingle at *East/West Network.*

In Japan, as a matter of small talk, I was repeatedly asked, "How many people do you have on your staff?" My interview subjects were usually horrified to learn the answer was zero. Perhaps they would have understood the situation better had I explained how much I relied on family members and friends. My wife, Julie O'Connor, functioned incomparably as a one-woman total support system. Every important concept in this book evolved from experiences, interviews, research, and brainstorming we shared. My father, Leon Burstein, was a bedrock of wisdom and moral support, as he has always been. He contributed directly every way he could, helping with research and sharing useful reminiscences about the part of the U.S.-Japan story I didn't live through. Craig Buck, Arne de Keijzer, and David Kline provided a stream of good ideas, solace in the more difficult moments, and even looked after those parts of my business and my life I couldn't attend to. Julia Aires, Bonnie Burstein, and Joan O'Connor kept me informed of news reports I might otherwise have missed.

I would also like to thank the journalists whose reports I have cited. *The New York Times, Wall Street Journal, Forbes, Business Week, Fortune, Far Eastern Economic Review, The Economist, Newsweek,* and others are doing an outstanding job of covering Japan for the English-speaking audience. No one reading these publications can plead ignorance about the trends shaping tomorrow's financial world.

This book would not be a book at all without two of publishing's most straightforward, fast-acting individuals, Perry Knowlton, my agent, and Frederic Hills, my editor at Simon & Schuster. I only hope the public's interest will now justify the unwavering support I received from Fred and his colleagues.

Dorothy Burstein, my greatest teacher, won't get to hold a copy of this book in her hands. But her spirit, consciousness, and concerns about the world were with me every day as I wrote.

INDEX

About the Author

Educated at Reed College and the University of California at Berkeley, Daniel Burstein is an award-winning writer and journalist who has covered Pacific Rim issues for more than a decade. In 1982 he trekked deep into Southeast Asia's jungles to write a highly acclaimed five-part series, "The War America Left Behind," published jointly by the *Chicago Sun-Times* and the *St. Louis Post-Dispatch*. His 1985 cover story for *Omni* magazine on Chinese science won an award of excellence from the Overseas Press Club. His articles have appeared in *The New York Times*, the *Los Angeles Times*, *New York* magazine and many other publications. Daniel Burstein lives in New York and West Redding, Connecticut.